COLLEC... ...

Mimi Khalvati was born in Tehran, Iran, and grew up on the Isle of Wight. She has lived most of her life in London. After training at Drama Centre London, she worked as an actor in the UK and as a director at the Theatre Workshop Tehran and on the fringe in London. She has published nine poetry collections with Carcanet Press, including *The Meanest Flower*, shortlisted for the T.S.Eliot Prize 2007, *Child: New and Selected Poems 1991-2011*, a Poetry Book Society Special Commendation, *The Weather Wheel*, a PBS Commendation and a book of the year in The Independent, and *Afterwardness*, a book of the year in The Sunday Times and The Guardian. She was a co-winner of the Poetry Business Pamphlet Competition 1989 and her *Very Selected Poems* appeared from Smith/Doorstop in 2017. She has been Poet in Residence at the Royal Mail and has held fellowships at the International Writing Program in Iowa as the recipient of the William B. Quarton International Writing Program Scholarship, at the American School in London and at the Royal Literary Fund, City University. She is the founder of The Poetry School and has co-edited its three anthologies of new writing published by Enitharmon Press. Her awards include a Cholmondeley Award from the Society of Authors, a major Arts Council Award and she is a Fellow of the Royal Society of Literature and of The English Society. In 2023 she was awarded the King's Gold Medal for Poetry.

COLLECTED POEMS

Mimi Khalvati

CARCANET POETRY

First published in Great Britain in 2024 by
Carcanet
Alliance House, 30 Cross Street
Manchester, M2 7AQ
www.carcanet.co.uk

ISBN NO 978 1 80017 333 0

Book design by Andrew Latimer, Carcanet
Cover image by Christina Edlund-Plater
Typesetting by LiteBook Prepress Services
Printed in Great Britain by SRP Ltd, Exeter, Devon

The publisher acknowledges financial
assistance from Arts Council England.

CONTENTS

In White Ink (1991)

Mirrorwork (1995)

Entries on Light (1997)

The Chine (2002)

The Meanest Flower (2007)

from *Child: New and Selected Poems 1991-2011*

The Weather Wheel (2014)

Afterwardness (2019)

for

Maitreyabandhu

IN WHITE INK (1991)

'In women's speech, as in their writing, that element which never stops resonating ... is the song: first music from the first voice of love which is alive in every woman ... A woman is never far from "mother" (... as nonname and as source of goods.) There is always within her at least a little of that good mother's milk. She writes in white ink.'

– Hélène Cixous, *The Laugh of the Medusa*

WOMAN, STONE AND BOOK

And I woke one night
in tears from a terrible dream
of a small stone house
with a central chimney, a spiral
staircase and grapes on the windowsill.
I later learnt: *you are describing*
a peasant cottage of the sixteenth century
to be found all over Europe – France,
Poland, Germany. That puts a different
slant on it. The hologram again
adjusting angles of vision receding
into history asserting the right
to unfold itself, perhaps being
itself a section, a skin some godly
presence is peering in to learn
something of what it is to be human.

And I woke one night
in tears from a terrible dream
where I said to the old woman writer
beside me *I've been here before.*
For some strange reason
the woman's name was Katherine.
Katherine? What does Katherine
mean to you? Katherine Mansfield
was the only name that came to me.

I lived in a house called Mansfield Place,
a small brick cottage in peachy pink
where my children were raised,
a spiral staircase painted blue

holding faces adjusting angles
to my line of vision. I was the big one
in those years. From the turn of the stair
that one about Tom when he was little:
Tom fly he yelled and he flew,
landing on my back in the hall
bending to pick up wellingtons.
Accidents of life preserving it?
Or patterns' interferences, mute
as the backs of angels who break men's fall?

And I had been there before in dreams,
playing games of hide and seek
through currant bushes and neighbours'
gardens, forgetting now what I was
searching for if I knew it then.
Something to do with infidelity
I think. In those years these were
things we suffered from, with our hands
in each others' pockets striving
to become one skin. Letting go,
struggling now to fill our own.

And I asked myself
why are you crying and answered
I am forty-three and have understood
in a dream of woman, stone and book
what all those people mean
and why they mourn
and how clean I have been
through all those years of innocence.

Two camps. The lover and the beloved.
The innocent and the betrayed. Meaning
that to move out of the oppressor's camp
is to forfeit innocence. Meaning
that to catch oneself at the point
of crossing a line is to wake in tears.

There is the fence. There is the wood.
There is the hunter by his billboard
for trespassers. Here is my face.
Scents of trails criss-cross the undergrowth
dense as twigs. A bird's hopping is enough
to turn tail for, only to come out at night
sniffing the air clean, criss-crossed by moons
and witches' brooms and cries of women
pricking the wood's seven layers of skin:
drops of berries beading a trail
of witness, where the enemy has been.

THE WOMAN IN THE WALL

Why they walled her up seems academic.
They have their reasons. She was a woman
with a nursing child. Walled she was
and dying. But even when they surmised

there was nothing of her left but dust and ghost,
at dawn, at dusk, at intervals
the breast recalled, wilful as the awe
that would govern village lives, her milk flowed.

And her child suckled at the wall, drew
the sweetness from the stone and grew
till the cracks knew only wind and weeds
and she was weaned. Centuries ago.

AMANUENSIS

Mirza, scribe me a circle beneath
the grid that drew Columbus
from isle to isle, tipped the scale,
measured a plus and minus

in our round lives. Amanuensis,
do you hear me? Look at the tree
holding the sky in its arms, the earth
in its bowels. Oh, draw me

the rings in its bark, a beaded spiral
where I may walk on Persian
carpets woven in dyes from sandbanks
where goats graze and the melon

cools in the stream. Have you seen the dome
of the mosque? Our signatures are there,
among galaxies, infinities: an incredulity
that leads even infidels to prayer!

The pool in the square is green with twine.
The tiles in the arch are floods
of blue brocade. And those painted stars
in the vault, this hive of hoods

and white arcades, are the stars and the sky
I saw on a night in Spain:
coves of milk and stalactites; the very same.
So leave your sacks of grain

my Mirza, your ledgers and your abacus. Turn back
to brighter skills than these:
your mirrors and mosaics. From each trapezium,
polygon, each small isosceles

face, extract me, entwine me. Be my double
helix! My polestar! My asterisks!
Nestle in my silences. But spell me out
and rhyme me in your lunes and arabesques!

STONE OF PATIENCE

'In the old days', she explained to a grandchild bred in England,
'in the old days in Persia, it was the custom to have a stone,
a special stone you would choose from a rosebed, or a goat-patch,
a stone of your own to talk to, tell your troubles to,
a stone we called, as they now call me, a stone of patience.'

No therapists then to field a question with another,
but stones from dust where ladies' fingers, cucumbers
curled in sun. Were the ones they used for gherkins
babies that would have grown, like piano tunes had we known
the bass beyond the first few bars? Or miniatures?

Some things I'm content to guess: colour in a crocus tip,
is it gold or mauve? A girl or a boy… Patience
was so simple then: waiting for the clematis to open,
to purple on a wall; the bud to shoot out stamens,
the jet of milk to leave its rim like honey

on the bee's fur. But patience when the cave is sealed,
a boulder at the door, is riled by the scent of hyacinth
in the blue behind the stone: the willow by the pool
where once she sat to trim a beard with kitchen scissors,
to tilt her hat at smiles, at sleep, at congratulations.

And a woman, faced with a lover grabbing for his shoes
when women friends would have put themselves in hers,
no longer knows what's virtuous. Will anger shift
the boulder, buy her freedom, and the earth's? Or patience,
like the earth's, be abused? Even nonchalance

can lead to courage, to conception: a voice that says
oh come on darling, it'll be all right, oh do let's.
How many children were born from words such as these?
I know my own were; now learning to repeat them, to outgrow
a mother's awe of consequences her body bears.

So now that midsummer, changing shape, has brought in
another season, the grape becoming raisin, hinting
in a nip at the sweetness of a clutch, one fast upon another;
now that the breeze is raising sighs from sheets
as she tries to learn again, this time for herself,

to fling caution to the winds like colour in a woman's skirt
or to borrow patience from the stones in her own backyard
where fruit still hangs on someone else's branch… don't ask her
whose? as if it mattered. Say: *they won't mind*
as you reach for a leaf, for the branch, and pull it down.

FAMILY FOOTNOTES

My arms in the sink, I half-listen
as someone keeps me company:
She's such a sweetiepie, isn't she?
I pause and to my own surprise

realize, seeing her suddenly through the eyes
of guests, how small she seems;
like a robin redbreast perched with other
mothers I thank god aren't mine.

My father cracks a joke on the transatlantic
line, misreading my alliances;
decades of regret still failing
to make her an easy butt.

But his laugh is warm bubble, a devil
to slip into, like the fold of his cheek
and the film of his eye, film that I know
my own before long will look through.

My children are with me, as always, my son
even now sleeping under covers
I have no more to do with. He is always
loving. To say this, to think this

seems suspect in a world such as ours.
How have we escaped it?
My daughter is about to bumble in the door,
late as usual, and be sweet to me,

nattering on as I clatter in the kitchen,
her breasts within an inch of my arm.
Nothing seems to rattle her: embarrassments
that floor me, still, at my age.

She is chock-a-block with courage;
fresh air on her cheeks like warpaint.
Pooled in this – this love – and this – and this –
what has riddled me to long for more?

SHANKLIN CHINE

They lit lanterns down the Chine
in the summer season, or on Hallowe'en,
down winding steps through liverworts
and horsetails, past narrow banks
of watercress and up the final slope
that ended so abruptly at the gate.

It surfaces at moments, unlooked-for,
when the little crooked child appears
to bar your way: demanding no crooked
sixpence as she stands behind the stile
in her little gingham frock and the blood
she has in mind drawn behind her gaze.

Are you the Guardian of the Chine?
(Perhaps she needs some recognition.)
Of course she never talks.
She only has the one face: dark and solemn;
the one stance: blackboard-set;
and a wit as nimble as the Chine

stopping short at forgiveness
that could only come with time or power
or a body large enough to fit her brain.
Is there something I could give her?
Some blow to crack her ice?
Some human warmth to make her feel the same?

Genie of the Chine, she reappears at moments
when I am closest to waterways, underworlds,
little crooked streams through hemlock

and dandelion that end so prematurely –
though *she* is there, like Peter Pan,
or the barbed-wire children who bang tin cans,

or the child you would have loved,
like any mother, any father, had you been
an adult, not the child with no demands
for sixpences in puddings, pumpkins
on the table, or any pumpkin pies
gracing homes that had you standing at their gates.

Genie of the Chine, she reappears
from time to time, when I am closest to myself.

SICK BOY

In the shallow, like a dog, between the sideboard
and the sound of breaking water,
his fear curls.

From the high road by the stove
whose smoke is scenting speed
outside his travel –

Swish! A figure stooping
in the corner rinses fruit
beyond the peel,

places three magic colours,
dots, a water-wand to name them
by a bowl of tangerines.

Under the covers it locks him in:
the rod, the rail, the storm.
Oh Mum. The sea.

Sand trails off the shells,
feet going down, the brambles'
pale green store.

BLUE MOON

Sitting on a windowsill, swinging
her heels against the wall as the gymslips
circled round and Elvis sang Blue Moon,

she never thought one day to see her daughter,
barelegged, sitting crosslegged on saddlebags
that served as sofas, pulling on an ankle

as she nodded sagely, smiling, not denying:
you'll never catch me dancing to the same old tunes;
while her brother, strewed along a futon,

grappled with his Sinclair, setting up
a programme we had asked him to. Tomorrow
he would teach us how to use it, but for now

he lay intent, pale, withdrawn, peripheral
in its cold white glare as we went up to our rooms:
rooms we once exchanged, like trust, or guilt,

each knowing hers would serve the other better
while the other's, at least for now, would do.
The house is going on the market soon.

My son needs higher ceilings; and my daughter
sky for her own Blue Moon. You can't blame her.
No woman wants to dance in her Mum's old room.

CONFUSING ARRIVALS WITH DEPARTURES

Small and scuffed behind the sheet-glass pane,
I plant my feet, my shoes worn thin the way
I wear them thin, below the presences in aeroplanes

for whom I am not
the presence I would wish to be
ineradicable

as the naked girl who has walked through glass,
punched the shape of what-I-was to a pentacle in shards
and walked away

(unaware how waterfalls of blood must look
– from cheek to chest and so on down – to someone by a pool
who reluctantly removes their shades).

★

I wish to plant my name
on lips that circle in the airspace
of my loss; have them mouth me,

mutter 'Mimi, all those houses, is she down there looking up?
Going about her business as the landing-strip approaches?
Watching me cross tarmac with baggage from the clouds?'

I scrape the ever-widening bowl for succour, for sweetness,
as all I stand to lose spins centrifugal,
only to find that sweetness part of what I stand to lose

while I so strong,
so centripetal,
grow from strength to strength.

★

I am a safety-pin
on the end
of the elastic distances of aeroplanes.

I spread my arms to the land's thin rim
only to find a wireless sky and lines like
'and will my fingers never smell of sex again?'

Someone taps me on the shoulder.
It is not the lover I would wish for.
It is a man who flies in aeroplanes;

spreads his papers in his lap;
looks down on earth's receding map and mutters:
'Over… Over… Over…'

IN SEARCH OF MELODRAMA

Where is the pain they only saw
when drunk as a lord she howled
obscenities? Even death,
the mourners hinted, eyeing
detachment on diagonals in space,
demands more decorum than this.

Why all the melodrama – her lover
used to say as though it were a form
of female illiteracy, plugging his own
speech with war and blood and scars –
can't we just talk this thing through?
Is that what she does then, as she sips

asparagus soup with friends who saw her
grief stripped bare in the wolfdog fangs
the devil laughs in? Talks it through
in her head with the room where for years
he sat half-teasing, elegant knee draped
over elegant knee, the freckles on his hands

tap-tap-tapping a long, slow message
forming in the hangman's game a name?
Where before the game was finished
the message came, cut short the thought
that had kept her going: *you'll see,*
he'll come to his senses in the end.

Is it there then, in her monologue pitching
into silence, queered by a presence who has
learnt to acquiesce? She's not about
to take yes for an answer, she will whip him
back to life, make him tell it like it was:
No, my love, no! Time and time again.

THE POULTERER

His card shows nothing sinister. He stands
against a background sky, a farmyard scene:
against the duck-egg blue and fawn, his hands
are pale as vellum, sleeved in acorn-green.
His name, though scrolled in black like other names
from higher decks – The Hanged Man, Hierophant,
rich in papal gold, The Tower in flames –
his name, though less arcane, is more extant.
He deals in lower echelons than they:
in women, mad in chains, who hoot like owls;
in men who line the fence like ghosts in grey;
in little girls who dream of ginger cowls:
     of claws that pierce the railings of their beds
     where father stands; who dream in coxcomb reds.

'YOU MUST LEARN TO MURDER YOUR DARLINGS'

And we did, we did.
Hid them under tree and bush.
Now I run. And wake.

Remember how he never called
me darling, never even wrote
my name in full.

And how I, too,
stopped spelling out sweet nothings.
How I kept my cool.

Beat him to the red.
Lopped these little limbs
and threw them to the wolves.

A 'POST-FEMINIST' DAWN

There are dawns of stone and pit: dead ends
whichever way you turn. A lover's note. Friends
who run in grooves our mouths should have sucked,
rooting for the teat of depressions they have licked,
hungry for the milk, the empathy to spurt from it.

We who live in limbo
fungus, fern and fallacy
We who lie in utero
waste-products of phallocracy
We who dream of dawns

submit: crazed with the flog of directives
crumpling our anger like cupid's missives
under pillows to corrupt our dreams, to make us
doubt the dawns our sisters wake to, out of focus
on a shore we cannot swim to in our reluctance to admit

the dream, the light, the ocean
how much has failed to fit
the picture painted for us children
the picture as We painted it
We who were framed.

And I ask myself, I ask you, is this it? All
that we were raised for, groped for, from the first bawl
at our mother's thigh, to the last clambering in?
No, there is more, you would answer, thinking in
terms you would hate me to think of as *making it*.

What are We to make of it?
We who are womb and foetus
We who see both sides of it?
Must we swing, celibate, in the hiatus
of the dusk, till mother calls us in?

Or, loving women, have a better time of it? Invulnerable,
penetrable, in an age that breeds without us, the reversal
of what it means to have power or be powerless, to have blood
without a wound, to have seed with a consequence, to have food
for mouths not our own; even now, in the thick of it

fixed by those who frame us,
spayed by a fear stronger
than the urge to love and to fail us
canker We are not; and larger
than the dawn's small stash of it.

THE WAITING HOUSE

'Tem Eyos Ki went to the waiting house to pass her sacred time
in a sacred place, sitting on moss and giving her inner blood to the
Earth Mother... she smiled, and sang... of a place so wondrous
the minds of people could not even begin to imagine it... But
sometimes a woman will think she hears a song, or thinks she
remembers beautiful words, and she will weep a little for the beauty
she almost knew. Sometimes she will dream of a place that is not
like this one.'

                    – Anne Cameron, *Daughters of Copper Woman*

And I will bring you sweetmeats of stars
                    and four leaf clover
and plait your hair in grassknot braid
                    that maidens weave
on holy days when streets are strewn
                    with widows' weeds;
and I will rub your spine with persian essence
                    rose and thyme
and stroke the down that tingling purrs of home.

And you will sing me songs my mother
                    used to sing
of pomegranates' stubborn juice sluiced
                    off silver trays
and rounded limbs in old hammams; and tales
                    of Taghi
at the kitchen-gate, gaunt and thin, slung
                    like a tinker's mule
with children's billycans, the smell of onion
                    taunting him.

And you will numb my rootless moan in murmurings,
                              bird of my breastbone
quieten, its sobbing still, its flailing wings;
                              and we will sit
in the waiting house, latticed by the sea,
                              in purdah drawn
by our sheet of hair, your cheekbone's arc
                              half-lit;
and we will croon and whisper till the hardening
                              yellow dawn

strikes on the mud where crabs peer out to pan
                              like periscopes;
then laying down on curling moss our ghosting
                              shadows' twine
in sieve of nature's palm, you will give me
                              your dreams
and I will give you mine and dreaming still
                              your blood
will live, as mine in yours, in mine.

JASMINE

If you find
the end of the root
in the scent of jasmine
and bind it through

till your sight
is amnesia
and your breath
love's wound,

you will wake with blossoms
starring your hair,
the will
to live more sweetly

girdling you
in ebbing rings,
like Titania
smiling at an ass.

ROOMING

This window holds the Aegean
on white-washed brick
I painted on a piece of garden
where I used to look for robins;

   this the terrace,
   smooth and silent,
   an open arch that disappoints me.

Under a white mulberry tree
Persian polo players
are spraying cries of flit
on photos of my family.

   I hardly recognise
   wood, ringed with
   melons, vowels, limes

or the Coronation Coach
on screens of thick dun paper
where my children swim; or best of all,
the nice brown egg I did.

   How real the speckles look!
   Long and many windows
   my lover is around to cut out.

This my lizard patch
peppered in the dust
of poppies and nasturtiums
you can tell is much too small.

I can smell the sea,
her bed at night,
ink horses on the curtains.

The fridge is humming empty pinks
or green of sweet william,
throwing nightstocks on fingerprints,
some of whom are dead.

Cross-legged, the word-processor
– a Malaysian boy-dancer –
sits: gold and intricate.

With her saffron in the rice,
only the widow on the wharf
and I now know
any book I wish in seconds,

half-open to the sky,
may rain down bruises
– marrowflowers – on my thigh.

NO MATTER

No matter how green the fields,
how wide the moors,
how steep the silence as they lean
against my door;

no matter how openings fill
with birdsong, spring as pale
in golden arms as a feint
along my wall.

No matter that air smells of air,
that time leads nowhere like the brook;
that pen and paper sleep beside
a willow cup, an open book.

No matter that the empty chair
where first I saw you sit
sits still angled to our ghosts;
no matter that my mind can lord it,

have it fill again, your open
shirt still open to the greed
that would steal a hand inside its store.
No matter where my fingers lead me,

I am lost without their cause.
I see, I hear, I taste and smell
but failing touch – your touch, my love –
my sensing makes no sense at all.

IN LIEU OF A POSTCARD

What is it that your absences have nursed
in me? What 'quiet grove'? What 'dreamy view'?
No odyssey perfects those scenes of you
I ramble in, rehearsed and re-rehearsed.
No information bureau better-versed
in catalogue, no lace whose cutwork grew
in shocks of spider-margarita dew*
can map my moods' terrain, her pocks of thirst.
And only habit, yours. I wonder if,
late at night, the cricket over, a criss-
cross rain outside is drumming while you snooze;
and wake to closing scores to find its riff
reminds you, not of deadlines you may miss,
but songlines more insistent than the blues'.

* Spider-margarita: a traditional pattern in Cypriot lace

REFLECTIONS

i

In the autumn garden

all the bedding plants are brown.
One might have guessed
how it would be, how it is,
the 'clockflower' vine
that is at its best
when the gardener's blinds are down!

ii

Even as I miss you now I know

that were you with me even now
to share my hours,
the hours I would miss far more than ours
would be my own!

iii

Since, when I am near you

you croak, old lizard,
in silt and reed,
let a river pass between us;

a footbridge spring by lotus-
flower, orchid hang from bark,
bark of willow.

On the far bank,
let a soft grey form
be conjured...

Through mire and film,
wonder
to think she is your mate

and your sigh like a golden lantern
carry
across water...

iv

The light of the thief who steals by night

outshines the moon!
But where is the thief who steals his light
from love's dark eyes? Out of sight,
stealing inside the glow of trust
she spills in every room!

LA BELLE DAME

Why brood on willow water? Surely hope
is something more than rope to hang a mood
on willow. Hang garlands on the stair! Come.
(Wainscot mice will steal a swatch that dwarfs them
in their lair, quick as any water rat
to spot the knot or head of pin to show
with monumental wit what good design
can do with trophies from the tide...) Come in.

I'll sweep the hearth; you make yourself at home.
Let's close the shutters: we'll mull things over
and leave pale knights to loiter where they will
(moon along the banks where dreams of virgins
hold them in thrall to their own misgivings...)
We'll call the squirrels in: let's have a ball.
Here's my store I'll share with you: an apple,
a loaf I baked myself, a nut or two.

Dusk will soon be gone and tonight we'll see
how big the moon is. Come here by the fire.
Let me smell your hair. Weeds are hanging there,
I'll pick them out. Next time, you'll know better
than to brood. Those banks of sedge and sorrel
never did do any good... water's filthy...
Come on, there's a good girl. Keep your head down.
(Look! I told you! Here they come, scurrying.)

A THANK-YOU LETTER

How lucid every arc, every plane, every mote
on lacquer's ebony. The ivory keys are quiet.
Space reflects me in its symmetry. A light.
A wall. A shadow. And I alone in it.

Here a cushion. There a rug. A picture
hangs, the name of her who gave it; the names
of all these people, those who chose it or wove it,
reflecting facets I have lived, earning the gift.

Here is Mahmoud dead and gone, Simin lost
in the backrooms of Tehran and what happened
to the girl who wove kelims? She named her daughter
after me, sowing me in someone I may never see.

How loved I have been. Come and see my room.
The stems beneath the surfaces are as fine
as old calligraphy, but feel how carefully I laundered,
smoothed, placed in perfect harmony the names

of those who loved me, like portraits in a shrine
of all who have died in a family. As I near the alcove
someone has reserved for me in the iconography of memory
for my children to turn to from the horrors of their day,

I am grateful for the gentleness of losing
flesh-and-bloodness in gifts I will leave like gravestones
or, less grave, in songs that will age into elegies
if I choose to play some music, to remain oblivious.

P.S.   I remember now the name of the girl
        who wove kelims: Mundegar.
        It means: she who remains.

'The mighty mountain-sentinel Demavand... becomes so familiar
and cherished a figure in the daily landscape, that on leaving
Teheran and losing sight thereof the traveller is conscious of a very
perceptible void.'
 – George Nathaniel Curzon, *Persia and the Persian Question* (1892)

> This grey
> is made more bearable
> by the thought of sun
> on your own brown skin
> just over the horizon
>
> and this loneliness,
> looking over its shoulder
> at its own old absence,
> looks forward too
> to a merry death
>
> and the lucky West Indian
> in a language that can be,
> when all's said, at least read
> by oppressors, hopes
> to honour his grandmother;
>
> but what if every time
> the thought was struck dead
> as the tree where you kissed
> in the mule-shade
> of a glade in Damavand?

What if the city
that gave credence to your sickness
were as vanished as the home
you took for granted you would bless
with success and happy children:

were now as alien as the dun
of another tongue, of freckled skin?
Would you turn to the dying –
take a leaf from their book?
To history, Russia for example?

How dead would a page be
without the smile you drew
(in brackets) on the face
of a sun, of a country
on the other side?

EVERGREEN

And I have lived with green in playing-fields,
neighbours' gardens seeping poison
through the fence: ground-elder flaunting
height and health where colour should have been,
the colours of my childhood, needed more than ever
in a land that adopted me, that turns me grey;

while the dress my mother danced in, golden
polka-dots and flounces, circles on its own,
sad as olde-time vaudeville, and camel, camel-
lilac of the slopes where shepherds' lives
meet poppy every day, has settled on the leaves
of war, and every leaf has turned.

Even blues are not the same: of tiles,
of domes, of skies too dazed for blue;
or of shadows, mulberry-blue, in the room
you enter blinded, learning how to see again
gloom becoming someone dear, a grandmother
who gives you grapes she has quietly washed.

And white, like all the colours of the world
raising home, hazy as the verandahs
you half-remember, is something to avoid
in a land where no one's hands are clean;
where dust is never sand but more a mirage
no one even yearns for, intent on lawns.

THE BOWL

'The path begins to climb the hills that confine the lake-basin.
The ascent is steep and joyless; but it is as nothing compared
with the descent on the other side, which is long, precipitous, and
inconceivably nasty. This is the famous Kotal-i-Pir-i-Zan, or Pass of
the Old Woman.

Some writers have wondered at the origin of the name. I feel
no such surprise... For, in Persia, if one aspired, by the aid of a
local metaphor, to express anything that was peculiarly uninviting,
timeworn, and repulsive, a Persian old woman would be the first
and most forcible simile to suggest itself. I saw many hundreds of
old women... in that country... and I crossed the Kotal-i-Pir-i-
Zan, and I can honestly say that whatever derogatory or insulting
remarks the most copious of vocabularies might be capable of
expending upon the one, could be transferred, with equal justice, to
the other.

...At the end of the valley the track... discloses a steep and
hideous descent, known to fame, or infamy, as the Kotal-i-Dokhter,
or Pass of the Maiden.

...As I descended the Daughter, and alternately compared and
contrasted her features with those of the Old Woman, I fear that I
irreverently paraphrased a well-known line,

O matre laeda filia laedior!'
– George Nathaniel Curzon, *Persia and the Persian Question* (1892)

i

The bowl is big and blue. A flash of leaf
along its rim is green, spring-green, lime
and herringbone. Across the glaze where fish swim,
across the loose-knit waves in hopscotch-black,
borders of fish-eye and cross-stitch, chestnut trees

throw shadows: candles, catafalques and barques
and lord knows what, what ghost of ancient seacraft,
what river-going name we give to shadows.

Inside the bowl, in clay and earth and limestone,
beneath the dust and loam, leaf forms lie
fossilized. They have come from mountain passes,
from orchards where no water runs or fields
with only threadbare shade for mares and mule foals.
They are named: cuneiform and ensiform,
spathulate and sagittate and their margins
are serrated, lapidary, lobed.

My book of botany is green: the gloss
of coachpaint, carriages, Babushka dolls,
the clouded genie jars of long ago.
Inside my bowl a womb of air revolves.
What tadpole of the stream, what holly-spine
of seahorse could be nosing at its shallows,
what honeycomb of sunlight, marbled-green
of malachite be cobbled in its hoop?

I squat, I stoop. My knees are either side
of bowl. My hands are eyes around its crescent.
The surface of its story feathers me.
My ears are all a-rumour. On a skyline
I cannot see a silhouette carves vase-shapes
into sky: baby, belly, breast, thigh;
an aeroplane I cannot hear has shark fins
and three black camels sleep in a blue, blue desert.

ii

My bowl has cauled my memories. My bowl
has buried me. Hoofprints where Ali's horse
baulked at the glint of cutlasses have thrummed
against my eyelids. Caves where tribal women
stooped to place tin sconces, their tapers lit,
have scaffolded my skin. Limpet-pools
have scooped my gums, raising weals and the blue
of morning-glory furled around my limbs.

My bowl has smashed my boundaries: harebell
and hawthorn mingling in my thickened waist
of jasmine; catkin and *chenar**, dwarf-oak
and hazel hanging over torrents, deltas,
my seasons' arteries… *Lahaf-Doozee!*…
My retina is scarred with shadow-dances
and echoes run like hessian blinds across
my sleep; my ears are niches, prayer-rug arches.

Lahaf-Doozee! My backbone is an alley,
a pin-thin alley, cobblestoned
with hawkers' cries, a saddlebag of ribs.
The Quilt Man comes. He squats, he stoops, he spreads
his flattened bale, unslings his bow of heartwood
and plucks the string: *dang dang tok tok* and cotton
rising, rising, is snared around his thread,
snaking, swells in a cobra-head of fleece.

* *Chenar:* plane-tree

My ancestors have plumped their quilts with homespun,
in running-stitch have saved a legend's lining:
an infant in its hammock, safe in cloud,
who swung between the poles of quake and wall,
hung swaying to and fro: small and holy.
Lizards have kept their watch on lamplight: citrus-
peel in my mother's hand becoming baskets.
My bowl beneath the tap is scoured with leaves.

iii

The white rooms of the house we glimpsed through pine,
quince and pomegranate are derelict.
Calendars of saint-days still cling to plaster,
drawing-pinned. Velvet-weavers, hammam-keepers
have rolled their weekdays in the rags, the closing
craft-bag of centuries. And worker bees
on hillsides, hiding in ceramic jars,
no longer yield the gold of robbers' honey.

High on a ledge, a white angora goat bleats…
I, too, will take my bowl and leave these wheatfields
speckled with hollyhocks, blue campanulas,
the threshing-floors on roofs of sun-dried clay.
Over twigbridge, past camel-thorn and thistle
bristling with snake, through rock rib and ravine
I will lead my mule to the high ground, kneel
above the eyrie, spread my rug in shade.

Below me, as the sun goes down, marsh pools
will glimmer red. *Sineh Sefid** will be gashed
with gold, will change from rose to blue, from blue

* *Sineh Sefid*: Mt White-Breast

to grey. My bowl will hold the bowl of sky
and as twilight falls I will stand and fling
its caul and watch it land as lake: a ring
where *rood* and *river* meet in peacock-blue
and peacock-green and a hundred rills cascade.

And evening's narrow pass will bring me down
to bowl, to sit at lakeside's old reflections:
those granite spurs no longer hard and cold
but furred in the slipstream of a lone oarsman.
And from its lap a scent will rise like *Mer**
from *mother-love and waters*; scent whose name
I owe to *Talat, gold* for grandmother:
Maryam, tuberose, for bowl, for daughter.

* *Mer*: Egyptian goddess of mother-love and waters

A PERSIAN MINIATURE

(Shirin committing suicide over Khusraw's coffin)

She told us: take a picture, an art postcard
– I took this Persian miniature – then take
the top right-hand corner and describe it.
Well... it looks like a face; two of the arches
that march across the background look like eyebrows
– not Persian eyebrows meeting in the middle –
but intersected by a nose, a pillar.
The nose has peeled and left a patch that looks
rather like a map of The British Isles.

The top left-hand corner she said to use
for the second verse – here I am on cue –
is also a face, only this one's nose,
believe it or not, sports a large pink map
of America, or at least, the West Coast.
As if to banish doubts, a sea of stars
beneath it waves the flag. You see how hard
it is, how far away one gets from art,
and sixteenth-century Persian art at that.

Well, the third and final stanza – although
I can't imagine how I'll ever get it
all in one – is to take the two-inch square
at the bottom centre of the picture,
describe it, wrap it up and there you are,
you've got your poem. O.K. Three lines left:
Shirin and Khusraw (Romeo and Juliet)
are dying: he's in agony but she,
though spraying blood on him, seems quite at peace.

So. That's hardly the place to end a poem.
It's interesting, though, to think: here is England
on the right, America on the left
and caught between the two, like earth itself
twin-cornered by the eyes of gods, Iran's
most famous lovers lie, watched and dying.
How could a painter in Shiraz have known,
four hundred years ago, of this? Has time
rewritten him? Or was it always so?

Has power always called for sacrifice,
the dream of love on earth to trade itself
for paradise, the 'Rose that never blows
so red as where some buried Caesar bled'?
And still the fountain flows from bowl to bowl,
from lips of stone to fields, from mines to graves;
and there, in Zahra's Paradise for martyrs,
still bears the 'Hyacinth the Garden wears
Dropt in her Lap from some once lovely Head'.

RUBAIYAT

for Telajune

Beyond the view of crossroads ringed with breath
her bed appears, the old-rose covers death
has smoothed and stilled; her fingers lie inert,
her nail file lies beside her in its sheath.

The morning's work over, her final chore
was 'breaking up the sugar' just before
siesta, sitting cross-legged on the carpet,
her slippers lying neatly by the door.

The image of her room behind the pane,
though lost as the winding road shifts its plane,
returns on every straight, like signatures
we trace on glass, forget and find again.

I have inherited her tools: her anvil,
her axe, her old scrolled mat, but not her skill;
and who would choose to chip at sugar loaves
when sugar cubes are boxed beside the till?

The scent of lilacs from the road reminds me
of my own garden: a neighbouring tree
grows near the fence. At night its clusters loom
like lantern moons, pearly-white, unearthly.

I don't mind that the lilac's roots aren't mine.
Its boughs are, and its blooms. It curves its spine
towards my soil and litters it with dying
stars: deadheads I gather up like jasmine.

My grandmother would rise and take my arm,
then sifting through the petals in her palm
would place in mine the whitest of them all:
'Salaam, dokhtaré-mahé-man, salaam!'

'Salaam, my daughter-lovely-as-the-moon!'
Would that the world could see me, Telajune,
through your eyes! Or that I could see a world
that takes such care to tend what fades so soon.

RICE

i

Ten years later, I recognise his profile in a Tehran cab.
You see these teeth, he said, leaning across the passengers,
what became of me?... I see him silhouetted in dazzle
as the tunnel ends on the last lap to Frankfurt, his hand
on the window's metal lip, his cap in the other circling
like a bird then, loosed on the wind, beating a tattoo

against the wires as I watch him reach to the rack for his case,
send that too struggling through the window, socks and all.
I have come, he declared, *to start at the start!* Now, a decade
later, he asks: *You see these teeth?* He bares them in the light
to show how short, how straight they are. *What became of me:
you wonder why?* His fist emerges from his pocket, clenched.

*I eat it all the time. My hand is never still, like a swallow
at its nest, going in, going out. Not a grain escapes.*
He fingers his moustache. *I even check in wing-mirrors.
See how it's worn my teeth right down?* His hand unfurls,
dabs at the back seat space between us. *Please, have some.*
What, raw? I ask. *It's rice,* he urges. *Rice.*

ii

I have fled on mules, the star of Turkey in my sky, to start
at the start. I have come like sleet with Mary in the dark; swum
into hedgerows by the line. Gifts of weave and leather tucked
in polythene for friends, already fled or free, are dry.
Will they harbour us, we wonder, ten years, a revolution later,
towel us from swollen rivers chanting MARG BAR ÉMRIKÁ*?

* Death to America

iii

The cabs still carry passengers: my mother in her black chador,
my sisters among soldiers, now and then a face
blasted like a cake. They have granted me asylum. I write plays.
A friend I love in London has hung the Kurdish mules I brought her
on the same hook as an old sitar she never plays.
When she dusts them she thinks of me, and of rivers.

I told her of the man I met twice: once in a train,
once again in Tehran in those early days… what days they were!
Ah well. Her sister lives near Washington; the husband – Iranian –
works for the Department of Defence, and in real-estate; comes home
to scan The Post, its leaders on Japan: po-faced as she snatches
victory from jaws set ever closer as they wing towards Potomac.

HAIKU

On the verandah
the wet-nurse thinks of her own
pomegranate-tree.

I brush my teeth harder when the gum bleeds.
Arrive alone at parties, leaving early.

The tide comes in, dragging my stare
from pastures I could call my own.

Through the scratches on the record – *Ah! Vieni, vieni!* –
I concentrate on loving.

I use my key. No duplicate of this.
Arrive alone at parties, leaving early.

I brush my teeth harder when the gum bleeds.
Sing to the fern in the steam. Not even looking:

commuters buying oranges, Italian vegetables,
bucket flowers from shores I might have danced in, briefly.

I use my key: a lost belonging on the stair.
Sing to the fern in the steam. I wash my hair.

The tide goes out, goes out. The body's wear and tear.
Commuters' faces turn towards me: bucket flowers.

A man sits eyeing destinations on the train.
He wears Islamic stubble, expensive clothes, two rings.

He talks to himself in Farsi, loudly like a drunk.
Laughs aloud to think where life has brought him.

Eyeing destinations on the train – a lost belonging –
talks to himself with a laugh I could call my own.

Like a drunk I want to neighbour him; sit beside
his stubble's scratch: turn his talking into chatting.

I want to tell him I have a ring like his,
only smaller. I want to see him use his key.

I want to hear the child who runs to him call
Baba! I want to hear him answer, turning

from his hanging coat: *Beeya, Babajune, beeya!*
Ah! Vieni, vieni!…

BABA MOSTAFA

He circles slowly and the walls of the room,
this Maryland cocoon, swirl as though the years
were not years but faces and he, at eighty,
in his warm woolly robe, were the last slow waltz.

'Children', he would say, '*truly* love me!
And I have always, always loved children.'
'It's true', she'd say, coming through the arch.
'Sarajune, you love Baba Mostafa, don't you?
D'you love Baba Mostafa or Maman Gitty, hah?
Here, eat this.' 'For God's sake, woman,
do you want her to choke! Come, Sarajune, dance…
da-dum, da-dum, da-dum, da-da…'

He circles slowly, the child on his shoulder
nestled like a violin and the ruches of a smile
on the corners of his lips as though the babygro'
beneath his hand were glissades of satin.

Wunderschön! Das ist wunderschön! He lingers
on the umlaut he learned as a student on a scholarship
from Reza Shah and on the lips of a Fräulein
whose embouchure lives on in him, takes him back
through all those years, through marriages, children,
reversals of fortune, remembering how in war-time
foodstuffs left his home for hers – manna from Isfahan,
sweetmeats from Yazd, dried fruit from Azarbaijan.

He circles slowly, on paisley whorls
that once were cypress-trees bowing to the wind,
as though these 'perfect moslems' were reflections
of his coat-tails lifting on a breeze from the floor.

'I swear to God' he blubbered, only days before
his laryngotomy, 'I was a good man. I never stole.
And if – and who can say? – you never had the father
my other children had, God knows it wasn't in my hands.'
'How is he?' they whispered in doorways as I buried
my butt-ends in beds of azaleas. Months later,
he writes: 'I can't eat *gut* and sleep *gut.*' He never could:
holding up *Der Spiegel,* in the small hours, to the lamp.

And now he circles, from room to room,
with a grandchild for company who step by step
outstrips him as he learns – relearns – to talk…
da-dum, da-dum, da-dum, da-da…

CHRISTMAS GREETINGS

i

Who is it sits at the top of the stairs?

Is it wise Sophia
who has wrapped the wind around her
aching tooth?

Is it Moira blind
who greets the air in her shuttered room
like pleasantries?

Is it old Doc Moon
strapped in her iron bed
with a broken neck, estranged
from her only daughter?

Who is it, then?

It is I who sit at the top of the stairs:
I who am blind and bent and broken.

I am your neighbour, you saw me last
with armfuls of children and notes I pinned
to your door.

She is a bundle, she is a shawl.
She is the spoon that turns in the bowl.
She is animal.
Her fur is spiked from the rain.

ii

The lift is a cage and they come and go
on leashes. She sits at the top of the stairs.
The woman downstairs, the one with the child,
stops to say Salaam. They have the sort of conversation
you and I might have in Highgate, or Victoria.

Have you ever been to Isfahan? Tabriz, or Shiraz?
The roses of Shiraz! Or were they only in Sa'di
on a shelf in Hornsey library in bad translations?
Where are the roses of Shiraz? I asked, long
before the revolution. Shiraz is not what it was,
                                    my mother said,
but there were rose gardens there, yes, I remember
                                    when we were children
Baba Sayeed used to take us. Beautiful! Of course,
                                    nothing like Regent's Park.

iii

The iron door, the lion grille clangs shut in your face
that still seems sweet to me. You had no daughter
but your womb was young and full of fancies.
                              You never guessed
that loving me like your own was the closest you'd ever get.
Let me pray for you. As you prayed for life.
No one has the right to fight so hard.
I say no one, no place on earth, no poor old woman
should be expected to endure a life that is pain on pain on pain,
you'd think it would stop, you'd think there are limits,
you'd – and this is Christmas, that's the joke –
you'd think that sound itself would tear the heavens
                              and smash it all to bits

but the reality is, the woman on the stairs sits there
plucking at her sleeve, pulling bits of fluff out of it
as though the skin of her arm could grow soft and plump again.

iv

'With best wishes for Christmas and a happy New Year.
Give my love to the children (the strangers on the street) –
God knows when we shall meet, I pray for you all...'

When and if we ever do, at the top of the stairs,
God knows what scrap of skin or shawl will take me
                                    under its wing,
change me into child again, saving butter for my bread.

Above the hearth, on Christmas Eve, the mantel gleams.
Snow is falling; porchlit cherub faces dear to someone,
dear as only ours can be, eye the wreath and sing.

In the Day Room, in the sunshine, the TV's on,
Lithuania, Romania, East Berlin grained
behind the motes, the haze of anaesthetic.

Do you live in Holloway? No, I don't,
but it's not too far away. To tell the truth,
she says, dropping words into the silence
we offer like a plate of soup held still,
I don't know where I live any more. I know
it's silly, she wipes her tears, folds them,
blots them out in her shredded hankie,
but I don't know where I live. Her nightie's
stencilled, stamped: ISLINGTON HEALTH AUTHORITY.

The men lie in rows like parsnips.
You say you've got some cream, black cream?
No, no, *anaesthetic* cream. Ah, *black* cream you say?

Are you going by bus then, or driving?
Perhaps you'd give me a lift? No, Ethel,
we're walkin'. They shuffle back to the ward,
minus tubes, gallstones, ectopic pregnancies.
Where was that we just had lunch dear?
She plonks her frame a good two feet away
from her own two feet. That was the Day Room,
Ethel, and now this is the Ward. Yes,
I can see that, she says, inching, inching.

It's smoking did it, her husband said. First asthma.
Then her leg went weak. Then gangrene.
Now this. Two inches above the knee.

Well over a hundred she was, fit as a fiddle,
did her shopping, her cooking, you name it,
no problem. But she'd *never* step into a car.
Then one day she opens her door – and you know
those villages, no pavements or anything – and bam!
a lorry comes along, slices the top of her head off.

…No, she didn't die. Heart like an ox she had.
No, in the end they had to turn the machines off.
Well, she'd have been – you know – poor thing.

3 a.m. they're smoking by the loo, in the alcove.
Out of sight, two nurses press their heads
together, like a Renoir, in a pool of light.

Can you credit it? That's what he said.
She says, so if they're female, it's curtains
for me, doctor, is that it? And he says,
well, we've all got to go sometime.
I don't believe it. Honest. That's what
he said: we've all got to go sometime.
Her daughter came, had a real go at him she did;
well, there's ways and ways of putting a thing
like that. Ooh, she was ever so upset.

Nurse, there's no hot water! She says there's no
hot water, Sister. That's odd. They must have turned it off.
They did that last summer when it got so hot, remember?
                              Unbelievable it was!

THE PROMENADE

Apt. 1719 North,
Pooks Hill Road,
Bethesda, Md.

i

Even the surgeon's name – Mr Quick –
must be a joke, a trick death plays on us.
You know he's dying, don't you? he asks.
I nod. He sits on the edge of the table
like a shooting stick and as guestimates
and sympathies run out proceeds to pump me
about public schools for his baby son.

At The Promenade, they take me for a schoolgirl.
Are you doing your homework? I'm – working.
Are you working or loafing? I'm working.
Are you bragging or complaining? Neither.
Why do you dye your hair like that?
Why not colour it all over? That was a mistake.
A mistake, huh? This is a bigamy club.
You gotta have three wives to be a member.

I am a member! I hear you! (I eavesdrop everywhere
like Puck.) All you have to tell me is look, Miriam,
I'm not a member. Why, how many lies've I told you?
That synagogue turned into a church, why'd you tell me that?
It never was that, I lived there thirty years –
I believe you, whatever you say honey, I believe you.
Now I know how it is when you don't nap in the afternoon.

You're the type, I said so to myself, you're the type
who throws up whatever she does or gives. That's not nice.
That hurts. Why'd you throw up that you gave me a novel?
Now you're crazy. OK, I'm crazy. When *I* say you're crazy
I say it with a smile on my face. So why do you think
I got my ears stuffed up with cotton? Alright, tell me.
OK, I don't have anything stuffed in my ears – I have *dust*!

ii

If it weren't for that woman I'd be dead!
His finger jabs at her or the kitchen
but it's all the same. His finger jabs
across the table: And where will you be?

Your father gone, your mother gone, your children
this one here and that one there and here I am,
a thousand praises, all you children round me here
like butterflies and where will you be?

A child is crying in the stairwell the concrete
stairwell where the smell of smoke and torchsongs
mummy's out and daddy's out and concrete walls
have big black pipes and *come to me my mel*

ancholy baby... Hi, how're you doing?
Belted and buttocked, in guard-dog blue,
a Security man asks for a date. Cleaners don't,
hauling on leviathans, recalcitrant on chains.

It's Cool to Pool, a diamond logo says.
Outside the library: Press Selection Button;
Stamps. Inside, titles I choose at random:
Gramophone; My Mother/Myself; Contacts.

Henry is a Jew from Poland. Where are *you* from?
When I tell him, leans over, conspiratorial.
My mother was hurt very bad – one look and he's talking
broken English – because she wouldn't tell them

who in the street had horses. There's no such thing
as Persian I tell Iranians. You know, like Canaan.
They only call themselves Persian because they're ashamed.
No! You must not feel ashamed! That man was crazy,

a little crazy and maybe you didn't agree with him
but now you're here, to be American, like me,
a Jew from Poland. He gives me a story to read:
Bernard Malamud's *The Magic Barrel*.

iii

ROSH HASHANAH
WE WISH ALL OUR JEWISH RESIDENTS –

> I got some good news for you!
> What's the bad news? Bad news? Never!
> How'd *he* get so lucky?
> He had a bypass three months ago July.
> Little chilly out. Today the first day of fall?
> Where are you, *South?*
> They got a treadmill and a step thing there,
> I'm going to call my GHA and see if –
> I picked up a good book the other day.
> Take one of Henry's stories!
> I like the stories about the movie stars.
> Big game today? Same size, same size.

Daddy, did the morphine work?
There was a man, he said,
a man who went to take a piss
and a wasp stung him on his prick
and it swelled and swelled.
Oh, doctor, doctor, he cried,
give me something quick
to take the pain away
but let the swelling stay.
God bless the doctor,
the pain's completely gone, he said,
and the swelling's still as big.

> I'll fix it. You fix it.
> They used to call you Dick the Torch, right?
> You want tickets, Dave, tickets for something?
> How come they sell that to you Dick?
> They mail that to you? It's a Nazi thing.
> I don't know how I get this shit.
> You must have registered communist one time.
> No, these guys are Republican. Elight.
> Elight? Elight. Oh, you mean elite.
> Every day I get two or three of these things.
> Against Jews? No, they're selling you something.
> They have them against Arabs?

A great land and a wide land was the east land,
A land without snakes, a rich land, a pleasant land.
Great Fighter was chief, toward the north.
At the straight-river, River-Loving was chief.
*Becoming-Fat was chief at Sassafras land.**

> Think there's going to be a war Dave?
> George Bush wants it. Sure he does.

* 'Who Are They?' Delaware Indian Song (Transl. 1885)

Makes the money huh? Sure. Sit here.
Have a party every day.

I am hung in a doorway but no strap slips,
no slip shows, hung only on a sentence…
He-Makes-Mistakes was chief, hurriedly coming…
Coming-as-a-Friend was chief; he went to the Great Lakes,
Visiting all his children, all his friends…
with any luck, till Christmas…
Don't get so hot! I'm not hot!
How long have I got, doctor?
till Sitting-by-the-Bedside rings the bell.

You know why my wife's happy with me? Dolores.
Dolores? My wife, you know why she's happy with me?
You said she was a liar. A prefabricator.
A prevaricator? A prefabricator.
How about a procrastinator?

iv

I do not want to write of death.
I want to write of what is easy
but what is easy? Juanita,
the deaf black cleaner who talks the pants
off vowels? Bowls of fruit, plates
he cannot eat off? Or this small, used knife?

Only children, toddlers passing in the park
animate the life in him,
the sudden smile, cracked
and reminiscent as the very ground
we walk on, barely visible
through acorn cups.

v

Today he teaches me:
$\frac{9}{5}C + 32 = F$
writes it on the margin of his crossword
where aleph, bé, pé, seen, sheen
spell words I cannot read

and that American football
    is something to do with yards.

vi

There are more ways to enjoy life
than as a 'temporarily able-bodied' person
or as a 'walkie' says Ms Letters Page.

Down corridors with even numbers
on the right, odd ones on the left.
The left side is the weak side,

sinistral, impotent. I have sat there.
Felt the smoothness of his jaw –
feel here, you see, no hair…

Kindness would have been a shoulder
if it could, could have snuck inside
the shoulder of his suit, become

flesh and blood, his own,
grown to be the cry-place
they cut away.

I have framed his face instead,
at Security, like an overlay,
a thumbprint on a lens

your fingers of their own accord
feel for, revolve around,
and rub away.

THE BLACK AND WHITE COWS

The black and white cows
hold centuries of use like china;
transfixed on downs, at home
in chiaroscuro and gilt frames.
Death is on their trail weaving
through the air of horns and apple boughs,
raising farmers' generations in the pail.
Pacing the hearse in a dumb
and destined task to cart it
back into the landscape, they wait
by the stile at the end of the lane.
And beyond, the empty pastures.

ACORNS

The pigs have come and gone;
the shepherd, too, with his fist of cups.
A handful every day he sowed
like seeds we know we'll never see
grow in our children's gardens:
his gift of oak to France.

My days are strewn with calls and bills
and hopeless thoughts of forests;
my nights with dreams of stunted bone,
the sudden shock of dwarf laid bare,
deformities my daughter wears
without my knowledge.

And near the grove we walked today,
like a dragon in the folly, a cigarette
glows red at night. No move to rape
but self-contained: some local dressed
in olive browns, determined not to miss
the promised comet.

'THE POPPY SIGNALS TIME TO
SCYTHE THE WHEAT'

I quote my mother though I don't suppose
she put it quite like that but found a brief
and simpler way to say that poppy grows
when wheat is ripe, like anger, love or grief.
For anger cannot foster change when dumb
to fault a man, or love that cannot scythe
his pride fulfil him; grief will not succumb
to guilt that bears a grudge to bear a wreath.
No anger, love or grief will harvest good
till men can learn to listen, women learn
to speak, and turn their dreams to likelihood
of change and peace, redress and union.
  The day he died my mother cried all night,
   her tendrils round me, wound towards the light.

PLANT CARE

A Poem for The Change

As the wasp turns and turns against the pane
I trap it in a lid, contain its tones
of panic, now dulled, now deathly quiet
as I scrape it up against the glass,
shake it out above the street to fly
to where it most belongs…

I strain to catch the nub of what is small,
world of tadpole, sperm on glass,
the prince who croaks on lily pads –
our algebra of shards.

Fingers wait for words. Heart for love.

I strain to catch a hemstitch in the dirndl
                                    of the gods.
See, they raise their arms
and in my yard and in my pond
blanketweed is raised on rods!

Man's slipstream as he warms
to his business would have me follow.
My mouth is library and grotto
where angel-fish swim in and out.
My hair is root and rush.

★

Cacti need little water; miniatures
barely a drop. A teaspoon each, she said,
or fill the tray. It waits on the melodeon
crammed with tiny pots that are all in flower
– pinwheel yellows, tousled fists of red –
so light, so dry, with a touch they topple over.

Lack of oestrogen makes women shrink.
While tall, thin, white women like Beverlie
are prone to osteoporosis, small women
like myself shrink even smaller. Our line
of nonagenarians cobwebs our family tree
where small old women hang like drops of dew.

> Feed me stew and stock of marrow,
> beetroot sliced and sweet to swallow.
> Veil me white in flowery lawn,
> meadow eyebright, moth mullein.

> All bones and bones from yard to bed,
> all knuckled knees and lolling head,
> and when I move draw back the veil,
> let death fly out and sing its tale:

> Left fist, right fist,
> which is the fist I hide it in?
> Sweet and joke and tethering-rope,
> your navel-chord and na-ame.

> Left fist, right fist,
> fool's gold, wish-bone,
> who's to know where the devil to dig,
> the ground all looks the sa-ame.

Odd that she hasn't noticed the dye, the glue.
Perhaps she has but never said. What could
she say? *Of course the flowers aren't real, darling,*
how could cactus possibly grow in England?
What do the English know about such things?
God, if you could see them in Arizona...

★

I wish to make tall statements;
to say that sea is time, that time
has many voices, that dead men and so on...
like Tom did. Not my son.
He, too, is Tom; is tall.
He, too, would like to make a statement.
Perhaps he does. Silently as seeds in rainfall.
I wish to say that life is... dot dot dot,
blue polka-dot, forget-me-not... I cannot. All
I can say is, that as a child...

and the voices are lost... lost...
and the word that is said
                    said twice, said twice
since we, the infant opening eyes
at the left breast, at the right breast,
heard once, then twice, the gobbledy-gook
of her twin-drum sighs: *Bokhor! Bokhor*!*
and drank and drank as we rose and sank
on the housecoat, on the houseboat, as the clock ticked
    and the groundswell shrank to a plea...
then we were children running past
on the lawn (oh, the lawn where they sat at cards!)

* Bokhor: Drink/Eat

who heard on the left and heard on the right
– the engine near, the ocean far –
the one, the two, the nation cry:
Go slow! Go slow! *Yavosh! Yavosh!*
and laughed and wheeled and ran on fast.

By the water's edge where they sat at cards,
fruit on the baize and amber in the glass,
no-one was queen, the red queen of hearts,
no-one the knave who stole her tarts, and aunts,
though childless, cried aloud as we pounded past:

Why, dust on my head, they'll break their necks!
My measle-child! My beetle-black!
Elahi, sister! Brother, run!
Oh, hurry and catch-as-catch-can!

Nahzi, nahzi, gol-é-piyahzi!
There, my love, my flowering bulb,
Allah be praised, she's only grazed,
fetch me a drop, a watering-can.

★

The cloth is spread, the table laid,
our heads beneath the vine are cool
and my place is next to one who asks:
How old are you? In my dream I answer:
Sixty-four... *Will you still need me,*
will you still feed me, when I'm...
Not sixty-four! You're forty-six, she says,
this smiling stranger in her anemone dress,
and I was born an hour before
or after you.

I have albums, too,
in my room back home, in my purple chest,
but were I to show her photographs
she would smile and say: Oh, that was the day...

laughter rose like a bird in the room
as I flew to tag it, bag each feathery
drift as our mothers billed and cooed.
I was the waist-high child, not you.

I was the one who stood nearby
as our mothers' hands, ringed in gold,
were snapping the pod and cutting the cloth
that opened wide, sweet and straight as an avenue.

While you in a land of airmail blue,
ruling your lines with p's and q's,
were doing sums, staining your thumbs,
racking your brains for news...

Mother, I stand in a garden.
It is a wild garden.
Of course I know that flowers can't talk
but through your tears their faces blur
then bring you back to where you were
as though they spoke. I pick them.
I dry them in a big, fat book.
I fold them in this scented paper.
It will keep them flat and bruised.

★

My mother's postcard shows a carpet-stall
where men in long white tunics, short blue waistcoats
are staring at a *farangi** in a trilby
and a Philip Marlowe trenchcoat. Above them
a plaque reads: FARSH FOROOSHI AHMADIAN**.
Pleasant and peaceful flight, arrived safely.
Happy I came. Haven't been round the town yet –
a town whose peeling skins of war await her,
as Ahmadian himself might once have stood,
deferential, in his fraying cuffs
beside the beaded curtain:

                                    *Befarmayid****.*
Gholam, bring tea, a *ghalian****…* Welcome.
May your shadow at my door ever lengthen.
Here is a sanctum, serpentine and cushion-
cool where guinea-fowl and golden hind
wind on the banks of silk between us, leagues
of flowing patterns please us, heavens themselves
descend to earth where stars may catch our heels.
Sugar? May Allah bring what Allah wills.
I tell no tales. May God protect your children.

Behind him, stacks of carpets ceiling-high,
pancake-thin, conceal within each a flaw
no human eye can find or finger feel,
small as the pea no true princess could sleep on,
a single flaw only the devil can,
and will, divine to flee its gape of silk,

* *Farangi:* Foreigner

** *Farsh Forooshi Ahmadian:* Ahmadian's Carpet Stall

*** *Befarmayid:* After you

**** *Ghalian:* Hubble-bubble

leaving a ground as pure as ash, a field
where all that grows is blessed and washed of sin.

In an older dream I had, the wash-basin
was in a room but also under trees
whose lower branches hung along the soap-ledge
so when I ran the water it took colour
from the petals: pink and gold. And the water
fanned carnelian-pink and saffron-gold
till pink and gold ran pale and spectre-thin
and petals, drained, now lay like cabbage-whites
and nothing I could do, no urging, willing,
could make the water colour. Later, waking,
I thought how even in my dreams I mutter
magic runs in holes they know nothing of in England.

★

You can drive the devil out of your garden,
you can scold him away like a loon,
but down by the pool where the eggs float, the frogs croak,
you will find him again with a jam-jar, a crowbar,
where the raspberry staked is pulped to a stain
and strained for a raspberry fool.

You can drive the devil out at the gate,
brandish a spell or a spoon,
but down by the hedge with a knapsack,
with a switch and a swash at the flies on his legs
you will find him again with a matchbox, like a magpie,
with a pebble or two for the straggling branch
where the tyre swings, the raven brings Bad News.

You can flush the devil out of his lair,
hang garlic and sprig on the wall,
but deep in the heart of the rosebush, the canker-bud,
the run of the blood that is silenced by
the fear of the clock in the hall,
you will find him again in a snail-trail, a fairy-tale,
where the gold of his hair is the Holy Grail,
a myth he will make his own.

But when sunlight falls on the lavender-walk
where the trail of the scent is as frail as the dent
in the sweet-pea, the sweet-talk,
he will flutter a moue of a mothwing, a white lie,
that flies in the face of the truth that is plain
as the nose on his face that defies you, denies you,
turning away to a shoelace that strays to remind you

the devil walks behind you,
in the garden of your son.

★

A teaspoon each, she said. I'll do them soon.
I'll breakfast in the garden with the children.
The golden pads of lion-cubs, the shrub
we can't name, are in full bloom.
The fountain's on; birdsong; a fading siren.

When I was young my mother bought me apricots.
We walked along the clifftop. I jawed one open.
Sunshine rose from its smell like something landlocked,
language in an orange garden, its laughter
spangled for the first time against ocean gray.

Later, gazing at the brooch on her furred
lapel, whole seconds must have passed
before I saw it as an M: flamboyant
where I was homespun, walking with my bag,
my paper bag of stones and fraying ends.

Squinting up at the sun, now all I see
is an emerald orb set in a diamond spray
so bright I close my eyes and see it still:
swimming on a blood-red sea of sandstone,
purple head and sperm-tail, world of tadpole.

★

Behind the careless slipper-talk,
glass slipper-talk of the fountain in my yard,
I hear their felted feet pad, ghost-clad,
ankle-deep in widow-walk.

One stands across the pond from me.
She stares right through me through the spray.
In Albufeira, in Jerusalem,
she stands on surf-blown quays, looking out to sea.
Or where the loose plank jars
her scarf slips, her basket jolts
her silvery fish,
her bright, bright yolks for Madeira cake.

On flagstones, as the cock crows
she knocks on the ancient door
where lovers, through the summer storms, play chess.
She brings them broad beans, *favas* fired
in olive oil and garlic, day in, day out,
till the season's change.

Nameless,
she is the chorus where the drama lies
though lovers, loud as the peal in the eye
of the storm, strut the stage.

She comes in pairs:
bulk and shadow, cry and echo,
fire and water, earth and air.

(She is the sigh as the ship sets sail.)

★

A dragonfly is nosing at the vine.
Like all my dreams, it looks for landings...

I prop the broom against the shed, come in
and later see through my favourite window
how morning gloom has dappled not its handle
but its hair, placed it in a ring of sun
as though it might transform, leap up and dance...

    Look, Ma, the trees are all so pretty!
    Look, Ma, at all the people!
    And all the pretty dresses have little flowers!
    And all the pretty trees have little dresses!

They gave me dream-clothes that were all
too small, except for one: an old thin frock
with flowers on. You can't wear that at your age!
my mother said. I can if I want and I will,
I thought but didn't say. I wore it, wore
my rose, my sex, and all my ego's field-days.

What it really means, I wailed,
smearing tears on my lover's chest,
is no-one will ever love you, not like that,
not like they did, ever again.

And of course they won't. How could they?
God knows they try, but hardly in the way
we'd like, the ways she tried to teach them.

No, they bury her instead with violets,
cutting her down to size with sentiments
they have bred us to crave for, in the hollows
of withholding, the gulleys of castration –

smooth-downed dells where the one-eyed horse's coat
has glossed, grown over – stroke it, see? – the gaunt
scaffolding of a socket's seerless hell.

So let us look for landings, gossamer:
meadow eyebright, moth mullein.

★

Atal, matal, tootoolé!
Gav-é-Hassan chejooré?
Na sheer doré, na pestoon,
Sheeresho bordan Hendestoon.

Yak zan-é-Kordi bestoon,
Esmesho bezar Amghezi,
Dowr-é-kolash ghermezi!
*Ochin-o-vochin, yek pahto varchin!**

We sat in rows, our legs stretched out
as she patted all our knees.
We slept in rows, mosquito nets
near marigolds and heart's-ease.

In the midnight rush of sudden flood
stampeding in the ditches,
we heard the bull-god: WHO HAS SLEPT
WHILE I SLEPT? WHO HAS DONE THIS?

On other nights, velvet nights
of stars and pinetrees, his smile
would glisten moonlight, his finger snake
a rectum smoothly, slyly.

But nothing came to mark us out,
no crosses on our doors,
branding on our brows or knees,
no telling mine from yours.

* Atal, matal, tootoolé! / What is Hassan's cow like? / She has no milk, she has no breasts, / They've taken her milk to India.

Take a Kurdish wife, / Name her Amghezi / And braid her hat red! / Ochin-o-vochin, take one of your legs away!

And nothing comes between us now
save home, sweet home;
hard to tell which sock should go
with which, as we switch and roll.

★

I meet my sister in the garden; her barrow is alive with plants:
    shrub and herb and creeper.

I know what you have carried all these years, my sister cries:
    like the running of the loam across my nails.

If the plant is left unstaked, shoots must find their own mouths:
    prayers turn inward on themselves.

As she has been my water, so I shall be her cane:
    on the seventh day, on the fortieth day, in one year's time,
    on known and unknown anniversaries of death.

Her clothing smells of pollen:
    all the years are flaking in her veil.

O save her from the lions:
    my darling from the power of the dog.

But who is the God who wields the sword, who blesses those that
take our children and throw them against the stones:
    who is the man that said, *If I had only two loaves of bread,*
    I would barter one for hyacinths to nourish my soul?

Remembrance shall be the food on our plate:
    of what became of us; what we became.

Remember how we walked the beach, sister, looking for our mother's
openings:
> how we combed the caves for driftwood, whorls of beetroot colour,
> evidence of what the sea reclaims?

How we turned to find the deckchair empty, our reference point
long lost in the crowd on station platforms:
> the milling of the bellboys in foyers of hotels?

Who paged so many names but ours:
> any name but hers.

Now we are the shortest line between two points:
> ancient brackets on either side of earth's long shelf.

God's big book is all that stands between us:
> where mother would have stood, her arms around our shoulders,
> the scent of death's-head honey in her hair.

Let us lean against her shrine, light our cigarettes:
> smoke is rising through the dust, curling like a vine above
> our heads.

We have heard the falling bombs, sat far away from breaking glass:
> here, on the sofa, where I held you in my arms, your voice
> at my feet calling through the clay.

Let us take our turn together:
> let us die as we have lived.

And neither live to live alone:
> fire without water, earth without air.

★

In heaven my father sits, babbling with babes.
On earth he sat in profile, like Whistler's mother,
on a Polish chair in a courtyard,
trepanned, too innocent even to notice:
blood spurting like a fountain from his head.

Oh, earth's red fist! Left fist, right fist!
Now she spreads her palm, her henna'ed palm,
her widow-psalm, her graphic red umbrella!

Grandfather, look up!
Stop dribbling ash, look up, look up!

Here is Ma'mad come to wheel you in,
to peel you of your shirt.

Baba, stroke my hair,
as you used to, by the sideboard,
where the urn that turned a thousand tricks
beneath the potter's hand may still
distil a curve, a tremor in the air.

He calls out names.
Any name will do – Maryam or Ma'mad –
to penetrate the cloister, the thick
stone archway… any name but hers:

she who took him to the bathroom,
stood behind the fountain,
looked up through the window,
saw the rainbow's glistening arc
not in heaven but in his pride,
his lion-head of hair.

★

Cacti need little water, but laced with cobalt,
terre verte, chrome oxide, even miniatures
can dominate a desert, dwarf a sky
of sulphur, rose madder, Arizona's
dusk on fire and its glory all still hers.
Snowscapes, seascapes, walled-in gardens – the rest
are gone. Gone up in flames, the coppers said.
They'd find it hard to sell them, Madam, I'm afraid
they've likely burned the paintings, sold the frames.

Spared, her cacti hang where her gardens were.
On the dim wall where absence plays with mirrored
lights on wardrobes, mothproofed, hanging fire
till the season's change, they raise their arms
like trident gods, cut swathes through lemon skies,
her nameless scrub of succulents and burrs;
while, on an Arizona Highways Calendar,
locoweed, goldenflower, paintbrush are names
brought back for me and stashed like souvenirs.

This time, she'll bring me back the 'scissor-sweets'
I asked for – edges flared where blades peeled back
from the drop of caramel, snared a seed
of cardamom, of *hell*… Farsi words
I haven't heard for years… sounds, smells
of avenues… the blue of street-name plaques;
she'll bring me back, as always, from the air
of childhood lobbies, a motto reinstated,
reinterpreted: *Je Reviens* from Worth.

★

Now we are the album-bearers,
wondering who and where
is the one who left the fresh black square,

whose two-year-olds, three-year-olds,
come back to us, exactly as they were,
only in dreams. They pose in sharp white frills
on breakwaters, scoop eddies into sky-blue buckets
at our heels, now we are the breast-milk dreamers
who wake with words unformed... where is the tongue,
the air's wet mouth, dear Lord, where is
the mouth, the clamp to take me in?

It is a dispossession, a market we are led to
not knowing what to barter, bid for, value more
than blood's red witch or the snowqueen's wealth...
though centre-frame, from mouths of distant tents,
like triumvirs in the desert, crones beckon:

    Have you come for oral history,
    a final heaping of your plate?

    Come to sample wisdom's wine?
    Or burn and pray for rain?

    Are these your fists whose ink runs dry
    when it comes to stake your claim?

    No. Let go my elbow.
    I, too, have stood my ground

    dreading to become
    the dreaded figure I became.

There is a dip in every dune where the urn
takes shape, sand begins to caul protecting
foetal forms and the gorse quickens...

I hear no footfall, see no change.

MIRRORWORK (1995)

MIRRORWORK

for Archie

Of course the serendipity of it moved me:
    a mirror-tree as metaphor become a
    mirror-tree as mural; a cherry outside
    my window become a willow in a tableau.
    The real become imaginal and vice versa.

Fooled me into forgetting, as I stopped just
    past the newsagent's on sunny days to
    see it glitter, how excitement, tempered
    by dismay, had first become, like the
    tree, asymmetrical.

Dismayed not so much that the willow-tree of
    England should deck itself in mirrorwork
    but that mirrorwork should lend itself to
    partwork, curvature, rising and falling
    as diadems of light on the willow's rise
    and fall, highlight, finite,

the inextricability of light and shade,
    infinitude of subject and reflection
    compromised by paint, ceramic, broken
    tile, glass used as decoration.

It marks the Silver Jubilee 1977. Below
    the roofline is captioned: THE ISLAND.
    I know nothing more about it. The area
    is still new to me but, as the mirror-
    tree seemed to suggest, somewhere to
    come home to, on my own terms.

You know all this, or some of it. Who
    never asked of me a poem, but a dedication.

★

You remember half the story: the mirror
   side that glitters. But the cherry-
   tree in Highgate fed through all those
   years with blank looks behind glass,
   my smoke, your smokescreens, silences
   disclaiming even argument – you forget
   how I gendered her, mirrored her.

She hangs my bedroom lights like globes
   against her throat, recycles snow as
   blossom when I am retrograde with
   childhood, still wearing winter clothes

and like a jaded lover levelling eyes across
   a road, cares little how I summer, what
   ornamental fruit I find to match her own.

I saw in her indifference yours. In her
   blossoms my bitterness at England. I
   never saw the cherry-tree. I'm not
   interested in trees. But in matching
   your indifference.

I refuse the natural detail to tell you how
   things look, how sky would look without a
   tree to blot my view of an avenue through
   cloudbanks like the genie from the bonfire
   growing longer, quieter, skyward.

★

Standing in its plot, its absence of a
   paving stone, my cherry-tree dissembles
   intimacy in echoes, seasons I think
   mirror me like the bric-a-brac of homes
   that took me in but were not mine

though I knew as well as they where biscuits,
   string or dog-lead lived and could be

seen – by strangers walking past – at
    a dresser, drawer, brutally at home in
    the world as any back view in a window

or frontal view of cherry, dogged as a
    greeting card with yet another Eden,
    yet another plot of fruit, cat, bird.

You chose red for the bedroom carpet.
    How were you to know how much there
    was already in duvet, pillow, curtain,
    kimono? How was I to know, agreeing,
    the fights ahead?

★

Yearning for a metaphor to do what mother
    never did, lovers tried and failed,
    childhood sends its feelers out, finding
    dreams, clay figurines, to grub around,
    nose against.

Other nights it floods, dams burst open,
    sluice-gates slither rushing into
    blood, first blood: *My Queen is here!*

And tiles are floods of faeces, rooftops
    dropping into halls where aunts, like
    knights at an odd remove, appear in
    slants of light as though life were
    merely doubt and not disaster.

So childhood finds a cherry-tree, a tree
    of flimsy blossoms.

Feeds this tree through every fork with
    terrors, motherless.

★

I've curtained off the tree today,
    pretending that her half of sky is
    greyer, wetter, more opaque. The
    half I see through, where no tree is,
    is lighter, actual.

My mother has gone on a coach trip with
    the Royal Academy and of course it's
    pouring down with rain. Her glasses,
    some days dark and some days clear,
    are pressed against a dream of heat
    behind the pane.

Beyond this cul-de-sac is a no man's land
    where a clutch of trees in shade, water
    in a bucket still rocking from the rhythm
    of a back that halts to stretch, droplets
    on a forearm shimmering with pinpoint suns,
    reclaim

energies of land, water, sun from scrutiny,
    assert their own economy, impervious as
    nature is to human dialogue and pain.

My tree is nothing but the thought of something
    not itself: a bare land that throws its
    own desire for shadow, orchard, rain.

★

What was that crow that came and went?
    Jagging a star like brick through glass
    first in blossom, now in air...

My mother on a coach trip, the Queen anointed
    in her golden coach stalwart in the heart

of England, I in my room looking out through
windows as gales of rain go past in light

crowd fractured dreams against the glass
while rivulets outlast them, splayed
like bony handprints on either side of
faces we have worn, outworn, birthdays
still tried on for size but never quite
grown into, in the flurry and the hurry,
our rows of fallen birds.

It is the bird on the one note stabbing the
air that carries the morning.

I wait till dusk for someone else to tell me
Live!

★

*I used to look for you in books, divine you
in Susan Griffin's* WOMAN AND NATURE, *find
you in* MATTER, SEPARATION *(Where He Begins).*

*I'd close my eyes, place thumbs against the
first half (where I knew you were), will you
out of the margins of this strange I Ching.*

*Mathematician, archaeologist, astronomer,
something to do with husbandry, marquetry,
dressage, optics, you were all these things.
You spoke in number, weight, measure, myth,
from chambers, mooncraters, 'time itself,
gathering speed'. Your tools were bronze,
their points fine as pins.*

*Once in a blue moon you were soft and vulnerable,
'one hand awake even in sleep'.*

'Foolish, crazy'? Perhaps. Seeing you
was always easier when you could have
no hand in it. Perhaps seeing you was
secondary. Never seeing you, lonely.
Or without the comma, and not never...

At no time does the private bond between
mind and mind speak with greater clarity
than when one loneliness speaks to another.

★

For days I've tried to trace its jagged
outline in the air: the crow that came
from nowhere, left its black impression,
crowstar on my brain.

But each crowstar in this series – angled
vacancies in space – is larger, vaguer than
the one before, the first I saw, till today's.

Today's is the air itself: beyond these walls,
ceiling, swollen to meet a force that has
taken hold of angles, starpoints, streamed
them into prayer ribbons whose aura I sit
crowned in, like a hermit in a cavern,
a ledger-clerk at some heavenly gate.

Opposite, the cherry-tree with its small
grey gaps keeps scribbling across my sky
while the crowstar gap that took the
shock, black on white, has disappeared.
Only the greys are left. I approach them.
Through memories of crowstars, each held
like a Qur'an above my head.

★

When sun promises a patch of sky bluer
      than the rest, I remember as a child
      looking up at sky, never seeing the
      legs around me, things tied to earth,

faces of carol singers, chapel readers
      oblivious to the company of angels.

Always above, beyond, were pathways of
      desire rising like lost balloons ever
      higher, higher. On an ottoman of cloud
      were no Gods, Kings, Olympians, but
      old men nonetheless, in cloth of gold
      with fruit and feast, ranged in a
      long, light wait.

Walking back from playing-fields with vows
      held like bonfire heat warm inside my
      blazer, I would then see, as if for
      the first time, figures round me,

alpines, flaking bark, and place myself,
      precise as any living thing, among them.

In every flower, blade or cloud I willed
      my longings into, is a memory of power,
      access to a short cut I can't name.

★

Where has it gone, the eye to eye, flank
      to flank, the same word of the same
      sentence said together, stopped together,
      unseeingness of arms around, eyes behind
      each other's backs?

A boy from Basra, numbed and being in a cell
    too dark to see, imagining that his arms
    had gone, kept asking where they had
    taken them, kept asking where we keep them.

Where, in a world we tear apart, a world
    we cannot share imagining that submitting
    to the test of glass and what we deem as
    glass we might see ourselves in him and
    him in us, might use our arms to hold him,
    touch his own and tell him…

We are the thought of something not itself.
    Each fragment whole, each unit split, but
    dovetailed, one wall, one dome, in whose
    muddied lakes of colour swim the blues
    of a bag, green rings of a skirt. We
    are the hall of mirrors, fine mosaic,
    the mirrorwork in which not even Kings
    can see themselves.

★

Yards from the mural, through the trees:
    glimmerings of silver, glints you might
    mistake for sunlight on a frontispiece,
    optical illusions.

Disclosed, willow branches bifurcate into
    angels' wings, epaulettes amassing,
    dripping silver.

Look up close: back into its splintered
    eyes! Retinas of leaf look back at you
    in unison. Living green in painted,
    living eyes in eye-slits. Voices
    thrown, disowned. Ventriloquism.

Tree in glass recoils from you, leans to
     orbit, stars. Shine without reflection.

A celebration. Faded to a fresco by
     breakage, refuse, accident. Pick one
     mosaic: crock from Turkey, blue on white,
     shop-surround in Ankara, Stoke Newington.

Hair of waterfall on brick, leaf-flèche, braid.
     There's no escaping silver. Mercury's
     plunge downwards. Running crests that
     leap: *The Great Wave off Kanazawa*.

A sea so bright with moonshine that it blinds
     its own horizon. Awed at the power of
     motion. The power of awe to still an ocean.

★

Under the green canopy are painted locals,
     mostly children, festive at a table.
     In geometrics – jellies, cakes, the usual
     bright concoctions. A photographer,
     black-suited, unnaturally large, with his
     right arm raised. Two boys with a spade.

CLEARING THE RUBBISH NOV 78, lettered on
     a wheelbarrow, stirs a memory of people
     who, catalogue to hand, captions, dates,
     stand in galleries and gardens asking
     factual questions, filling in the context.
     The English are good at this. Iranians
     hopeless.

Coming upon mirrorwork in Hackney, my father,
     for example, might shake his head (denoting
     in Iran admiration), note differences between

theirs and ours – mirrorsmiths, community –
and feel, without expressing it, a severance,
a loss of context.

Around the corner, from behind his shop-window,
the dry-cleaner waves to someone passing.
No-one looks at the mirror-tree. It has
grown on them, from birth for some, drained
its dazzle into eyes grown tired of dazzle.

I glance as I pass. Not with indifference
but an incipient sense of the customary.
Seeing things as they are. You, me.
Accommodating difference. On its own terms.

VINE-LEAVES

Even the vine-leaves shot with sun
have shadow leaves
pressed close on them.

Even the vine is hanging
ones that seem like twos:
a top leaf
on a shadow leaf, its corner slipped,
like invoices in duplicate.

If I stood to look from the other side
with the light behind me,
would I still not see
how the top leaf shot with sun
might be the one that fails to fit
its duplicate

instead of
– standing where I do – seeing
how it is the shadow leaf that fails to fit
and failing

makes the one leaf seem like two
and being two, more beautiful?

AU JARDIN DU LUXEMBOURG (detail)

after Henri Cross

If summer had its ghosts, gifts of wind
wind blows to you and whisks away,
then these two small girls

in pale pink flared
like two sweetpeas
I would take for mine and twirl them
to the balustrade…

Look how, squatting, peering down
they think the ground a river,
a winding in the gravel

whose underwater mysteries
like gaps between our memories
appear and disappear…

Like gaps between our memories
that reappear through tow-ropes
seemingly in reach, then, far out

where leaves are light
and light is fish
persuade us with a colour,
dissuade us with a depth

twirl them back through leaflitter,
parkland, crossroads, up and over
chimneystacks, birchsmoke, lavender

till, like gaps between our memories,
seed and dust and all wind carries,
they are seen at such a distance

we think them elemental
light, fire, air!

COMA

Mr Khalvati? Larger than life he was;
too large to die so they wired him up on a bed.
Small as a soul he is on the mountain ledge.

Lids gone thin as a babe's. If it's mist he sees
it's no mist he knows by name. *Can you hear me,*
Mr Khalvati? Larger than life he was

and the death he dies large as the hands that once
drowned mine and the salt of his laugh in the wave.
Small as a soul he is on the mountain ledge.

Can you squeeze my hand? (Ach! Where are the hands
I held so tight to pull me back to the baize?)
Mr Khalvati? Larger than life he was

with these outstretched hands that squeezing squeeze
thin air. Wired he is, tired he is and there,
small as a soul he is on the mountain ledge.

No nudging him out of the nest. No-one to help him
fall or fly, there's no coming back to the baize.
Mr Khalvati? Larger than life he was.
Small as a soul he is on the mountain ledge.

WHAT SEEMED SO QUIET

when I listen hard
is bird to bird, wheel on rain,
what you say, I say.

How tall the pines are!
Heads thinned, as though to hear what
heaven says through wind.

The harder grey falls
the brighter grows the dream of
light, and wind (like rain

that is only heard
as it meets our world on water,
stone or pane), wind

itself a silent
thing you think would drown you out
well might, but also

carries you the more
to blow through open windows
like my own, in Highgate.

SANDPITS

Sandpits from long ago sadden me.
I will give them topsoil, John Innes No 2,
bring them in like seedtrays, water them
from moon rivers springing even here,
trickling in a stream between my fingers.

What will grow? Miniature palms?
Poplars rustling in the ebb and flow
of shallow river-beds fed by snows
from Anatolia? Where two waters meet,
hedges rolled round turquoise pools? A pear?

I shall grow here; from patience, solitude,
vision old-fashioned as a cottage garden
that keeps a hold on history, a slower way
of doing things and pays the price by being
hard to get to, overlooked by motorways.

My own oasis; surrounded by what is sloughed,
grown into and grown out of: womb, clothes,
marriages and friends, and now, body,
losing elasticity, inch by inch
discarding me, as I do it, to self.

This shall be my birthplace; where nothing grows
for those who think to see a shoot, a tip,
a thin white stem that curls up like a question
only gardeners, head gardeners can answer.
A coffin then; earth you peer on, wondering

what death is like, where one goes, when you
yourself will go there. But I cannot rise
above my body, find answers in my self.
I, too, can only see this earth and somewhere,
not close by, but hanging immanent in air

or in a taxi still weaving in and out of
traffic, the smell of marigolds eludes me.
The driver said he had bought ten pounds' worth
of marigolds that day and hours later,
still in their trays, had nothing left but stems.

I've been at it since 3 o'clock, he said,
putting plant pots out. They like to crawl
up inside where it's damp and muggy. The dustmen
won't be happy – they'll weigh a ton those bags.
Thousands upon thousands of live snails.

Have you got ivy? Funny you should say that.
I thought to myself just this afternoon
that's what it was. Perfect breeding place.
I've got ivy, too, I said and thought
of Jane, who told me off for killing snails.

She thought me heartless and I thought her amateur,
like a parent who only sees his kids on Sundays.
Yet we both love flowers. Love that can't be weighed.
Yes, sandpits sadden me…
And so, come to think of it, do seedtrays.

DEER DREAMING

Ten years of sweetness on a small scale, sleeping
on her father's jacket, my daughter's face,
her dreamface, is one window of a dreaming.
Scalds and sandhills, meanders and petroglyphs
have no bearing on this pastoral, bark
flashing signals on my eyelids. However,
two journey lines drive into me: a dream
with no horizon line, no body marking.

Facing backwards on a train with the landscape
drawing away from me, I travel only
a short route into its sadness, wire-fencing
distanced into aerial dots, deers' antlers
into stands of trees: a lost settlement,
a broken spirit galvanised to tracks
draining from the body through windows, windbreaks,
diverging into flatness, greyness, fields.

Deer make horrific noises when they mate;
wake you at night, to impotence and fists.
A baby in the carriage cries. A caged deer,
frantic, filthy, an enclosure, back garden:
another window of a dreaming. Stroked,
how it clung to me, rubbed my leg! Mucus
strained across my hand, how I rained those blows
on indifference, his face, hers, still sleeping!

They refused to take the doe back – pointblank –
back to where they took her from, to a time
they cared enough for deer to make her captive.
I wanted to be shot! of her. But violence
only woke me, to impersonate the deer
in me, or dear, not knowing what either means.
The meaning is not written, the disguise is.
The deer sits upright; wears its mask and munches.

BOY IN A PHOTOGRAPH

The wind is up and as we
wind down it grows harder, colder, harsher.
He is the boy

arms around his knees
like a shepherd in a loincloth
dappled under trees

who gazed out to the hills
where life somewhere else raced faster.
His watchface even now

is skudding on his wrist,
tracking like a ninja-cloud
following its master. (The wind

was up but has changed its mind,
only leaves in close-up
are blowing harder...)

What was it he was gazing at
across those hills, eyes trained
on a flare, ears keened to a call

of horizons? We have captured him
and blown him up, in shade, in youth,
while his unseen flock

– what flock, what fleece? –
grows larger, smaller, larger.

THE NORTH-FACING GARDEN

for Jill

I have never seen her in the garden.
Never heard her gardening. Only heard her
talk of moonlight walks, perhaps tonight,
if the clouds clear.

I have seen her white carved girls, yawning
in a gentle stretch, outcrops where Himalayan
balsam drops its caramel in berries
loved by birds.

I have heard no-one in the garden.
Heard nothing but the waterfall, fountain,
the pitter-patter in steamrise, after rainfall,
that dribbles off at seven.

Yet someone must have gardened it. Hours
every day for years. The evidence is there –
barrow, cuttings, a ladder in the wood – someone
who did it all before we came.

Like the Indians before Columbus.
Like nature before woman stepped,
hair dripping like a seal, with her infant
out of water.

Or the invisible footmen of our childhoods,
shadow hands that served us, we
who were Beauty, at the table of the Beast
we also were.

Here, shadows are where colour grows
though only rose, all shades of rose
from the palest of anemone to dogwood, wedlock
or heard in hart's tongue fern.

The garden facing North takes its colour
not from sun but from her face: deepening
in the evenings, stove-flushed, lamplit, waking
to a bedroom facing West –

Why I'm no good in the mornings, she says.
Behind the eyes, smile, dip and rise of features
that apologise for the poverty of words,
stones speak, spirits prove

and with time on her hands, she makes Eden hers:
re-entering through a backdoor stone-propped open,
unseen behind an arch, hovering like a shade
of our former selves.

WRITING IN THE SUN

is a kind of blindness:
blinded by the sun
and blinded in the shade

in a vague abstractedness to leaf
– like a library of words
heard dimly or forgotten –

writing in the sun
is what would make

re-entering a room
as cool, hushed,
as walking into sleep

if sleep were
a marble void
on the threshold of cathedrals.

For a moment it seemed easier
to walk towards the park
purposeless

than to take my life in hand,
become, if only for an instant,
someone writing in the sun

when one instant of imagining
walking into people's prayers
might be answered
with another and another.

PRAYER

has nothing of the grandeur
or the violence of crowds
but circles stockinged
in its own quiet sphere

like lamplight sealing off what gloom sees
by its cone against the dark,
an interval when, weightless,

the body loses cut and thrust,
rises like a plume of smoke
to add its grievances to air's.

Prayer
is like watering the plants,
popping out to get the paper,
a trundling, pottering,

an audience for dust
that settles even as the duster's hand
moves across the grain.

Prayer can interrupt itself – fling
instructions over a shoulder, offer
delicacies on a shelf;

resume itself, its murmuring,
like berries, herbs
left drying in the sun

as, moving out of earshot,
you find your own momentum,
your freedom not to pray.

Prayer is not a scourge.
Though the head bows, back stoops,
it is a lifting, a soft and drifting
spiral like the echoes of a string plucked,

a sky to feel alone in,
how small one is, how packed
the earth with people;

how far the neighbour's radio
– as skin meets stone – recedes
and amber beads count amber suns
that are still to rise, still to set.

Prayer is a time of day
that, on a winding stair,
greets itself.

INTERIORS

after Édouard Vuillard

Édouard Vuillard (1868-1940) lived with his mother until her
death when he was 50. Mme Vuillard was a seamstress and her
workroom, like his studio, was part of the home. 'The home and the
studio were one, and the honour of the home and the honour of the
studio the same honour. What resulted? Everything was a rhythm,
a rite and a ceremony from the moment of rising. Everything was a
sacred event...' (Charles Péguy, *l'Argent*).

My own mother was a dressmaker and my grandmother (who
bears some resemblance to Mme Vuillard!) presided over daily visits
to her home by seamstresses. This poem is intended as a tribute, not
only to Vuillard's art, but to the art of these women.

Much material is drawn from *Vuillard, His Life And Work* by
Claude Roger Marx (Paul Elek 1946), to whom I am indebted.

I. FOUR INTERIORS

THE PARLOUR

Between the saucer and the lip,
the needle and the cloth,
the closing of a cupboard door
and the reassertion of a room,

in those pauses of the eye
when the head lifts and time stands still

what gesture flees its epoch
to evoke a crowded continent?
What household conjures household

in the heterogeneity of furniture,
rituals that find their choirs
in morning light, evening lamps,
in cloths and clothes and screens?

This woman sewing,
man reading at his desk,
in raising eyes towards the wall
do they lose themselves in foliage?

Sense themselves receding
to become presences on gravel paths
and, in becoming incorporeal,
free to be transposed?

Do they see themselves and not themselves
– have any sense how manifold
might be their incarnations –
in the needlepoint of walls and skies
so distant from their own?

For this profile hazed
against shutterfold and sky
has as many claimants
as there are flowers on the wall,
in a vase, on a dress, in the air

and everywhere, like leaves,
recognitions drop their calling-cards
on a mood, a table set for supper,

disperse themselves as freely
as the mille-fleurs from a palette,

settle unobtrusively
as her to her sewing, him to his book,
lowering eyes from vistas
that have brought them to themselves.

THE WORKROOM

It was in the whirring of a treadle,
biting of a thread,
in the resumption of the treadle

while eyes were closed
and shadows of the scissors
like the noon sun through its zenith
were passing overhead

that allegiances were fed their rhythms,
loyalties first given shape.

With a lever sprung, a length released,
launched in its wake on a sea of stuffs,
flecks of wool, waves of walnut grain,

receiving food, receiving drink, we gave
the thanks we never knew in time
we would strive to give, to keep alive
in words, in songs, in paint.

It was in these gestures, the day's devotions,
with a pockmarked thumb, pinheads
jammed in a mouth that held them safe,
that an inheritance was slowly stitched,

a paradigm to give body to
like a second life to curtains,
a lining to a dress. And now,
when prayers we never knew were prayers

in the guise of silver bobbins,
machines we never mastered,
are once again in currency
in the hands of daughters making light

of the partnering, unpartnering of threads;
when voices caught, then thought lost
in transit while ours, in vows,
were still keeping faith

return in transpositions,
in a dream like a revelation,
familial as they were in life
to orchestrate our states of grace;

how can we not fail them?
What sacraments can we find but these
poor leavings of a memory
of a home, a time, a place?

THE STUDIO

Moving into an attic with skylights
that reflect
this attic, skylight,

this self-portrait that rises
from refuse round an easel,
refuse round a mirror, concretions
of a life fallen from the body,

concrete images by which we thought
to reconstruct our layers;

caught in an upper angle,
the triad by which light
consecrates mirror, wall,
the forehead's lobe

– a tightening of tension
between sky and thought
and where thought falls –
with an instrument at hand and memory
transfiguring, holding up prefigurements

of all the hand creates…
we move into a chain, a series of removes
like dinner guests at table recessive
in glass, like the painting of a painting
retracted to a sketch.

With skylight overhead
where birds divide their paths and cleave
its compass point as cleanly
as leaves cleave stems

or with fielded gold below
in those voids for interleaving,
becoming, ceasing,

and sounds of playing children
too far to be intrusive
like seabirds in a bay,

we are complicit in a subterfuge,
this series of removes,
diminutions to a dot

but cannot lose, nor even
drown in the grand design, that moment
when the eye lifts, the hand descends
to a description of itself.

THE BEDROOM

Sewing at her window,
leaning her head on a plane of light
like a cheek against its pillow

or watering her hyacinths,
whatever was passing through her mind
light from the lamp recorded,
light from the window guessed.

The room she had come to tidy,
tidied and left alone, embroidered it;
the air outside with its hooves and bells
indoors almost mute

spread it to thin in squares and parks
while flowers downstairs
on divans and chairs
rumoured it back to borders
flowering at her nape.

In doors always left half-open
she is suspended in mid-sentence

like a thought
too generous to express.

Entering, exiting
as part of the same slow motion,
gliding profiled to the right,
older, to the left,

hers are the two stooped figures
behind the scrim of childhood,
parentheses we are caught between,
stalled in their vague arcades.

Might they not be our muses?
Our covenants with absence?
Greys that are never storm and cloud
but oyster, dove and snail?

Might they be spelling a secret,
in codicils a condition:
if art is to nail a butterfly's wings
and a prayer for flight be the nail…?

If only it were a question of will!
But will, mourning our own mortality,
forfeits the gift of pity
art earns in mourning theirs.

With an arm along a table,
a head against an arm
and the sensation of an eye

from the highest corner of the room
that looks down, sees only

our right side laid
in falls of light
while shadows on its underside
pulsate against an ear,

how childhood in its timelessness
like a fishspine between sun and moon

in this laying out of halves,
this pool of concentricity,
luxuriates!

★

And though the head stays still
while the mind, listing against currents,
logs driftwood on its way,

on frequencies faint
as lilacs in a beige

is such a weightlessness of objects,
scumbling of their outlines
that volition, like a craft

fazed by would-be voyagers
– colours and their offspring,
rhythms and their cargo –

is arrested at the rivermouth
while on the deck the masts,
long antennae of a daydream,

frame a stillness that might pass
for idleness.

★

While journeys made, or broached,
are left hanging in their harbours,
left hanging in farewells,

journeys daydreams sail on
surprise themselves with atolls:
an atoll in an Indian ocean

where birds that have lost their power of flight
because they have no enemies

make scissor-runs across sand and tide –
poignant, being flightless,
more poignant, being safe.

★

The eye is on us.
The eye is on a vertical
from the oilstove to the cornice,
ground floor to the upper,

lamp-post to the clouds –
anywhere we might be seen:
a shop, a park, a bed.

Seeing with neutrality
that small of a back, nape of neck
our familiars seem forgotten in

it rouses us to run to them,
wrap arms around the waist,
kiss the neck bowed over work,
have them turn to face the light

for where light strikes
the eye sees only
face or hands or hair.

★

Water makes things dark
but in the sprinkling bowl
it's red – a different red
from the bowl itself, yet red.

High on the mount of Venus,
on the flowering bulb where the thumb
still flowers,
a vesica once opened up

a bloodshot eye that cried
in blood, sweet melon-blood
it took hours of holding high,
of pressing hard, to stem.

Now closed in a thumbnail
scar, tiny scar inspected
on the train of red,

like an eyelid seeing inwardly
or a sickle moon
from its vantage, detachedly

it poses as a palmline,
records as any palmline would
how small the threat to life was,
how near the knife the vein.

★

The lever of the Singer
is a long slick thumb:

like saintliness
stern
on its own small world.

Under a human thumb pocked
not in rounds but triangles
of vanished skin like sails,

it sets the eye in motion:
level with an upper world,
a lower world, whether

an empty eye,
threaded eye,

eye that sees no difference
between function and futility,
action and mimicry, riding

gaily on its open plot,
its silver pole, its carousel.

★

Through flowerstems in water
drawing vowel-sounds of ghosts,

cousins' voices
drifting out of space,
through liquid slugging into jugs

and the smell of olive oil
– tomato pips like frogspawn
pooled on small glass plates –

comes the punctuation of a reverie,
a summons arcing over chairs.

A disc of air, bright or warm
to walk towards

forms when they call one's name.

★

But where, among figures stooping, stretching,
in tigerstripes and polka-dots,
working, sewing, sweeping,

women flattened into vase-shapes,
the ins and outs of drapes,

women always floor-length
whose elbows might be objects,
profiles air,

where, in a play of particles
is the figure centre-stage,
actor with his laughlines,
cardinal with crucifix,

the great divide
from which all distances, certainties
irradiate?

Here are two heads at an angle,
one woman cutting cloth
and both heads at an angle that suggests

an intimacy, rapport,
a solicitude

but may only be the one
from which
they see straight.

★

Drops of sweat fall on lawn, go grey
and white again under the iron's nose
as steam clears.

It clears on fields,
sewn one to another,
braided with a hedge.

On the far side of the hedge
is nothing:
no life except one's own,
the sky's, the trees', the clouds',

nothing where ought to be
the promise that was given
when one thought of looking there.

Tacking in an armhole
flashes semaphore and sunray.

★

Out in the park it is lighter
than it was, lighter than expected
as though the afternoon
reversed itself.

But here indoors, we're solid
as clocktime, any segment of a day,
any going in and out of rooms

that hold each other's voices
on the measures of a thread.

Over doorsills, tiles,
from the intensity of borders
to the middle ground and back again,
taking carpets at their own speed,
we move along their pathways;

even in the circle measured
to our own span, not alone.
Even when tonight, in our room,
voices silent in the thick of walls
talk among themselves, we will feel,

lodged long before we enter,
like a bass note to the moonlight,
a memory forgotten that will not go away,

the ceiling of a presence,
a company, a solitude,

like hearing in the dark
intermittent rain.

★

Under an eye that casts its threads
we duck, we weave, we cast our own,

marking time until, on growing points
of verticals, that height is reached
from which

an eye might think it reasonable
to negotiate,
from which an arm might reach
to adjust the shutter gates

so that light pours down in a wider
sphere for those who now, penumbral,
taking up such little space,
weigh only lightly on the earth

to extend their own threads in,
their yards of worn elastic,
tethering ropes of sun and moon
between

the basin and the yard,
treadle and corridor,
conception and flowering –

anywhere they need to reach
with slack to spare.

★

Once the wheel is turned,
articulations of the lever
folded under cover for the night

and the need for counting stops
as blankets open up their triangles,
tartan rugs their squares,

those whose closing eyes rely
on an eye that keeps its vigil,
empowered in the dark to see
brighter in their stead, know,

relinquishing without resentment
their weight beneath its power,
how darkness can illumine

what day hid, life hid, to eyes
that grow accustomed to its glare.

In the play of parallels, sightlines
reminiscent of a child's
cut off above, below
borders, banisters, picture-rails

are the verticals of harmonies,
horizontals of melody and inbetween,
where the ground shows through
in florals, filigree,

fleshtones
that are merely space for the eye to skim
or inadvertently alight upon

as a bird between two chimney pots
in the breaks between foliage,

as a life between polarities
now here, now there.

★

As the ear is to the orchestration
of sounds near and far, mingling, overlaid,

an orchestra in which the human voice
is an accent as a bird's is, the ring
of cutlery on glass, trowel on brick,

so, too, the eye,
seeing wallpaper as fabric,
a baby's cheek as millboard,
a butterfly
large and white above a path
that turns out to be a passerby
receding down a lane,

is, to the hierarchies of vision, blind
but, by some law of mimetism
able to convey

not only sounds and tastes and smells
but the workings of memory itself,
short-circuiting, choosing what it will

to light on, without a thought
for boundaries, vocabularies
that distinguish the substances
our world and we are made of,
landscape from the flesh.

★

Inside seams, colours never fade;
they have the heartlessness of furnishings
that have never known the wear and tear
of sunrise, sunset.

Feet phantom under hemlines know
no depths, wandering bodiless in rooms
where a girl is first the blue,
blue shape she represents.

The process of perception
– squandering of time, elasticity
of space – is all we recollect
of detail we once drowned in:

its anchorage so strong, faint,
luminosity so near the edge
as we dizzied off to galaxies
through the exactitude of parts –

left their workings in the pulse
of a flowerface.

★

Counting beads, apple pips, tiny things
only we are small enough to count on
– investments they know nothing of
in their indulgence of our games –

or colours by their nuances
stained, fatigued, in sun-leached lengths
reds no longer red;

turning marbles to the light
and marking indentations, the surface
scratch that tells us where we are
and were before is still the same,

we hold tomorrows solid in the promise
of growing powers, days to come
when pips give way to orchards –
apple-green, prune-violet, gooseberry-red.

Little do we dream, though,
that larger minds at ease
with magnitude, expansion,

will be as nonplussed as we are
by the small become dimensionless,
the infinite nonsensical,
by particles as fuzzy

as the kitten in the parlour
collapsing like a star
as it turns to catch its tail.

★

In the run behind the piano
where a pencil fell,

fluff collects, spiders die
and lead, having long ago
lost a train of thought or the point
of a calculation,

finds itself accepted
by a community of objects
oblivious of our own

in which the human element
is as leaf is to the branch,
pencil to the page.

★

Who is in the room then? Behind us
as we gaze into the mantelpiece, glass
behind the mantelpiece, seeing

the smoky backs of daisies, cards
that curl away from us, from unexpected
angles the closures of a room distorted
by dimensions meeting, repeating,
rising up their gradients, redefining

not who we are but the space
we thought familiar, the room
inside the drapes?

Do not turn round.
Count the petals of the daisy.
Between three and four, seven and eight,
sense

who passes in the corridor, enters
on their slippered feet and tidying up

not only cloth but vibrations that
might betray their wake,

folds the angle they have entered,
the hidden diptych in the corner
and, with linen on their arm, leaves you
to the daisy, the backward writing
in the mirror, pollen on the marble
you will smell but not disturb.

★

Caught between desire
to enter sitting-rooms illicitly,
huge among the ornaments, chairs
we dare not sit on in the presence
of the air's thin wraiths,

and the line of least resistance
to rooms we have the run of
among the largenesses of elders,
whose bustling is our luxury,
our leave to be ignored in,

we hover on a landing
between the handle and the stairs:

for stowed away with odours, whispers,
mirrors where the souls of those we love
are skyed like chandeliers,

dimensions we know nothing of
– of lives played out before ours began,
games too human or too pitiable
to let us see, with the same eyes,
the world we saw this morning –

will lure us in with stories,
feed our hunger for the evidence
of crimes we cannot name.

Sauntering back through doorways then,
with an innocence no sooner lost
than reassumed, we take our place
at table, lift our eyes to faces

knowing nothing of our loss
but betraying, for the first time, theirs.

★

These were rooms
we should not have entered;
or entering, not taken fright,
fright at their premonitions,

the story with one ending
we would fight against
and in fighting

corrupt the spirit
that is outside the scope of stories
or is the one that has no end.

★

Behind every keepsake we touch or wonder at
through glass, is a world curtailed,
a household lost to history, a darkened room

where youths betrayed mark time
till they can reinhabit bodies
strewn again with roses,

be claimed again as integral
by the parenthood of death: deaths
that will leave these sitting-rooms
for us to light, too late.

It is now that we want them lit.
Now that we need the dancing. Now,
while a rosebud framed in a cream
of skin, black velvet on a neck,

little dreams in its dreams of dancing
of lives lived at such a distance
to those dreams as our dreams now

are to this life lived,
these daisy chains, thumbnail slots,
this small wild life that we ourselves curtailed.

★

Take a theme, an object near at hand,
near to heart and hand
and play it over again.

Each successive time you play
within it will be
the last time that you played it

and in this dialogue between the last
and the one before or after
your contribution, your part
in how a century sees itself.

Take a motif from a carpet,
the intimacy that kneels
at the foot of something larger,
too large to fit the frame

and again repeat it till,
flake by flake, glance by glance,
you have a covering of a corner

majesty throws light on
and, by reflection,
becomes aware of the concept of itself.

★

Though morning light and evening light
come, like echoes, friable as gunfire

and faith, in a weakening tug-of-war
between the reality that bombards us
and the will to give a body
to the latency inside us, wilts,

the memory of tables
vibrant with refracted light,
objects now forgotten
on their plastics or chenilles,

the child cluttering up the doorway,
the hand that eased her in,

the evocation of a lived-in grace
that continues to sustain us
however gracelessly we live

still connect with a source of love,
that sudden shining open space
to which words, conjoining as they near,
float in.

★

It was those glass-sprigged afternoons
the best part of us was born in.

Now, in a fading light – condensation
rising on the panes, snowing us in –
through a veil of milk

it aches, it glows, it passes…

NEEDLEWORK

Within the lamplight's radius,
within the frame the flowers,
my name within my lifetime
handed on to no-one dies with me.

My knots are neat.
My cottage gardens will be stretched
with the ones my daughters stitch.
My youngest keeps me company.

On an upper landing where my work
is hung, in another century,
some strange and foreign woman
may try to picture me

and fail. Or is it that I fail
to picture her? I cannot think
what she would want with me.
With hollyhocks and bonnets.

THAT NIGHT, AT THE JAZZ CAFÉ

everything about her was beautiful:
skin and hair and eyes proving
clichés holding true.

Was it fluorescence on her cheekbones,
kohl that made her eyes shine, silver
on a thong against her throat

or something in the way she held me
as though no skin or hair or bone
could ever come between us

that made her
– lovely as she'd always been –
that night, so much, much more?

No lover I, to name my love a rose!
No nightingale, old feather-dustered,
grey one I, in my daughter's cast-off clothes.

But if I were
I'd wing it to some stained-glass aisle
and, trapped between two musty shelves,

take my feathers to the dust
on gilt-edged tomes; then as paeans rose
from powdery skins, showered in a firefly fall,

I too would throw my lot in, give vent
to the songs heard no more in a world
– God keep her safe –

in a world so pleased with its own distaste
what head would lift, librarian stop
for the nightingale and rose?

ON READING RUMI

Earlier, to be ready, I hoovered the carpet.
Fluff from your socks has strewn it like cotton-flowers.
I pick them, spin them to thread between my fingers.
Short threads. Where are you now?

Night is not the death of day. It is
her lying-in, her waters breaking. Why
not stay then? Ease her way? A new day,
stillborn, will only multiply our miseries.

Night, so you let us sleep *like fish in black water!*
Sluggish, I slow-nibble, stare. When I move,
my Master's line moves with me. Far above,
he is sleeping like a rock; too drunk to stir.

If, as you say, when I feel my *lips becoming
infinite and sweet,* when I feel *that spaciousness inside,
Shams of Tabriz will be there too,* please tell him,
graciously, two is company, three's a crowd.

My friend has broken up with her own friend –
and he's no Guide, whose lines might make amends.
If guidelines could, I'd give her, as a token –
the egg is whole, though the shell be broken.

Why should I listen when skin is more persuasive?
Or touch, when looking without touching can give
a taste of love so unlooked for, and so rare?
Today, your scent. Gratefulness rises on the air.

GERANIUMS

The geraniums are still alive, and fuchsia;
lobelia, daisies ready to uproot
and in Tom's room
dwarf nasturtiums trumpet up a red
borrowed from some other flower
while one brass-orange hangs its head.

They do well here facing South whereas
those I saw trailing from the top floor
as I came back home
in my absence have been on a green rampage.

It's twilight in the kitchen – rather
twilight between the leaves outside,
a light grey over the dark of slates.
Gold inside the kitchen – an anniversary
kind of gold though none and none with whom
to celebrate.

I'm eating proper meals now, the fridge
is full of yoghurt, melon, raspberries,
I've even bought a plastic box for fetta,
at the same time strew
books, papers, clothes anywhere I like
for the luxury of meeting them as I might
the self I was two hours ago, later.

Twilight deepens: geraniums' red
fluorescent, fuchsia's tiny buds
running their pink down leggy stems –
buds unlikely now to open. September.

The window is a mass of leaves in
silhouette and the window-box, so bright,

so lit, almost a part of the room, itself
part of the night outside, one open door,
reflected, open to another.

I too am both in and out. In glass,
like an Indian movie star fronted
by geraniums. Indoors, smoking,
looking at flowers, the me my children
love me for, letting them go, still loving them.

LOVE

When someone sits on your bed
and strokes your hair for a long while
then quietly leaves,

though you feel the mattress
relinquish weight that anchored you
and float unsafe on a surface

that is even but seems to tilt,
though you hear him go, your loyalty
is now less to love than to night and day

whose death and resurrection
you are made
implicit in.

THE DEER'S EYE

is not an eye for seeing with;
mahogany, smoked glass, globed
wing mirror that inflects

a world of sound, scent, measures
the speed of flight against a veld,
the deer's eye is unchanging:

a spirit-lamp that does not guide
but follows where the will goes,
its level never changing

not even in a flat-out run
slow-motion disentangles into
splits, vaulted, folded,

or at dusk when those two lamps burn
as sight fades, dawn when they catch
the limb of a gibbous moon,

obscuring, reflecting
or radiant to the point
flame dies, light implodes.

To bring the deer's eye level
with your own, across bedclothes, nightroom,
like a newsreel, thriller,

brings you where you should not be:
unbeliever in a temple, voyeur
in a playground, armed, defended

in an arena where fight/flight
is a bolt through grass, judder
of a shin, gold of an eye with a pupil,

dark of an eye without,
its intelligence within.
To cheat this eye, steal from it

– be it with awe, tenderness –
intimacy, sensation, the right
to draw our metaphors,

superimpose, magnified, our vision
on an eye that cannot see
its own death filmed, is to justify

lives we cannot change,
lives that, left unchanged,
themselves change nothing.

REACHING THE MIDWAY MARK

reaching, for some reason, out for it
only to wake in a darkened room
where chair and clothes and bed

have no more weight than air has
in the daytime when all these things
are solid... mother, tell me.

Poet-mother, born of another
generation speaking through its own
veil, have you told me? I cannot find it.
Not the marrow, not the heart of it.
Is it

like daring to fill a room with light
when the house is dark...

how silence thins...
how sounds rush through in a sudden flood
but nothing breaks, not one thin strand
of silk? Is it

like prising open a fruit to find
torn ligatures of strawberry? Blue,

a blue that goes with Egyptian gold,
the bluest of blues the minute before
night thins itself with morning? Heavy,

disembodied? How the first time feels
when you ask a man *can I kiss you*, is it
how day and night change places?
To do with articles of clothing?
All the things I could tell you mother?
All the things they tell me.

THE FACE

Apart from – under the line of the eyebrow –
a line of olive swelling as an olive swells
to a glint of cream, two round black eyes
like two black cherries and those two plucked lines

surprised to find themselves so high above her eyes
no dialogue takes place
in all that space left in between,

nothing, as you pass her in the street,
of her face remains

except a certain light, a clarity,
a reflection not of sun or cloud
but of an image of desire,

an image of becoming
she has placed like God in sky
and though she thinks it private, preceding her
like sun, cloud, clear to any passerby

it pours across her face, unwritten, bare,
the force of all those futures
we have in mind, had in mind
and some we failed, some we now embody:

not an inner light, not an outer
though the sky glares and her face
is turned towards the place the sun should be

(and yours towards the station
with the light behind your back where motorways
span farmland, ring roads, open country)

but on her skin, an emptiness that glows
the way an empty morning
clarifies to an urgency, an image

whose name or face you do not know
but feel its tug, its urgent wish
to meet itself on paper
and by being seen, by seeing warn

the emptiness so filled with light, dream, hope
it cannot know
the worlds between

the beacon and the lines
that will get written
as they did on mine
on a face that passes in the street.

CHRISTOPHER ON FOOT

Stepping out of his poems and into his
prose, is it freedom he steps into,
a kind of travelling on foot

where once he covered desert, tundra,
aerial views, now slowing by a verge?
Or something he steps out of –

not a suit of clothes, habits,
stanzas and modesties, but
out of the very thought-before,

its cartography, history, even
its family members?
Whatever it is – in reach now –

let there be no early frost,
boundary, no sign that points
the one way back;

let no-one spy on it, pull
or push at it, let it not be
tended brutally, impassively

but escape him, keep its distance
beckoning while he, hot and laughing
struggles, stumbles to keep track!

APOLOGY

Humming your Nocturne on the Circle Line,
unlike the piano, running out of breath

I've been writing you out of my life
my loves (one out, one in).

I've pushed you out of the way to see
what the gaps in my life might look like,

how large they are,
how quickly I could write them in;

and not (at least till I've lost you both)
rewriting you only means

that the spaces I'm not writing in are where
I live.

A VIEW OF COURTYARDS

As though a courtyard were the pedestal
of a column – set in stone –
of air and sunmotes, winter draughts
that, ambushed in its paths of light,
struck canopies and eaves
with gloom, with gold…

as though cornices and lintels,
                    parapets, window-jambs
etching shadow-teeth on terraces,
                        skiagraphs on brick,
were starclocks, sundials,
henges that were homes…

the way herdsmen move from slope to slope,
swallows wing from shelf to shelf,

at the equinox they moved
lugging bedding, bundles, samovars
across the yard, past the pond
(holding heatwave safe behind their backs,
sunlight warm along their laps)
as the season turned
and the weaver's shadow
altered on the loom.

As sunrise spins itself in barberries,
dusk conceals in jams,
so kitchens faced the east
(for morning sun is good sun),
storerooms west
and in between, bicameral as the heart,
living room
changed hands.

★

My lover phones to say he's had enough of this
– this never knowing what the time is –
and has bought himself two clocks.

North and south still chiming in my head,
the bond between us tightens

and here we are again – though miles apart –
bound in our parallels, as he sets
bells ringing, times
a coincidence of paths.

★

As though sherbert vials, waterjars
were to think of dust, downtown,
roads going south where the Gulf lies,
vacant, under defunct oil-rigs

(where the urchin's light green eyes
are of thinnest glass, frontages
only fronds could ever wave behind,
no homefire burn in…)

and the insistent phrase
in search of its outlet song
could not escape so wide a plain
or the flute breath's holding,

undoing what damage the old view did
I place myself at thresholds
                          – vernal, autumnal –

garden
where my heart is.

★

But – paths running parallel – solstice
came and with it another separation,
so I brought the garden table in,
wiped web and rust, lined it up
with a sill whose outer half,
dark in the shade of a rampant vine,
will later catch its raisins…

Seldom used it. Used
the stones of my yard so well
– lying under lavatera – they buckle
even more now, splinter, tip dangerously
on the very step where my mother fell,
fractured her pelvis – first
in a line of hairline cracks
becoming broken cradles…

Moved back in. To my old desk,
an upstairs view of the Archway Road,
next door's rose failing to get a grip
on lace, across the road, my neighbours.

Having lost the power to move at will,
not my own, but the seasons',
encumbered with belongings
as though fixtures and fittings
were my metaphor for roots,
I function where my habit is

far from rooms determined
by the gold along a wall,
the alchemy of ponds
turning memory of water
to ice and back to water,

tied as I am by fear of loneliness to a man
whose contract with mobility

has shunted me off flightpaths,
passed me like a caravan.

★

Lacking southern sun
to leak from an unseen source
behind thicket, cloud or cornstack,
light to make it finite,

my shadow
is all ground on which I walk,
sky to which I turn,
no Mecca, no Jerusalem,

no weft or warp
in brickwork or basketry

to say I am, am not, I am.

★

Facing the Archway Road,
an older lifeline teases, thin
as a single hair but strong as fishing-line,
something going backwards
on an airpath between spine and door,
door and newel-post, that curlicues
the stairwell, exits into garden,
frazzles loose ends into air
that will snare them in illuminations,
the machinations of the zodiac.

Now love and light stored up in me
coincide with what went before,
before I lost my bearings,
coincidence of earth and sky,

past and future sibling grain
in our elders' sifting hands.

For divisions we have come to prise,
earth a house and garden we inhabit,
sky a bafflement of maths
despite moonwalks, space probes, sky labs,
they did not: saw themselves as underbelly
and sky a slender frame like Knut,
lid for sarcophagus and land.

★

As though an *eyvan*, meeting-point
of greeting, parting, verandah boards
over which a household trudged
or came to rest while an infant slept

were the locus of the soul
between the spirit that is garden,
body that is home

(where leg-bindings loosed
even as a journey ended
would let the heart go out,
the soul repair…)

I undress walls, pull
carpets back and forth
to redefine the focal point,

stoop to pick up mail.

★

Bedrooms were no battlefields,
no single parents' boxed retreats.

'Don't let the child sleep by herself!'
                              the women warned
as though night were a stranger offering sweets.

But night was a sling of bedrolls
                    flung this way, that way,
on terraces or carpets, wherever day had landed
childfalls, summer-calling cousins,
a bridegroom from the city

and bedrooms only latitudes
to give them bed and board
with every night a new – however fabulous –
configuration, ever redefining
what yesterday found fitting.

As for dining-rooms?
There was no such thing.
A tent, perhaps, in the orchard
of a house where you spent long summers,
remembered best its boiling vat,
globe of morning milk;

or the cooling length of a hallway
where the barest draughts slinked
in and out, reared at the door
as the cloth flared up
and rice came steaming in.

Spines that reached with ease for bread,
even the old, crosslegged,
thighbones lying flat on earth,
hipjoints opening down to earth
as though to help her
take them in.

★

As though on some dazzling noon verandah
an oil-lamp flame were left, like Cinderella,
still burning in its rags,

every year the stars rise later,
emerge in half-light
when one's relation to the half-seen plants,
marrow under giant leaves, seems sacrosanct.

★

In a summer-house of six rooms,
in every room a fireplace, my mother
as a child scissored to their covings
cardboard floors, walls, interiors

she furnished with matchboxes, wire,
seashells, felt scraps; even
tiny rugs that bore, like exports,
the weave of a small girl's hand.

When inhabitants of the real rooms,
curling up on mattresses, in moments
before sleep, let their eyes fall
on sofas, bureaux, bedroom suites
any western home might have,

it must have been as though
falling through a looking-glass
into daughters' lives where fires burn,
wood gleams, bedrooms where in every
nook and cranny is a turning in cocoons,
a learning and unlearning –

the past a cold stone fireplace,
oil-lamp with no wick,
journey into sand...

as though a doll's house with no dolls,
a dome within a dome
could have prophesied a shrinking world
where the soul mistakes
its yearning for migration
for freedom to cover earth's span;

even while furniture is being placed,
carpets tacked and the saw, screw,
unpartnering our seasons,
nailing down the flux,
the vagary of maps.

★

As though this loss, this giving away
of the shirt off one's back, discarding
a love that no longer fits

were only a pupal stage
and this flick of the pink, fireflash,
only fright colouration
before the moth takes wing,

with a click of the latch
I take to the bark,
fly my colours,

survive
on homegrounds wings can match.

★

Ham- is a Persian prefix meaning -mate,
so *hambazi* is a playmate,
hamclassi a classmate
and our word for neighbour

is *hamsayeh*, meaning
one who lives in the same shadow,
a shadow-mate.

A good word
is as a good tree –
its root set firm,
and its branches in heaven;
giving its fruit at every season
by the leave of its Lord.

I wish to learn the good words
in Gur'an or Bible,
in women's words or man's.

I wish to find their offspring,
the shadow-groupings in the fireplace,
this family or that *fameel,*
madar, pedar, dokhtar.

Learn how to set the future
newly-bathed upon my lap,
bring sky down to wrap us in,
feel myself as human as I am.

Have David at his desk across the street,
Karen in her kitchen
feel as close as fist to fist on rope
or gazing up the starclock chute
as the tug on heel and hand.

Have skylight be to calendar
what soul should be to self –

vision
to these small repeated acts.

ENTRIES ON LIGHT (1997)

Knocking on the door
    you open, after every
absence – yours or mine –
    as our grounds and elevations
realign themselves, you
    on the step below me, one
or both of the kids above
    I'm struck again as you
face me, turn your back, stricken
    by how small you are.

Bird mother, busy woodland
    creature mother
beginning-small and ending-small
    I don't believe that it's only
a kernel blown to husk
    the great revolve and vanishing
point of our figure of eight
    as you cross the kitchen, lower
the gas and we, entering
    let the small shock pass

that is the shock: for
    watching your anxious steps
vanishing deep down corridors
    to return with gifts, it's more
with a sense of vastness, height
    that I see you shrink;
of radiance, like your candle
    lit in the daytime, that I notice
how pale your hair and skin seem
    beside ours.

Dwindling, as hollows
    deepen, brighten and what is
nearest catches light
    in the circle you inhabit and I
inherit, knowing my reach is smaller
    much too small to lift
and shawl you in my arms, fading
    you intensify, like candlelight
on scalloped lace, in the pink
    the very fabric of our lives.

★

Sunday. I woke
    from a raucous night of
seagulls, shafts of sun
    in old bazaars where motes spun

on an abacus for angels.
    Do you long
to go back to that childhood
    the angels asked

in a grown-up body?
    the everlasting blue enquired
as I woke
    to skies washed clean of dust

and churchbells.
    From the acorn of the blind
such seas came
    such tall grave oaks!

Acorn-greys
    of the sea, its pennant rocks

where cormorant wings
    are omens… *Do you long*

to go back to that childhood
    the waters asked
in a grown-up body?
    the everlasting shore enquired

with a cockerel
    to wake me in the morning
a dog to guard us
    through the night, one window

pink with sunset, one blue
    with dusk? I could go on and on.
But I am moving into the morning.
    I am making do with light.

★

Today's grey light
    is of
light withheld but
    softly
shyly like a sheltered
    girl's.

It's a
    light in gentle
motion
    like a young girl
sitting
    splaying her skirts

her listening smiles
    around her.

When
    barefoot
she disappears
    momentarily to another

sky
    gleams like glassware
we can hear not see
    we
contract but air
    expands

into a memory
    she has thrown
behind her.
    And in the memory is
light
    and lightness.

★

Scales are evenly
    weighed, inside
outside. Light is
    evenly poised
– blur to the gold
    glare to the blue –
it's twilight.
    In two minds.

Who can read by
    a lamp, focus
land's outline?
    But blue soon

sinks and gold
    rises. Who
can stay the balance
    if light can't?

★

Streetlamps
    threw battlements of
shadow on a lawn, somewhere
    a travelling

clock ticked; rockplants
    hung faceted
with lurid
    orange raindrops

dustbin lids
    gleamed
under gutter-pipes
    and eaves.

But given
    the minerality of
shorelife, rain's afterlife
    it seemed

with a moon in the sky
    tide going out – and
wave coming in on wave –
    a miracle

that the one should draw
    the other, as though

gravity were more to do
    with weightlessness than weight.

★

The heavier, fuller, breast
    and body grow, the higher
flies the thought, the more
    rarefied its air.

It is the law of action:
    the stronger a gesture, the lighter
its recovery. On a black sea
    how far the spirit sails!

★

Through me light drives
    on seawall, fencepost, brittle
spears of lavender. A light
    at its most inexplicable.
In reversals, shadows, replications
    of a ceiling light, table lamp

amber stars that now signal
    now don't, across water.
A world turned back-to-front
    where natural arbiters
of light, sea and sky
    are silenced. Light on

passers-by, dimpled on the gloss
    of windowsills and who knows
if foliage shadowed on stone

is from creeper or curtain?
Even our image in glass, like knowledge
    forgotten, startles us. How bright

the lamp is in the garden!
    Between this world and the next
runs a white rail to impede
    our fall, illuminate
our light-world's edge, the selvage
    of our small front gardens.

★

In the amber
    are the leather globe, quillpen;
bald velvet, Red
    Admirals, in the amber are their leaded

lines, candle weeping at the window
    a husband's shirt hung up
to dry, a crib
    and a child's turned head.

In the amber is the smell of
    fox, rosin, stale
tobacco, in the amber is the hallowed glow
    of something old, and male.

★

The air is the hide
    of a white bull, the light
as tame. But if a storm brews
    this afternoon

when bladderwrack will be
    black at his hooves
and the first white waves
    lather him up into seafoam

she will mount him, rein him
    in with the right horn
and as shorelights fade
    riding oblivion back into time
where the light of the rosehip
    founders, see
tameness
    reveal its astonishing face.

★

I'm silenced in.
    Bowled over. No
globe so round, star
    as silver, though I've
seen a thousand
    suns, ever rose
like this, a sun
    of grapefruit silver.

Ghostliest of
    beginnings:
a nocturne in the morning
    a Shangri-La
in the upper pane, turn off
    the light, let
acid glow
    from every angle.

One empty room
      can't see it, walk down
the street you'll never
      catch it, even the skylights'
gold denies
      a white eye holed
into the mind of heaven.
      For a moment I was

threatened. Depend on it
      the sun, the moon
depend on him
      who loves you, even
the moon can rise in the morning
      Shangri-La come to town
the beautiful
      be terror.

★

I hear myself in the loudness
      of overbearing waves, you
in the soft retreat, if-and-but
      of withdrawing sighs, the tug
that gets me nowhere.
      It'll never end. Sound
of the sea – still Sappho's sea –
      the yes-and-no of lovers.

Inland, I dreamt of hearing
      waves again but here
sea in my ears, watching reds
      of lifejackets, blues
of a hull and sails, recapture

in the yes-and-no of my own blood
only the to-and-fro of our endless
    drift – my bed a beach, you said.

Everything I ever said about you
    was true; but trueness
in that tone and at that pitch
    never helps. How could we help
having loved elsewhere too much
    and I don't mean other lovers
but homelands, other cultures
    pulling oceans in their wake?

★

Speak to me as shadows do
    where light comes through
perforations of snow-white lace

attenuating on a surface
    eyelets into ovals
softening prisms into flakes.

Speak to me as echoes do
    attenuating, softening
the thing first harshly said.

★

This book is a seagull whose wings
    you hold, reading journeys between
its feathers. It flutters, dazzles.
    Sings cleanly in shade. Sharpens
your ears to journeys life's taken

that scraping of a mudguard, tinkling
of stays. Its spine has halved the sun.
    Sun fired it with a nimbus.
A wheelchair passes, crunching on shingle.
    This book, set off by wind, makes you
long for the world, to take lungfuls
    of pleasure, save scraps on quick raids.
So that sated, you turn, blot out the world
    enter another, settle for words.

★

I'm opening
    the door of shadow
on a page. In the doorway
    stands a poem

like a girl in a dress.
    I see through her
to her feelings –
    absent on the page, absent

as a house might be
    through an overgrowth
of ivy – his
    heart, his despair.

She wants him
    not to talk of
leaves, or to stand
    in sunlight.

To close the door
    on strangers, lie on her

as a yellow page
    might close on grey.

Not a sheet
    between them, not even
the gap where a thumb
    disengaged.

★

One upper pane by a windchime
    her moon shines through;
plants, tall or hanging, are
    reminiscent of tunnelled trees
while a fern at eye-level
    confirms some forest floor.

Out there a dog barks rapturously;
    nearer home her cat, whose kittens
died in the litter, scrabbles earth
    with nonchalance, jet streaming
down her coat. How does one invade
    people's spaces with such ease

or people's bodies for that matter
    and is this bad or good?
As natural a brutality as is
    natural to commingle
breath, moisture, soil and seed
    in the underbrush of woods?

★

I've never been in a hurry
    to find you out, letting
you pledge yourself
    to the oracular. Once

I might have been
    a cabin in the woods
a patch of grass where you studied
    Latin verbs with a friend

who studied you
    so you began to have a sense
of friendship and with it
    loneliness.

I came to you
    through a woman once
who missed me, with you around
    and wanted the three of us

to make space and time
    for a taste
of my vernacular. Now
    with my name on your lips

and hers wiped off, she thinks:
    I thought you weren't
interested – you said you weren't –
    in *happiness*.

★

It's all very well
    for me you think and I
for trees and sky and wind;
    blind to the grief
beyond our walls, who can tell
    what shadow falls, or leaf?

★

Show, show me.
    But you see
only through the lens
    of your own eye. Light
strikes your bed
    differently
towerblocks I like to see in a
    cityscape at night
loose screams you hear
    differently – such
fortresses we are.
    Show, show me.

Let the blind lead the blind?
    But we're not. We see
a burnstripe on an arm
    mole, hair
utopias emitting light
    that strikes differently
or fails to light.
    Not isolation
but the singularity of thought
    – thought that freeze-frames
feelings
    we might have had in common –

is the fortress that I plead from
    and am heard
bell-like
    in the service of your own life
lovingly and with empathy
    but when it comes to mine
how should I
    have the heart to tell you, *show* you
that it's not the scream
    in my throat, or the thought
in my head, or the light of beliefs
    I steer by?

★

: that sky and light and colour
    cloud, clearings

should raise me, strip me down
    to the bare bones

of vocabulary – rise fall sea sky
    a tree and not a sycamore

flower and not a bluebell
    till the agony of daily life

falls away, like ground from a tilting
    plane, drops far below me.

★

I love all things in miniature
    – the blue tree whose sprigs
are like the lilac's in miniature –
    and small things too since they
recollect a child's eye view
    of a small world inside a large
in which small things might represent
    the large – acorn cup a cup, sprig
a tree – and because miniatures are
    fully-formed and in completion
futureless, as if childhood itself
    were arrested, made redeemable.

Lying belly down on grass, level
    with a sparrow's eye as it cocks
its head, engages without seeing us
    I remember how our first lessons
were tailored to a scale in which
    the child loomed large, creatures
small and therefore it was incumbent
    on our stature to feel tenderness.
I felt it for a moment and have lost it
    now that the mind has taken flight
left a birdless stretch of grass
    so much larger than itself.

★

In that childhood time
    of peering out
from a hut of leaves
    at the ebb and flow –

though little did
    sun perhaps on a glint

of straw, wind
    ballooning a shirt or branch –

each gust and pause, drift
    of skin between
warm and cold, was a source
    of mindless patience.

How a world could be
    changed from moment
to moment, broken
    by sudden entrances

a bumblebee, helicopter;
    resumed and our
solitude, brushing wings
    with its passing by

be, for the contact
    safer: this
was the ebb and flow
    we watched for

as though each shift of
    grass, flight of paper
float of shadow across a path
    weren't just earth's

response to a moving heaven
    but the heart's reply
shaping life
    and we its recording angel.

★

Light's taking a bath tonight
    in the sea's enamelled
blue-rimmed bath, lying along
    its length. Hair submerged
thighs and belly in mile-long
    strips showing through white
between limbs and fingers
    bluer depths.

Light's closing her eyes
    not once but twice – once
face up, once facing down
    from her ceiling mirror.
In rising steam, the longest
    bath earth's ever seen, closing
her lids on sea and sky till only
    mist and vapour stir.

★

Dawn paves its own way
    if what we mean by dawn
is sunrise. The sky's already
    light by the time the sun
comes up, rising on its own
    prediction of the day.
This is how art is made.
    And memory. And love.

First, the halo overhead.
    Next, the body. Last
the roots like the final
    rays of the sun spiralling
as earth pulls free of them

and they of earth. Then
illumination's width and frame.
    This is how love is made

rising into a desire
    for love, however grey
the outlook, late the hour
    hard for faith and fear
to pave the way. Love
    full-face. Preordained
as sunrise, chasing after
    the ghost of its own grace.

★

With finest needles
    finest beads
lawn and dew are making
    a tapestry of water…

★

When sky paints itself
    with daubs and puffs of
cloud-sponge, wrinkles
    the silk surface of the sea, trails
fingers of light on a misted
    ground to illuminate
its manuscript
    what should I do
but put down my pen, marvel
    at its changes before the marvellous
puts away its own pen and
    the sun, so small, so glorious

rising in a cone of light, sinks
    behind the grey again, leaving
a scar of rosy fire in melting pinks
    and vanishes?

★

There's no jewel
    we can think of
that's orange. But she
    has studded her hair
with clips and stars
    trailed from her fingers
chains and ropes
    hung from her throat
twin pendants
    in cleavages of water

flung anklets, bracelets
    to bob on circling floats.
She's scattered a fistful
    of uncut gems
over shore and hill, a chip or two
    dropped on a skyline boat;
set five ablaze
    in a row of lamps and saved
for her royal knuckle
    the brightest stone.

But we who pass by railings
    facelessly in twos
past necklaces of traffic
    glass cases banked with jewels
will have to choose

from local
topaz, tourmaline, citrine
    quartz for there's no
jewel we can think of
    that's orange.

★

Moons come in all the colours
    of the rainbow. Combine them
too. I wish I could see such moons
    parade themselves night after night
across my window. I wish I could
    keep awake to watch such moons.

And if I could, I'd wish words were
    inks, inks quills for lyres, wish
I could play and sing along with the words
    like Sappho. I'd stand at the window
stripped, take colour from the moon
    as it shone through cloud, marbled me

head to toe, in rainbow. I'd learn
    like Uri Geller, eyes closed, palm
on my belly, moon on my hand, to read
    colour through touch, open my eyes
to have the moon confirm, at a stroke
    the shades we'd been through.

Perhaps I could keep these colours
    under my skin, transmit them
the way you say my eyes change colour
    when we're making love, through
my entire length lying under you
    to your every pore. Then you'd know

know in your bones how to read me
    how to match my moods.
That'd be good. Better than clues
    most men I know are blind to.
Most men are colour-blind did you know?
    when it comes to grey & green & blue.

★

Why not mention the purple flower
    token of exchange
between this world and the next?
    Ignore the wind

and the wild wet light blossoming
    as the purple does
when you draw the curtain to inspect
    the light but your eye rebounds

from a flower, colour
    you can't quite name.
Purple will do. What does the shade
    under grey stone walls

grey underside of wings you saw
    when the sun blazed
turn blue, cornflower blue as gulls flew
    into the face of the sun

in another lightning exchange, matter?
    Mention the purple, stay close
to the heart: remember
    when the curtain is drawn

on the infinite blue that today
      is infinite grey
it's the heart that knows
      the best in its gift

to exchange for the gift of sky and light
      and though you can't place
its name or shade or hearing
      the cynic's groan at the mere

mention of flowers – oh not again –
      retreat like a snail in your shell
throw shame to the winds, gravitas to the skies
      and do it! – mention the purple.

★

One sky is a canvas for jets and
      vapour trails, one
Venetian. One a dawn that may spoil
      or bloom, the other
a perfection. On towerblocks or grand
      canals, roundabouts or
basins. Removal trucks, motorbikes
      icecream vans are gilded
in the one, in the other, silence is golden.
      On a moat in Dresden
there are swans, colonnades in water.
      In the Piazetta everyone
is dressed in white, everything is
      lined with copper.

Some will look for immanence
      in a shadow on the wall sinking

through water, or focus where the shadow ends
    on a bricked diagonal of gold
and remember how sun warms brick and linen
    in offices and houses
how glory that was general
    is particular to them.
One is the glory of the yet-to-be, one
    of a past that reminds us
how we've seen it in our own lives exactly
    as it used to be but were
blinded by those lives, distracted from our own
    perfections.

★

Black fruit is sweet, white is sweeter.
    Sweeter than any white grape, white fig
is white mulberry, too sweet to eat
    without water.

And water, catching casts of berry
    is bluer in its blue-washed pool
than any sky in living memory, boasting
    hot summers in England.

If England is small
    this corner of heaven
is smaller. Barely two bow-lengths
    but morning as long

as the Garden on the Day of Rising
    and evening the length
of a life so little wasted, little room
    has been left for regret.

Instead there is shade and silence.
    One as deep as the other.
Yet for all their depth, buoyant
    as a salt sea, more buoyant for the scent

of jasmine from four corners; only
    tuberose clutches more at the heart
when the heart's at home but home's
    where the heart grows greyer.

So if I were to tell you in future
    how sweet were the berries
left lying in a bowl
    dried and greyed and inedible

once sweet enough to bring tears
    to your eyes, I swear to God
not a word would ring true, for even truth
    lies in the face of the incomparable.

★

They go right through you, smells.
    Those sweet, back to old childhood
springs, churning your stomach smells.
    Lavender-scented writing paper, violet
Love-Hearts embossed with hearts;
    sweetness grown sickly on tongues
so free with bitterness. Tastebuds develop
    from sweet to sour to bitter but why
should one preclude the other, narcissi
    choking a room with scent, repel?

Let me drink you in, small yellow stars.
    Bury my nose, as children do in donkey's fur
in your blotted skies, your criss-crossed
    shadow lemons. Meet, in the depths
of my lungs, companion smells – bacon
    from boarding-school kitchens, damp from
rotting bridge-struts, juniper's gin and long
    before cowslip, primrose, daffodil –
hyacinth on the *Haft Sin* table. *Sombol*
    serkeh, somagh, seeb, seer, sabzeh, samanoo

seven symbols even Iranians puzzle over.
    They all relate to health, my mother
claims, for example, vinegar is good for
    arthritis, sumac is anti-cholesterol
apples are obvious, garlic, greenery, malt
    all stand for *Salamati*, S for health.
For sweet, salt, sour, an ill-assorted spread
    of comestibles nothing much to look at
but smell them, cook them, taste them… Ah!
    Salamat boshid! Blessings for the New Year!

★

He's tying up the gypsophila
    that lay like a snowspray
on his emerald grass. Dark emerald
    that reminds me of Rilke's
dark evergreen, *our hours of pain.*
    And has flung a bouquet

of dead daisies there. Uprooted
    like aftersmells of love they remind me
of Valentine's smell, *corn and milk*

coming through her tears.
Are those deadheads still on the pavement
    in that backstreet I think

is Tehran? The walled tree's
    whose mock-stars fall
out of its skirts to a shade
    the width of a smell: a white cocoon
I can enter, stoop in, bow my head
    to a guttering star, bridal-veiled.

★

And had we ever lived
    in my country
you might have asked
    had I returned

were backstreets cool
    in siesta heat
did hawkers call
    the mulberry thrive

on neglect?
    Who can I ask
of mulberry and mint
    courtyard shade

so alive with presence
    when no one's around
but a burning sun
    and grapes, walled-in?

Who can I ask
    to ensure a return
have me to stay, receive
    my gifts?

★

Winter's strains
    have surfaced to skin
under bra-strap, thigh elastic
    stone under skull and towel.

As wind blows, sun burns
    I turn to the ground's pull
record in every crease, every
    three-ringed knuckle

the ferocity of white.
    Tonight, against your knees
two shields of red when I
    near you, flashing moon-teeth

to your laughter, blackberry
    nipples to your lips
the nightsky we see by will see us
    by our eyes and teeth, like lamps

cut out on its own black skin
    sickle moons on winter
nights when we, worm-pale, sleep
    in rooms as black as ink.

★

And in the sea's blackness sank
     wreckage of the day
its faces, voices, stops and starts
     while to the surface rose
lights, lapping of waves
     squawks of invisible birds
we heard as apertures
     in a low dark sky –
the glittering crust that to an eye
     seeing for the first time
evidence of man's night on earth
     might be as intricate, luminous
as space to ours and wondrous
     in its buoyancy, littoral
between depths and heights, electric
     on its charts of glass
as peace might be
     putting out without sound or sail.

★

When space is at its emptiest
     an undervoice in which
songs of the sea, lamp, grass
     inside one's orbit sing

then space assumes a radiance
     an open throat through which
songs of the sea, lamp, grass
     sing not of themselves but of

something old, something new
     something borrowed, something blue
something, whoever it belongs to
     in which other lives begin.

★

Was it morning, night?
    I remember
only because I have it
    now – stamped when a baby
was born in those days –
    her footprint.

Blue-inked, small enough
    to fit a notepad
like the first
    inkling of a poem.
What time was it?
    I remember

winter light on that
    boulevard, some park
the Shah had planted
    opposite, how poor it looked
how poor the strollers
    were in their shabby coats

mountain light and rows
    of saplings.
If she asks again
    her time of birth, I'll give her
mountain light and her own
    loveliness, I'll even

give her the name
    of a boulevard, hospital…
Apadana… Pars… everything
    but the amnesia
before
    that footprint.

★

Curling her tail
   and staring
not quite sure who
   I was
how many kittens
   I too
had had, stalking
   past as
disdainfully
   as blackness
smallness
   warrants, this
is what she
   left me with:
curvature
   and silence.

     ★

His 18th. He likes Chinese.
   Café Rouge'll do. I've spent
a fortune on his lamp, lamp to light
   his future, throw light on him.

I see it on a piano, YAMAHA in gold
   torso in shadow, right hand
with his father's fingers – no his own
   plying up and down up and down

though only over a small stretch
   the way it used to drive me mad
make me tear my hair, get rid of him.
   A lamp to light him. Something

to keep forever we both agreed.
    The way my mother's mother
scarved and sunglassed in the sky
      would want it. No pyrotechnics.

While the fireworks in his body
    are what he himself once called
in between the keys. When I first read that –
    of a restaurant he'd have for jazz

he wrote, called *In Between The Keys* –
    something flashed inside me. Like
scattered light, his mother's skirts
     inside him. I dream of him

four years old, abandoned in a bath
    the tears on him. Squib, damp squib.
I taste the salt, his lashes' salt.
    My fingerling. My waterlips.

★

Staring up from his pram to the sky
    through mobile leaves that so
transfixed him, no matter who smiled
    and cooed, whose head might suddenly
block his light, those sea-washed eyes
    that had never yet seen sea
wouldn't flinch, barely blinked
    and when at last they panned from
tree to you, it would seem as if
    time itself had been scanned
so slowly did sight catch up with vision
    vision give way to a human hold.

And though he'd sit for hours, tearless
    and wide awake, you'd lift him
shoulder him with kisses, words, any
    bauble waved like a flag to bring it
home to him, him home to you.
    But even his eyelashes, so long
and straight, channelled his gaze
    outwards and onwards and irises
so light, so green, implied nothing
    but light behind them, as if his mind
had fled to the back of his skull
    and bled every shadowy lobe.

As you carried him in to a sunless
    hall, behind your back, were
those eyes trained down on a lane
    where the pram still stood?
A white sheet rumpled, an awning
    of leaves shadowed on sheet
and hood. As you shifted his weight
    and revolved to the door
between him and the light, did something
    pass – like a tryst, deferred
drawn up through those eyes to a sky
    he was saying goodbye to?

★

New Year's Eve.
    Under a sky as high as this
we are cut-glass, space-lattices
    for broken narratives, like
mountain cities left behind
    through the mind's eye, revisited.

Pavement weeds are faint with light.
　　Birds raucous in the bushes.
Perspectives in the High Street
　　lowered, lengthened, acquire
the clarity of paintings. Glass
　　animals of childhood, horses

seals balancing on crystal globes
　　are as we are to the sky
whose distance finds no measure
　　between cloud and cloud, this year
and the next, being the same high blue
　　we saw when we were small

and our menagerie of bright revolves
　　already broken narratives.
Against the unbroken blue, nothing
　　is not nervous, alive with light:
stream, swans, bicycles, elude our need
　　to follow one train of thought

of wing or water, adjacent roofs
　　throwing down a flock of birds
like a gauntlet to the wind, stand
　　impassive as it lifts, whirls
on a clap of laughter... and as we
　　on foot, happy to be human, move on.

★

In this
　　country
the brilliance of
　　sun on snow
is as though

not love
but belief in love
   laid its hand on you

you the adolescent
   whose world was always
gilded, warmed
   even on its highest
snows
   and now
every berried branch
   you look up and through

slopes
   of builders' sand
remind you of last year
   when it laid its
hand on you
   gentle
as the turning of a
   calendar.

        ★

Here's dusk to burrow in;
   doorstep light where children
going home from school, mothers
   at the open doors of cars
forms having lost their shadows
   when the sun went down

become them. Trailing to peer
   dim-sightedly at a glove on a spike
creature or leaf curled on stone
   coin or charm in the rubble

as if, too late, they were looking
  to learn a landscape they know

wind will shift, night remove
  they freeze, sniff air –
freedom just yards from the warren.
  But thresholds braved today
as tomorrow's beckon, will darken.
  So catch, in the last of the light

the last child, mitten and scarf
  ankle and calf from kerb to car
the snowberry-white last gesture
  for that tail-end of our darkening
forms – *entre chien et loup* – that
  mark and its marked erasure

is the theft and gift, fang and fur
  of dusk, this double vision:
a sighting of metamorphic laws only
  dusk affords with menace and grace
but eyes inscribe, mistakenly
  as last transitions.

★

All yellow has gone from the day.
  I'm left with the blues and greys.

Pool of light on the desk.
  Strangely content. Perhaps

night is more my element.
  How white white flowers seem

skin showered, oiled, and the day
    but a night away. The days ahead...

★

While the tulip threatens
    to lose one leaf
and a pigeon
    perched on a tile-red roof

grooms another, ruff
    to the light
articulating
    irridescence on its purple patch;

while a small girl plays
    with her football in a coat
as red as tulips
    and my son now smiles at children

being a man;
    as days pass, post comes and goes
without news, across
    empty lots, back gardens

as far as
    waterways to mill towns
these urban tracts between us
    spread

as if they
    could be our river now
and these desks where we ply
    a trade, riverbanks.

★

Even if I never said
    or said too often what was
on my mind and you wore
    new shoes in plum-bloom

purple I'd made you buy;
    even if you did
head north when we were both
    due south, *if only* was

our only melody line
    and for good or ill, any *even if*
says it's a waste of time, I'd still
    regret and regretting, lie.

★

Darling, your message on the phone
    made me cry. I phoned you back
to let you hear the tears
    in my voice but your phone
was engaged. On second thoughts
    I'll write you this with
tears gone from my eyes and cloud
    like smoke from smokestacks
moving across a lining of blue
    that is our sky, that no matter
how clouds cross, yes, my smoke rises
    – I'm not smoking now –
we've always known lies behind them
    as the heart and breath behind
your vowels – such a long ah
    in darling! – as tears behind these
words, not sad tears nor tears

to lay on you, but dried tears to
'open the eyes of the heart'
    as they say back home – and this is
back home – to beginnings we always
    dreamed of, now lay a claim to
not knowing if dreams come true.
    I'd thank you but *'it hasn't a thankyou'*
and I haven't words large and clean
    enough – the phone's ringing now…
it wasn't you… and this sentence
    if I go on like this is never
going to end as you aren't with me
    nor I with you. I wish I could slice
that bit of the tape and keep it forever
    but neither you nor I know how to.

★

Is it before or after the fiesta?
    Have the revellers gone in
that the sunflower leans
    like a bystander in shade;
with the bowl of the fountain
    empty, holding last night's
laughter, is the wedding, fiesta
    today? Who are the bride
and groom, sea and sun, heat
    and flesh, in a sprinkler's
arc, are the bridesmaids sparrows
    seen through spray? Why
does an air of expectation meet
    before its joy, regret?

★

On a late summer's day that draws
    to a close as summer does
– one closing within another –
    I remember tree peonies

deep in shade, globe within globe
    wearing colours on their sleeves
like doublets slashed with crimson
    and regretting how flowers

so gorgeous, luxurious, seemed
    destined to a half-life, even
in their prime only ever
    half-open. Not my kind of flower

I'd half a mind to say.
    Now summer rises, rises
then droops its head. The stem
    of the sky's too weak for sun

lolling its face in shade.
    Summer's a slipped umbrella
the melancholy
    when everything's been said.

★

First you invite me to tea under your appletree and now
    send me a photograph of where we sat, you, still ill
by your herbs in shade and I in a wedge of sun angled
    under apples. Let me not break the chain. Send you
a poem of your photo of the patio of your new home, wish you
    entirely better. The doorway's as narrow in its light
as shadow's broad and black in the kitchen. Blackest of all
    your bike in silhouette. And the appletree just visible

where bright light grows on a shrub I'd know, if it weren't
   for those clumps of flowering light you knew I'd like
has no flowers. But what can I write that's not in the eye?
   How something tall and narrow can suggest a yardage of sun
an L, one arm of which you'll plant, where drainpipes ask for disguise
   with shade-lovers? How, in a city's heart, Elephant & Castle
you can be in the heart of the country, how knee-high trellises
   fronting allotments whose tenants stop to talk to you, spell
an other worldliness? But you know all that. How memory
   speaks to the image, image to the word. How inadequate
we are in our borrowings, not knowing if by saying *I'm like you*
   we do violence. Thank you for the herbs, tea, the photo.
Think of this as a postcard but more than that, a short time
   spent in your company, after the event, a recognition of those
differences we run into now and then, alternatives we never chose –
   patios with loaded apple-trees, herb troughs, neighbouring
histories of architects and saints in the churches of south London;
   other people's knowledge vaguely interesting, vaguely boring
lifestyles, lovelives and sometimes even illnesses worn transparent
   on a face that brings it home: the equity no one has in common;
differences that now and then make us feel are of less account
   than an hour or two – and I hate that word affirming but –
affirming, the way women do when we say *me too*, each other.
   (And the facings of your bookshelves like an opening accordion.)

★

Everywhere you see her, who could have been
   Monet's woman with a parasol
who's no woman at all but an excuse for wind –
   passage of light-and-shade we know
wind by – just as his pond was no pond
   but a globe at his feet turning to show
how the liquid… goes topsy-turvy, how far
   sky goes down in water. Like iris, agapanthus

waterplants from margins where, tethered
　　by their cloudy roots, clouds grow underwater
and lily-floes, like landing-craft, hover
　　waiting for departure, she comes at a slant
to crosswinds, currents, against shoals of sunlight
　　set adrift, loans you her reflection.
I saw her the other day I don't know where
　　at a tangent to some evening, to a sadness
she never shares. She wavers, like recognition.
　　Something of yours goes through her, something
of hers escapes. To hillbrows, meadows
　　where green jumps into her skirt, hatbrim shadows
blind her. To coast, wind at her heels, on diagonals
　　as the minute hand on the hour, the hour
on the wheel of sunshades. Everywhere you see her.
　　On beaches, bramble paths, terraces of Edwardian
hotels. In antique shops, running her thumb along
　　napworn velvet. A nail buffer. An owl brooch
with two black eyes of onyx. Eyes she fingers.
　　But usually on a slope. Coming your way.

★

Don't draw back
　　his lilac said.
Don't pin me down
　　his blue and grey.
Whose tears are pricking
　　eyelids? asked his pink
on snow. Mine, black answered
　　mine that light can't shed.

★

Light comes between us and our grief:
    flushes it out with gold.
And when skies are overcast, still
    we collude with clouds, building
grey to a spur for light that will
    drive us to stand at a distance
from ourselves, small at the barricades
    clouds burst to let grief go.
Light leaves us bereft in one sense
    only to flood us with sensation
bleeding out grief in a bright dissolve.
    There's something I can't hold
in the presence of light, great light, or feel
    as a river might feel for its stones.

★

Why does the aspen tremble
    without a trace of wind?
Under its spire, close
    your eyes, listen.
Listen to Khadijah. Her
    big heart beating.
He is bringing a new wife
    home today. Half her age.
Twice her beauty. Aisha, Aisha.
    Listen to the leaves.
What the Bosnian Moslem women say.
    The story they weave.

Khadijah is not jealous.
    Under the lintel she
stands, arms folded.
    Arms she will open wide.

Large, generous Khadijah
    ample-limbed…
A horse pricks up its ears
    backs two paces, whinnies.
And a current, faint
    as the morning star, runs
through her, air around her
    ripples, stills.

Like an arrow shot from
    a quiver, that impulse
loosed from her heart
    is caught in the arms
of aspen, sends a shiver
    through every leaf.
And thereafter, though there are
    no aspens in Arabia
though there is
    no wind, this is why
the aspen trembles
    over the bed's thin stream.

★

Boys have been throwing
    stones all day; even
the youngest – barely two –
    could throw stones that reached

the water. Years ago
    you threw them too from a beach
or bank and I, whose throws
    even dogs disdain, valiantly tried

to skim them.
    I read in Sylvia's diary
of stones the colour of fox – and so they are
    from a distance.

Apricot stones, filters.
    I bury them under a red-fox coat
of shingle. Camouflage
    so much of the past in my rush

to near the future. Far away as ever.
    Whatever the shore, wherever
the blue, letters locked in drawers
    rowboats, wells

in dogeared snapshots, postcards sent
    but mysteriously
repossessed years later –
    hidden pockets of a globe

we once called home
    are still at home and will
when I least expect, resurface
    in the gap between

boy and girl, whose stones soar
    and sink without trace
or land, marked
    'return to sender'.

★

Foreshortened
    light claws out of the sea
skin-puckered. Reluctant
    to leave the great outdoors
– benchwood warm –
    huddles behind grey towels.
Light's eyes are blurry with
    salt, heels white with water.

Fists knuckled and locked
    against his mouth, scanning
a roughening shore, he squints, wavers…
    Makes to go then, dropping
his towels, shoulder-blades twin
    gleams of sun, he's back in the swim
to brave out the day as
    yours lengthens.

★

On a diving-board, against
    a centrefold of sky they queued:
eyes rheumy, hair plastered, scars
    whitening under welts of pus
and queue there still as if
    in the after-image, sparkling off
into scythes of light, were the gold
    and ground of every plunging replay.

Knowing replay is not countless
    that water and its breaking
close on a lap behind them
    was it for this that they
showed no mercy, shrieking, shoving
    the weakest from the highest board

clowning about with variants
    on the perfect fall from grace?

Wanting nothing less than a commandment
    for themselves to hurl, shatter, resurface
into their features, for this they held
    nose and breath, plummeting faster
than the speed of sight, fell and kept on
    falling until, in that last recall
higher than the highest board, they froze
    in that blue inhuman air?

★

These hills are literally blue.
    And ryegrass pink
not with a setting sun but
    in the lie of grain, underside
of plaited heads wind's wave
    combs through.

As night comes close
    this far north, nearly
two months after midsummer's eve
    still light at eleven and
enormous skies nowhere near the end
    of their travelling show, wind

whips at my hair, tugs loose
    my clothes. Wrenches
out of my eyes, ears, frozen pen
    a scene, like the line
a croft, a tree and a Highland moon
    cleared to stand alone.

★

I have removed the scaffolding
    from the Parthenon. In the city
of the mind's eye, acropolis of
    dawn, now scaffold it with rays.

I have turned its north face to face
    east, ramparts into London smog
and where blue begins its columns rise
    where blue is clear, they end.

As for height, I have left it where
    it was, dwarfed in the eyes of Gods
at whose feet my chimney pots are
    fat, terracotta statuettes.

In place of white Pentelic marble, I summon
    time as a counterweight. Time
in the guise of sun too high for rays.
    And imagination too slow to keep pace.

Summon them in the name of lightness
    for by their own dead weight
they make our images so weightless
    that even in this short span, despite

millennia stone survives, this
    atonement, my monument to memory
has gone up in smoke, left nothing
    but a few clouds to bar its trace.

★

So high up in a house
    being alone is ethereal
like a wind curled up on its ankles
    precarious in a tree

or lung-stain of a shadow
    in a corner of an attic
you can't inhabit as every breath
    must leave its branch

hoarsely clamber down
    to converse with what is real.
So why delay? Is being alone
    the greater love, the greater loss

the ineffable, unreal: touch
    of a cold cheek rosy
in a lower room too much
    the open sore that never bleeds?

★

These homes in poems –
    how large they were. Upwards
and sideways. How they housed
    in sun and gloom, those loved
unloving fathers' ghosts
    mothers medicinal as scents
that drifted in from trees
    with unusual names.

These homes had attics, tea-chests.
   Country or cathedral views
woodsmoke like epitaphs
   scrawled indelibly on air.
Air was always resident.
   Charged with the many duties
loss imposes on a habitation
   whose owners are elsewhere.

(Air must don its apron, dust
   shafts of light, shake out
camphor and cobweb, breathe
   rings on the bell.) Above all
there was singing. As if the mind
   had climbed to its highest
landing, from an upstairs room
   someone's voice.

And the house rose only
   that this voice should be
embodied, bulwarked against
   wind by walls, rooted
in nursery furniture, friendships
   only flyleaves know
married to its elements, skeleton
   and soul and carried downstairs.

★

For those who have no homes like
   these, no fork in the road to mark
their winding route from others'
   let the house that the song sings
into being serve as a stopping-inn
   to share a couch, pass the jug

resing the song that will carry
over wilderness and mountain.

★

For you, who are
a large man, a large
man and a delicate poet, whose
flagstoned hall I have
stood on the brink of, ice-blue
walls been warmed in

and learned, looking at your
wife, your beautiful
wife – and you think so too –
how warm ice-blue can be
like an aureole for eyes
of blue, Nordic hair of honey

and slept in white and blue
on an empty floor
at the top of your house
padded in socks on carpet
to a bathroom through books
and books you have lived through

and that living-through I catch
a glimpse of, too awed
to envy, empties me till I am only
filled with a sense of books
unread, life unlived, a span
of time and space out there

much too late for the taking
    but not for lifting
as I did the patchwork quilt
    of blue on white, a corner of…
for you, I felt like writing
    a line, out of the blue, a poem.

★

When
    against a cloth
of blue
    silver linings are
reversed
    then, unfrocked
like a single
    diamond drop
vested head to toe
    in blinding white
light enters
    as *Der Rosenkavalier*.

★

The gate has
    five bars and five
bars of song
    for whatever reason I might
want to sing
    as I climb the stile to a
solitude
    escaping from itself
in smoke-filled rooms
    would be more than enough

to swing me
    as the river does
white heifer on the hill
    from the
dark side of solitude
    to its light-starved
underside
    silver-fir green.

★

I'm reading with the light on
    though it's 4 o'clock in the afternoon
and the skylight overhead, masked
    with a calico blind, casts
a whiteness in the air as if a blanket
    of snow had covered the pane
and light was filtering through flakes.
    Outside, the freshness, suspense

of after-rain. So the reading-lamp
    behind my shoulder, casting
a small gold glow, is relegated
    by natural light to illumination
that only alters colour. But since
    I'm reading poetry, that small gold glow
having little to do with visibility and
    from a source outside my vision, seems

to have taken upon itself the task
    of a farmstead light at the end of a path
when you first emerge from a forest –
    light that the poem heads towards

or has come from, light you don't read
　　lines by but between them by, warming
as the page descends. And when the page
　　is turned, the glow recedes so that

lamplight, skylight, gold and snow
　　merge and the first words you read
The dandelion does not yet blossom here
　　pull you back to their own
gold, light, snow, sky, up on to a ridge
　　– the old road between farmsteads? –
leaving the poem out in the open
　　and the forest on the page.

★

Times are – thinking about new wine
　　in old bottles – when the mind
flooded with sensations only
　　the old words make sense of, tastes
as if never before, their delicacy
　　of invention, proof of the pudding.
Such a dawn was this: of promise
　　and illusion, birds' proverbial choruses.

I mourn the untold usages still
　　redolent of grape, of yeast, if I had
new eyes, ears for the daily round
　　they sprang from, mediations
between man, nature, beast, little altered
　　in a world as young as ours – evil
being no disease of age, corruption
　　no condition of maturing.

I mourn their number
　　and their ease. Reading
won't bring them back. Rather
　　drive them further back to the cask
the cave they were laid down in –
　　the mouth and mind that framed them
mouth and mind that now
　　consign them to the bin.

Unless, that is, we read the world
　　that informed them with the same
immediacy we assume when we read
　　or word our own, and by doing so
find how the same words fit.
　　John, at dawn today I read your book
– as I wrote you, and I'll write it twice –
　　caught between two sleeps.

★

Like old red gold welded
　　by rhythm where the words
have cracked
　　snatches of a poem
set behind my back, keep setting
　　as the sun does.

I recite them
　　not by memory, by heart.
The rooms of memory
　　are dark. Rooms of the heart
flared with dreams where
　　blur-faced as white pansies

children lining windows
    thumb their nose
at memory, go
    fishing about in the bloodstream
for slips of the tongue
    figures of speech, puns

that work both day and night.
    Work
and then run out.
    What heart knows is rumbled
molten, eroded, with nothing to cling to
    but love. Memory's

a bad mother, neither oral
    nor literate.
Heart has her number
    holds her to
her smell, bare bones
    the heart's refrain like rock.

★

An Iranian professor I know asked me
    the first time we met, as he'd asked so many
students: *Saheb-del* – how would you say in English
    saheb-del, can you translate it? And each time
he pronounced the words his fingers tolled the air
    like a bell, a benediction. Years have passed.

Saheb means master, owner, companion; *del*
    means heart. Heart's companion, keeper?
Heart's host? And in those years I've asked
    friends who in turn have asked friends

who know Urdu, Farsi, and no one has come up with
    the English for *Saheb-del*. Is it a name

for the very thing that won't translate? And why
    don't I remember having heard it said?
They say it of people who are hospitable, 'godly',
    I'd say it of the professor himself. Trust him
to keep asking, us to keep failing, and if we can't recall
    its tone, tenor, with what word shall we keep faith?

★

I've always grown
    in other people's shade.
Not for shelter
    in solidity, neither they
being spreading oak or beech nor I
    some shrinking violet

but when a face upturned
    towards frail light, a voice
that interweaves between
    dark leaves a space for
flower, path for thorn, catch something
    of light's reach and axiom

then lower on the stem
    my edges breathe, droop
through dust re-invents desire
    not for gloss but growth
from this common soil, that upward
    thrust from lateral roots

to a realm
    wholly natural, and radical.
When a face, a voice
    like new leaves on a vane
promise turn by turn
    a view, on a spiralling belt

towards that light, then
    being roused I know
while upholding the crown
    in whose shade I too
throw shadow, I draw
    a freight of light in tow.

★

…Human beings must be
    taught to love
silence and darkness.

But in silence comes
    the seepage of
a gas fire's breath

in darkness the pink
    of a child's
mosquito net – it seems

their very presence
    is that love
for how else can we invoke

afterworlds without
    voice, light
but through things that

breathe and move, obey
    an absence
that is deified because

absence is unbearable
    unless, in a residue
of breath and light

we bear the agony
    of presence, and do
call this bearing, loving?

★

Nothing can ruin the evening –
    car doors slammed, voices raised
in the last of the light, voices
    without owners. And that's
a difference between art and nature –
    art transforming – voices, traffic
tawdriness – but in a gathering-in
    an almost selfish motion; nature
extending outwards as the shore its arms
    night its stars, an open invitation.

The palace of a ship at night
    blinking stars like cursors;
those disembodied voices from
    who knows which shore, drunk –
why note them, fail them?
    Torn between life and art, why is one
without the other like a shore without its sea
    night without its stars, why am I
– still beautiful – so unable to contain
    the ugliness, my own, in either?

★

It's the eye of longing
    that I tire of
the eye of fantasy
    lost in the grey horizons.

Having neither the heart
    nor talent for
invention, why should I
    – no child of mist –

be party to this cold
    imagination, its cloak
and hood, smuggled goods
    its faery in the dingle?

Where are my sunlight's
    givens? Near the sun
and far from folk
    an albino child, skin clean

as silver, hair white as
    snow, under the Simorgh's
eye as she flies
    over the Alborz Mountains

years later will hear her cry:
    ...behold my might,
For I have cherished thee beneath my plumes
    And brought thee up among my little ones

before she ferries him home
    gives him a feather to light
as a signal
    in times of trouble.

But this is my borrowed plumage
　　language, more strange to me
than this foster-tongue, this English
　　fairy godmother.

★

To be so dependent on sunlight
　　– small desires on the lookout
gull feathers snagged on slates –
　　is to be, in a climate
doomed to cloud, its changing mind
　　a paler version of the story:
he whose glory flew away from him
　　three times in the shape of a bird
whose wingspan was so great that rain
　　could never fall but when faith
at last deserted him and falsehood
　　took its place, fall it did to prove
that glory goes back to God, resides
　　with God, by any other name.

★

What is he looking for
　　the great white sun
throwing the force of his search
　　like torchlight onto the sea?
What he looks for
　　will be present
only as long as his looking:
　　what he fails to find
absent
　　to the precise extent

of his brightness
    blinding himself by reflection
while the passerby takes in
    a high sun, a broken

and a peninsula of violet
    the translation between.
It's darkness
    the white sun looks for
the one thing
    by the light of his eyes
he'll never see; one thing
    the brighter, further
he throws his rays
    the more recedes: it's
his shadow that he looks for
    and will never know
if it is God or self, friend or foe
    if it follows or precedes.

★

It lives in crystal, flame.
    At night like any man
creeps into a cave; moves
    by stealth, coming and going
by starlight, carrying tatters
    in its mouth, nimbus in its hair.

Who can tell on water
    if shadow's nibbling into light
or light at shadow's edge? Thus
    it is mouth and tail, tail

and mouth, ice or thaw, none knows
    which way they face.

It scavenges on breath.
    It is ear and voice, voice
and ear, by these it mates.
    Eradicates, illuminates
hunches down to ponder
    how weak, how bright, its chain.

★

As wave comes in on wave
    so light on light
but the one being
    visible, divisible
the other a metamorphosis
    by stealth

serves only to remind one
    how the mountain of
a life, growing to its star
    station, moon station
sun station and finally
    to the utmost limit of the sky

has all the while
    been burning, there
where poppies rout
    the dust, a fire to keep
blood moving, on the foothills
    of an outlawed faith.

★

It is said
     God created a peacock of light
and placed him
     in front of a mirror.
In the presence
     of God, being so ashamed at his own
beauty, his own
     unutterable perfection, the peacock

broke out in a sweat.
     From the sweat of his nose, God created
the Angels.
     From the sweat of his face, the Throne, Footstool
Tablet of Forms, the Pen
     the heavens and what is in them.
From breast and back
     the Visited House, prophets, holy sites, etc.

From the sweat of his two feet
     God created, from east to west, the earth.
The sea is
     glistening peacock sweat.
Tarmac too.
     From sweat of the peacock's feet of pearl
comes my window view.
     Perhaps I am formed from a trembling

drop on his ankle.
     Cypress, sunflower, bicycle wheels
grass dried in heat
     to the colour of wheat, all, all are
peacock water, peacock dew
     shame and beauty, salt and light
God's peacock
     in his consciousness, walks over.

Too much light is tiresome.
    Knowing this, today's
keeps its counsel. Tight-lipped
    the sky has closed its door
against the sea which
    like an aimless child
spreadeagles on its bed. The day
    is set aside for function.

Every shrub, roof, windowsill
    broods on its own
injunctions. Even birds on errands
    forget to play on thermals
winging it straight across the sky
    as though time and light
were the same thing, same task
    and every bird and bush accountable.

★

Light's sharpening
    knives of water.
I long for the coolness
    of a room downstairs.
White grapes. A morning
    cigarette. To take
umbrage behind hessian
    blow on a glass
of tea, sugarlump held
    between my teeth, taste
how bitterness
    too quickly sweetens.

Light's packed its water
    of knives in drawer

upon drawer of
    darkness. Where sea's
banded in shadow. Laid
    smaller silvers
out in the calm: glimmer
    of tines, crests
salvers and scoops, flatware
    embossed on handles.
And that downstairs room
    never to have, never to hold

the way Proust says
    on meeting with colons
that inviolate pause
    when a gathering falls silent
before it intones
    has brought him, while
reading, the scent of a rose
    which has never evaporated
though centuries' old, there it comes
    with its teas and spoons
luminous fridge, against the light
    bowed silhouettes of people.

                    ★

I've stored all the light
    I need. Stored it
in the dark jars of my body.
    Light's in its phase
of falling. Souring, sweetening.
    Boring us with its constancy

polishing, straightening. Light's
    like a grandmother tiring
pushing a strand of hair behind
    her ear, knees aching, sighing.
No one looks up, the sky's too bright.
    Four boys on seaweed ledges.

We look at the sea instead or
    inward to reservoirs
four-handled jars, fats and oils
    seven-herb pickle, smoked fish, spice
down to the cold slabs of our stores
    under bone and cartilage.

★

I loved you so much
    I couldn't bear the thought
of cold water on you
    dripping from your chin, hands

running down your elbow
    as you lifted your face to the sound
of footsteps. Smiled at me
    through water. Even

when the season turned
    and no one walked out of shade
to burn in sun
    you'd run the cold –

how cold your hands were.
    Nowhere, as the season turns
and I walk from shade
    or the smell of shade on a sunless

street, in and out of the shade
      of trees to find
no difference, will someone again
      bowing a silvery

head to a tap, move me
      to the kind of love that registers
on skin's temperature
      every shade of difference.

★

Air's utterly soft, back to its habitual
      cardigans and greys. Relief or regret?
I think of Jane, how she must have felt
      once her house was stripped of visitors.
Of myself. In days when they came en route
      to the States, Iran, bringing
their lifestyles with them. How they left.
      Leaving the house like a house

shorn of heatwave. Where a suitcase
      had been, how amplified the space.
Turmeric stains, a pot misplaced
      how aftershave can linger. And voices
of our own lives, resentful, neglected
      beginning to call from far away.
Or in another language – theirs. Crossing
      each other's waves upstairs, downstairs

making the town seem bigger, smaller
      its centre somewhere to go to
every day. Jane and all the immigrants
      whose families come to visit, overstay

their welcome, leave us holding our life
　　in two cupped hands, bewildered at
its lightness, like a fledgeling's, wondering
　　why it is they who have flown the nest.

★

And suppose I left behind
　　a portrait inadvertently
like a showercap on a peg
　　of this seaview that is hers
and insinuated between its clouds
　　strange glimpses of myself
that would alter her view
　　not only of me but of the sky
her mornings open out on or
　　worse, something of herself

either way some hurt would unfold
　　open out its own cloud, like smoke
would streak her air. Her air of...
　　Seeing ourselves beautiful
also hurts. No longer what we are
　　what we were we love but cannot claim.
Looking up, each time we do
　　is a silver seachange pencilling
light, shading, erasing
　　each time, each time a change.

And where is the singular moment
　　unwritten, that's free of pain?
As if by magic, silver lines
　　of the horizon have disappeared.

A black ship rides on grey.
　　Between everything is a distance
by which we know ourselves, ever
　　smarting in the gaps, between
clouds, ships, a child and his unseen
　　parents walking on ahead.

★

'Going away'
　　is not so much
a going away as a
　　coming towards that

part of ourselves which
　　in our daily lives
seems so curiously
　　absent, distant, then here

away from home, in a snatch
　　of song from a beach
at dusk, so endearingly, so
　　agonizingly close.

★

Finally, in a cove
　　that cups thin fog
like a hand its thirst
　　this indivisibility of
sea and sky like a grey
　　pearl between two claws

makes sense: as if a bay
    waisting a horizon, woman
twining legs around a man
    were what were needed
to make the horizontal
    more beautiful, more felt;

to interpose
    between eye and sense
a possibility in containment
    of the infinite becoming part
of what the eye can never see
    but the sense can comprehend.

★

It can come from the simplest
    of things: a room
tidied, new folders slipped
    from cellophane;
how a ballpoint runs
    without smudging or
looking up through smoke
    blue spiral veils
how your eyelashes
    become nets for light
so wherever you look
    light can't escape.

What makes it shimmer?
    The irrational and static
glow that invades and
    expands a space till

like a bubble full to bursting
    poised, infrangible
skin meets the outmost
    reaches of its waves.
And the shimmering starts.
    Thickens. Radiance
solidifies to a volume
    you can walk in, wear.

Dangerous, being so sheer
    it's also safe.
You wear it like a mantle, aura
    a superstition
you must not name.
    You call it *the shining*
secretly to yourself.
    Follow it down the street
carry upstairs to unwrap
    so its perfume fills the room
like flowers waiting for water…
    Make it wait.

Inside its capsule, time's
    both a sentence you
must run with, grappling
    blind corners, pursuing
a flare, and a silence
    coiled, sprung to mime
every flicker and feint
    in an eye, an ear…
don't lag behind, don't rush it.
    All you have to go on
is how footfalls sound, shining
    dims, trust and prayer.

Who put it there? You did.
    Who can again at will?
You can. What are its talismans?
    Desire, despair. See
how it came this morning
    from loneliness, boredom
a hint of rain; a move to
    call it in as you might a boat
rise to it as if to dawn
    tell someone else what you
call it. Dare it to live up to
    rise above, such names.

What is the light we walk into
    bathe in, wake to?
Of the two lights that it is –
    one sky's, the hour's
orientation of a room
    riveting in slants, slow
pirouettes, the other –
    what is that though?
that comes to meet the first.
    As if our daily darknesses
half-felt had, sooner or later
    to see the light of day.

Our own light I mean.
    Some sleeping thing
that rises, like a fawn
    from bracken, half-dazed
at its own liquidity...
    what fusion is it made for?
Flesh with its source of being
    silhouette and sun

in the open hand of a clearing
    or occluded green
the heart's dissolve, to die in
    be stripped of flame?

What deaths of ego, cynicism
    cowardice must we undergo
clinging to those darknesses
    we feed like ravenous mouths
forego, to unveil the simple
    moment, that open hand
on ours, both fingering back
    the curtain to reveal
a single ray? Of truth maybe
    aligning its core between
two lights, their shining eclipsed
    as its own is newly named.

THE CHINE (2002)

I

THE CHINE

To be back on the island is to be
cast adrift but always facing the same
mother who stays ashore, is always there
despite the mist. My balcony's a crib.
Through its bars the waves rush in. Not a ship,
not a gull, and the sky in its slow revolve
winding the Isle of Wight with a giant key.

We are spinning backwards in a slow spin;
we are in a time warp, a gap, a yawn,
a chine that cleaves the mind in two, a line
on the land's belly. Shanklin. Rhylstone Gardens
where an old man rolls tobacco, as sparing
with the strands as the years have been with him.
Luccombe with its own chine, barely a stream.

Every childhood has its chine, upper world
and lower. Time itself seems vertical
and its name too implies both bank and stream.
To be back on the island is to walk
in both worlds at the same time, looking down
on talus, horsehair fern notched through the Ice Age,
Stone Age, Bronze Age and still here at our heels;

looking up like an elf, ears cocked to silence,
from a zigzag of silver and silt. A chine
is a form of urgency to reach the sea.
As coastlines have eroded, chines, like orphans
stranded in a high place without their slope
of history, have had to take a short cut,
make deep cuts into the soft clay of cliffs.

Childhood has its railings too. And its catches
of glove on rust, twisted wire with a slight give.
Playthings. For in an upper world that turns
beachfronts into toytowns, patches of moss
into stands of minuscule trees, no railing
is not a harp, no rung a wind might play on
something other than its maker intended.

Every leaf must be touched and tasted, holly
tested for suppleness, mimosa dusted.
The mind has its work cut out by the senses
and analogies must be drawn, the unknown
be known a friend by citing its kith and kin.
Shanklin: I know you as you were, the timbers
of your pier, now gone, of your tree-stormed bridges.

But in the lower world we dream. We listen.
Not for water which is the sound of listening
or for schoolgirls passing above unseen.
Under lawns, hotels, we sit hours midstream,
crouched under a hundred blankets. If eyes
were ears, we'd hear the very mud-bed thicken,
rise in little mounds where the water's clean.

Every path brings us back to the beginning.
Shanklin Chine is closed for the winter, both ends
barred with notices. But the mind is not.
Or memory. And time is spinning backwards
with the mainland out of sight and the great plain
where herds roamed the floor of the English Channel
and were drowned by it flush again with valleys.

I look down on them, my own that were fed
by chines, from the long esplanade of light
on Keats Green and seem to remember walking
with my mother here, running my hand on railings.
The beautiful inn on the corner's a wreck
and there, at the bend, where the light's so bright
and people walking down the steep incline

pause at the top before walking down, black
against the blaze before their torsos sink,
something vanishes, there, where the path drops
and a young boy comes running down the hill.
Never, O God, to be afraid of love
is inscribed on a new bench where I sit,
facing the headland with its crown in mist.

THE RAIN CHAPEL

We are roofed under rain. Rain so great
we imagine it a cave, a chapel of timber
drumming us to sing. Our breath comes short
and cranky. We are children learning hymns.

Rain stands over us, patient, obdurate,
rain has faith. Of unimaginable beauty
is the voice rain has in mind. Our part,
though here we are as quiet as mice, mutely

lifting eyes to the rapping of rain. Rain's eyes
are steady. So many eyes has a cave.
We look down, not abashed by our performance
but by our lack of faith. We try to believe

in the voice rain has in mind, for a soundboard
needs melody, melody man while we –
but we are children and children are afraid.
O who will sing the solo? She will, no she will

and someone always does. But in our heads
we hear a voice not so easily betrayed.
Rain eases off and leans back. Sways, pedals,
glances back to the exit. Shines on slate.

For every cave has an exit and even birds
sing better after rain. And there we file
to the music, gratefully, as the last chords
rise to the rafters, tearing off our veils.

WRITING LETTERS

After chapel on Sundays we wrote letters,
ruling pencil lines on airmails. Addresses
on front and back often bearing the same name,
same initial even, for in some countries
they don't bother to draw fine lines between
family members with an alphabet.

Those who remembered their first alphabet
covered the page in reams of squiggly letters
while those who didn't envied them. Between
them was the fine line of having addresses
that spelt home, home having the ring of countries
still warm on the tongue, still ringing with their name,

and having addresses gone cold as a name
no one could pronounce in an alphabet
with no *k-h*. Some of us left our countries
behind where we left our names. Wrote our letters
to figments of imagination: addresses
to darlings, dears, we tried to tell between,

guessing at norms, knowing the choice between
warmth and reserve would be made in the name
of loyalty. As we learnt our addresses
off by heart, the heart learnt an alphabet
of doors, squares, streets off streets, where children's letters
felt as foreign as ours from foreign countries.

Countries we revisited later; countries
we reclaimed, disowned again, caught between
two alphabets, the back and front of letters.
Street names change; change loyalties: a king's name
for a saint's. Even the heart's alphabet
needs realignment when the old addresses

sink under flyovers and new addresses
never make it into books where their countries
are taken as read. In an alphabet
of silence, dust, where the distance between
darling and dear is desert, where no name
is traced in the sand, no hand writes love letters,

none of my addresses can tell between
house and home, neither of my countries name
this alphabet a cause for writing letters.

NOSTALGIA

It's a night for nostalgia he said.
I felt I was missing something, some
echo of nights we must have shared
in separate alleyways, far off home

rain drew him back to, or clouds,
or the particular light behind rain.
I was nostalgic for words, last words
of a poem I would read on the train.

There was a power cut today. I lit
three candles, ate lamb and read
by candlelight. The beauty of it
was too lonely so I went to bed.

It rained then. In the daylight dark.
I lay there till I heard a click
and voices. When the lights came back
it was like a conjuring trick –

there they were, the animated creatures
of my life I had thought inanimate
objects. And I was the one conjured
out of their dream of a dark planet.

THE ALDER LEAF

It is perfect. And of a green so bright
no other green has a say in it, fine-veined
and tiny-toothed, in short, a leaf a child might
choose to love, remember. And later, name.
Children love what is perfect, the best catkin,
blossom with each whisker in place. But sometimes
on a path they will halt and bend to a matted
object strangely furred, spun with gauze but numb
to prodding and hard as rock, neither insect
nor larva, stone nor egg and troubled both
by choosing and ignoring it or failing
to find something on a nature trail, loath
to ask but asking, *what is it?* learn nothing
of shit too late to name in retrospect.

WRITING HOME

As far back as I remember, 'home'
had an empty ring. Not hollow, but visual
like a place ringed on a map, monochrome
in a white disc. Around it were the usual
laurel hedges, the chine, the hockey pitch,
the bridge. On one side, the crab-apple tree
with its round seat, whose name puzzled me, which
wasn't surprising since everyone but me
seemed to understand such things, take for granted
apples can't be eaten, crabs can be planted.

Writing home meant writing in that ring, mostly
to Mummy. Mummy had a white fur coat
and framed in it her face looked tired and ghostly.
I am very well and happy, I wrote,
meaning it. Sensing somewhere in that frame
a face too far away, too lost, to worry.
And why would I? Worry should keep, like shame,
its head down in dreams. Sorry sorry sorry
I can't write anymore goodbye love Mimi
I wrote after only four lines to Mummy.

There's no irony in that. I was six.
Right from the start, home was an empty space
I sent words to. Mapped my world, tried to fix
meanings to it. Not for me, but to trace
highlights someone could follow: Brownies, Thinking
Day, films, a fathers' hockey match, a play
called Fairy Slippers, picnics, fire drills, swimming.
Even the death of a King. When my birthday?
I wrote at the same time, dropping the 'is',
too proud of my new question mark to notice.

My mother kept all my letters for ten years,
then gave them back to me. Perhaps they never
touched her, were intended only for my ears
for I never knew her then or asked whether
she made sense of them, if my references
to the small world of a girls' school in England
had any meaning. It was the fifties. Suez,
Mossadegh, white cardies, Clarks sandals. And,
under the crab-apple tree, taking root,
words in a mouth puckered from wild, sour fruit.

HOLIDAY HOMES

It's that particular yellow of stone
I recognise, though this is Edward Hopper
destabilising, I'm told, perspective: a lone

house on a hill, its face to sun, a runner
of gold on lawn spilling down the embankment
on to sprays of cedar, I think they're cedar,

with their backs to me; a perspective lent,
not only by the train from which this scene
is seen, though without any sense of movement

bar those lightning stabs of an acid lime-green
striking the branches, but also lent by
the painter's memory to mine – one keen

and empirical, the other, like many
people's traumatised by displacement, poor
and generic. These people claim how happy

their childhoods were, paint pictures even more
static than this. Ask them the year, they flounder,
don't ask them to fit the pieces, their jigsaw

is made of sky and sky was never ground
pieced into fields. I'll take this home for mine,
it's like any number of homes I found

placed in the wind. Cypress, cedar or pine –
it's all the same to me. Out of the painting,
I'm out of here for good, leaving a line

of families I borrowed, mothers, siblings,
a railroad track that like all railroad tracks
keeps promising without delivering.

I hate this house on a hill; ocean, outback,
dark side wall where the man, like a cockerel
up at dawn, wheeling his barrow, comes tacking

back to the front with compost, potato peel,
his useless, toothless grin. Where are they all?
No one's out on the lawn. It's early still.

That yellow frontage doesn't fool me, level
horizon hiding sea: I know it's there,
I can smell it, hear cutlery, the table

groaning with ham and jam, tremendous stir
of family. Taste toothpaste mixed with toast.
I have lived their lives, been their daughter, sister,

dog-walker, skivvy, peeled potatoes, lost
days and weeks out of my life playing ping-pong,
hula-hoop in holiday homes, a guest

for Christmas, Easter, friend who tagged along
not for the fun but for the hell of it.
Hell was other people's kindness: belonging

served on a plate like someone else's favourite
food destined to become my own with each
plump sultana bursting against my palate.

It did no harm. Imagination teaches
the mind the same; and love of humankind,
recognising ourselves in others, reaches

from house to house, hill to hill: but mind
is not a heaven, bright blue dome to spend
one's days under, lazing; or any kind
of friendly roof when cedars sough in wind.

SADNESS

It is difficult to know what to do with so much happiness
                                                    — Naomi Shihab Nye

With sadness there is something to rub against —
these, your words, for unhappiness is speechless.
Sad air breathes, at whatever altitude,
recirculating air. Rub it against glass

and the shape it takes is nothing but the melt
of breath. Follow it with your eyes along
the patterns of the curtains and it will trap you
in a leit-motif you can't escape. You're wrong.

When the world falls in around you, there are
no wounds to tend, holes to fill, no prop
of stubborn plaster; tenements don't crumble.
I've measured the ceiling for the curtain's drop,

metres are where I left them. *When the world
falls in around you, you have pieces to pick up,
something to hold in your hands* you say. Like this?
this button? A grey that fell, just now, a trick

of heaven? No, it comes from my green pyjamas.
Happiness sews on buttons. Sadness looks for
sadness to couple with, not comfort. The minute
I lift my head from the page, my heart takes over.

ALL THINGS BRIGHT AND BEAUTIFUL

No sooner do I wish for the random than
some pigeon comes belting out of the sky
towards me, is joined by another who squats
on the parapet while the first flies off,
gulls wheel above and a third pigeon comes
sidling round a drainpipe to make a pair.

Thoughts they might be in a mind like a sky
sometimes empty, sometimes – for here comes a flock
filling the window – active, frantic, cluttered.
More is due to luck than we like to think,
fearing the random, out of control, the mess
life without consequence would leave us with.

Remembering how in chapel the idea
of goodness, justice, was as palpable
as the doe, hare, small creatures hung above us
in a Tarrant watercolour, how hymns
and their mystifying words nonetheless rang
true as I would be in the vows I made,

as the faith that they and their keeping would
be welcome in the world – remembering,
in short, innocence, I find it so hard
to let go of the verb 'to beget' – how good
begets the greater good – to believe in luck,
good or bad, and against it, helplessness.

Where are the birds now? Drifting in a loop
like cinders. Roofed, I am under their wings,
overhead beating, gliding, or above them –
my dark fat pigeon on the guttering,
poking that black head out of his collar like
an idea not sure if it can make the distance.

CHILDHOOD BOOKS

They always saw me through; kept me indoors
lying belly down on a counterpane,
stretching the hours on a single bed, poring

over cowboy annuals frame by frame,
The Famous Five, Black Beauty, Little Women –
scores of books remembered only by name

and the room, atmosphere I read them in.
It was a shared room and the maroon carpet
where I spilt black ink, the guilt of it, summon

a room-mate calling, *aren't you coming out yet,
when are you coming out?* and with it, all
the turmoil and agony books create

while a ball thuds against an outside wall,
the sound of sevensies echoes on stone,
I fall behind in coordination skills

but run ahead past endings to the questions
endings leave you with, answers you supply,
authoring every journey but your own.

For what was mine but a hole in the sky,
a non-event, half a wing in a window?
Did sun glint on its rivets? Did I fly

by myself, was there land or sea below?
Or simply a drop to the answers I wrote
too young to have answers, too long ago?

Today I'm infinitely sad. Afloat
with nothing to attach my sadness to.
Though it's March and nearly too mild for coats.

And ground is sad, sad for us who are no
gazelles – how long it takes to cover paving
stones. How rarely we run and then only to

catch or miss a train, I never liked running
not even then – long before I smoked.
You can't run and be sad I suppose. Being

sad's like finishing a brilliant book.
Becoming aware of the time, the room.
That tear-stained patch on the pillow. Stroking

the pillowcase, between finger and thumb
tweezering a quill that had scratched your cheek,
pulling it out to unruffle the plume.

Sometimes a tuft of balding down was stuck
to the shaft. Sometimes a blade, speckled, dipped
and blew, too limp to use. It all comes back.

How you tickle a feather along your lips,
lick them, balance moustaches under your nose;
stick with a snap barbs that cross over, slip

into troughs like a zip whose teeth won't close;
then with all the flight gone out of its vanes
how you drop it, knowing no one will know.

How a whole life, a whole childhood can drain
away without someone to see it go.
And yet, here's a hole I remember plain
as the day: a pinprick left in the pillow.

LYRIC

A lyric couldn't do what birds do, could it,
alighting at random, swinging from line
to line, driving at the reader. Some birds
against buildings, grey on grey, disappear
entirely, dying in and out of colour,
or white-winged, black-winged, differentiate
too briefly to inhabit the memory
of such a small three-dimensional plane.

Birds seem designed to be seen against sky.
As the lyric is designed to be seen
against self. Slanted on a background where
whatever matches blends and is interred,
whatever holds its own ground, black or white,
argues depth and whatever hovers, craves
descent, struggling to alight on a skyline
but failing, having to fly, flies out of frame.

SIMORGH

for Carcanet's thirtieth anniversary

Simorgh sat on top of the Tree of All Seeds,
beating her wings, causing the seeds to fall
at the feet of thirty birds. Of *si morgh,*
as we would say. But whatever the language,
however far-flung, birds follow the fling
of seed and so did they. Round the globe, singly
but in tandem, she led them to the world's end.
Who are you? they cried, from raven to wren,
and what are we that have journeyed in fog
and suffered these wounds on the way? And *Simorgh*
replied, rubbing her feathers on each wound,
not as we would salt but as healing rain would
plumes of glass: See, your wounds are wiped and with them
the space between *si morgh* that hides my name.

LISTENING TO STRAWBERRY

for Aubrey ('Strawberry') de Sélincourt

I knew it as the poetry I could never hear
without his voice to give it utterance
and the way it ran inside me was clearer,
closer, than the way it ran in others

though they loved it too, owned it too
but owning so much else, loved it that much less.
Owning so little now, I recall how he drew
it out with pipesmoke, through long crossed legs

out of the earth as if he, so long and lean,
were a brook for the vowels to run through,
knocking consonants like little stones
to quaver in their wake. Certainty can quaver too.

And still retain its faith. Outcast
in its deepest spells of orphanhood, the soul
can recall – through memories of grass
and place, a shaking hand on a pipe's bowl

that indicates a turn of phrase – an undertow
to weather, a companionship that being human,
echoing high in leafy woods, confiding low
when at our lowest, deprived of human company,

makes deprivation sweet to bear. And for
those of us who heard him, in our girlhoods
when girlhood was still a word to stand for
a kind of kingdom, a wreath around our heads,

it was a binding that netted us together
like wild strawberries never safe from bird
or hand; a murmur I can still remember
with or without remembering the words.

MIDDLE AGE

There are those who are radiant confronting
death in cornflower blues and violets.
There are roofs that kneel to large shapes of sun
submissively as cows to the sky's gait.
I protect myself from happiness, rooting
into the search for it, mourning its youth,
though it's the lesser courage that admits
to unhappiness, to gladness, the greater.
What did we vow we'd be in middle age? –
young of course. Immortal. Assuming process
reversible by that effort of will
only gods possess, protean, promethean.
Knowing we'd die but not knowing how tired
we'd get, even of loving, how we'd fear
emotion. No one tells us. How we'd get
our second wind from death and even then
only those who are charmed, transformed by grace
we think a miracle – who knows what strength
it takes, who only sees those blue eyes bluer,
who only sees apparel. No one tells us
about middle age. Forget teeth, sight, hearing,
what about the heart? You'd think it a dumb
organ, stones in its well, a clobbered clock
not knowing moments from minutes, stone itself.
I tell my heart to move, it doesn't. Look,
I say, what do you like out there, tail feathers?
It looks but doesn't see, sees but can't name.
It's middle-aged. I think of Keats and wonder
how one so young could feel it rich to die
till I remember illness, pain. And though
here I am healthy, knowing pain will pass,
from where I am I catch the drift of it –
a wind that blows the other way. Or rather,
doesn't blow but being ever more easeful,
makes me see, as if in a glassy surface,
fingers dragged in the shallows of its wake.

RIVER SONNET

Welling up in her fingers, water runnelled
seaward through stones. She wasn't watching water.
Or thinking of tomorrow – how time funnelled,
flows. Water was doing her thinking for her.
Draining down her thoughts till they ran as lightly
as leaves across a playground, rose to torment
branches that had borne them, betrayed them, nightly
blurred distinctions, daily held to their bent
and finally torn loose. She heard the river
babble, level, contradictions resolve in
a rush, out of her hands, felt quarrels fly
in droves. *Who-o-o* the river sang, *who-so-ever*
clouds rang round the sky, sky thinking itself in
river, river thinking itself in sky.

GOOSEBERRIES

Birds are chirping now rain has stopped, their songs
like the rain are silver. I hear the silence,
the music of panic, of loneliness.
Rain passes like unhappiness and birds
sing happily out of the same dull silver.
It is all the silvers of cloud and cold,
the white shine of illness. A friend lies dying
in hospital. The night I saw her there
we watched fireworks from her window, her window
filled with photos and dried flowers for real
flowers are infectious, fireworks at Christmas.
When two times meet, another friend says, stories
must end – by which he means, when day meets dusk,
the page must be marked, the book closed and children
while away their questions. I heard a story
of a child who, it was foretold, would die
when the leaves began to fall; when they did,
a sister, brother, sewed the leaves back on
but how the story ended wasn't told –
besides, the dying do not want our questions.
Today I bought a card with berries, currants,
each translucent as a small wineglass held
against light, each tiny globe marbled, jewelled.
The flurry of birdsong behind the curtain
has gone: now and then the trill of a latecomer.
Every morning I wake alone. Today
I find the balm and bitterness. The sweetness
of pulp, pop of a taut skin, gooseberries
a friend on the phone tells me a hen used to
lay eggs under, two eggs you'd have to slide
on your belly to reach so prickly was
the bush, with hairs sun shone through on the berries
fine as the hairs on the back of a child's hand.

Twice a day two times meet. Between the two,
like a prayer between two palms, the bookmark,
the memory, is placed. When day meets night,
night meets day, we must hold our breath, delay
our need for answers, live with what comes next.

II

THE INWARDNESS OF ELEPHANTS

The Wishing Tree

Where do those poems go, the ones
we wake from, take back to sleep and oblivion?
In what book have they been written?

How deep and dark the book, how full,
how cavernous – a book of all the ages,
grey fish crossing the open page.

It's Christmas Day. I've been given
a wishing tree. Wishes hang from its branches
like silver fish, wishing me stardust and linen

robes, golden moons and skylarks, bright
coloured sandals and tinkling sounds like Ariel's:
it's a poem, a red heart beating in a well.

Three elephants walk the rim and chocolate coins
I will never eat ring the earthenware. I'm caught
between the two – between air and water,

heaven and hell. I sing better
in the air. Underwater I am dream and agony,
sin and righteousness – who am I

in the ocean's depth? *And may your God hold you
in the palm of his hand*, one of my wishes
ends with. It went right through me. Something Irish.

Who is this God who holds my fields in rain?
I think of his palm. Of Iran. The gold
hand of Fatima I gave a friend on a chain.

My wishing tree's gone dark. Gone the way
those poems go. Underwater it bursts into flame.
On it is hung my God, my friends, their names.

Silhouettes

I've been reading Vendler on Graham
mornings in bed. They're blending together,
weaving in and out of each other

like seaweed through surf.
I don't know which road to take
into my daughter's flesh. And if,

inadvertently, I come upon a snapshot
stuck on a fridge of two small boys in shorts
– one small, one heartbreakingly big

for I remember slipping hands under his armpits,
hoisting him up and how T-shirts twist
and everyone thinks he's older than he is

in those great big feet – then my whole
week gets skewed and I'm guaranteed
bad dreams. Unravelling skeins, skies, bleeding

into water, over my head, under my hips.
This is how I lose a daughter,
how I make red water wield the whip.

These are the body's tokens,
this is how the spirit is broken
night after night, dream after dream.

I've bought myself a watercolour. A sunset
and silhouettes. A mother and her calf, two trees
and a flat horizon. Strange humps like refugees

huddle on their backs. They can't be towers.
What are those humps? I asked her brother.
They have passed one tree, they will pass the other.

Mammont

Long before the mammoth there was
mammont, an enormous creature
with feet resembling a bear's.

In Estonian, *maa* and *mutt*
mean 'earth' and 'mole' and indeed
mammont lived underground, ate mud

and sometimes on subterranean walks
poked its head above ground
only to duck back down for it found

sunlight hurtful, so hurtful
it perished in the open air.
Elephants still hate the glare.

But in moonlight
they spray themselves with water
and discreetly, under its fountain, mate.

Are you the year's last sun then,
husband? snow in your hair?
It's a long time since we've spoken.

Once, long ago, at the mouth
of the Lena river, a mammoth
was found with an eye and brain

still intact after isatis, wolverines,
foxes had fed on it and skinned,
the remains were sent to St. Petersburg

where they fuelled endless debate.
The body, however mutilated,
records what the mind forgets.

Elephant Man

Films about the British Empire
are invariably monochrome – sepia – the colour
of tea and biscuits my son says and we laugh

in one of my fields of tenderness.
He himself is a field. Taller than
the tallest grasses, higher than the highest

mast in a bay. He faces the horizon,
hides his eyes by facing the other way.
He has tried travel. The song of whales.

He himself is the music he cannot play.
I am the wrong note he says. I change
my tune but I'm no piper, and my range

smaller than my strength belies and my breath
smokier every day. Of all the songs earth's
creatures sing, I aspire to the elephant's rumble

too bass for man to hear. Because it covers
distance, because it moves the herd. Mothers
are always wrong. Whatever the song,

whatever the note of anger, love, despair.
And their song travels deep inside them,
down to their boots, down to the roots they tear.

My son stares out of his eyes as if to torch
his brain. He covers his head in a towel
for the world is covered with jawbones, burial

grounds the thaw reveals, I look like
Elephant Man he says. He eats his meal.
Potatoes mostly. Shovels them through the crack.

White Gold

Back from India, my daughter gives me
a carved filigree elephant, a baby
inside it tooled from the same grey flesh.

Is it ivory? I ask, as if chinoiseries,
chessmen, dominoes, combs, piano keys,
daggers, rifle butts, hunting horns,

inlaid pulpits and mosque doors, Zeus
at Olympia, Athena in the Parthenon,
Tutankhamun's chair, Solomon's throne,

weren't enough white gold plundered,
not to mention hair and tails turned
into fly whisks, ears into tables,

feet into umbrella stands and even
eyelashes sold to guarantee fertility
and the desired number of children.

No, she says. And my cow proliferates.
On boxes, bedspreads, mugs, cushions,
in jasper, wood, brass, ceramic processions.

My favourite elephants are on a black
glasses case: two calves embroidered
in shades of pink, one rose on powder,

the other reversed. I attract them the way
I do children: a whole orphanage of elephants
on presents, cards, surrounds me on my birthday

and from Oregon come cuttings – Chendra
has anaemia, Pet eye surgery, and in Kenya,
when there is no ivory, there are no orphans.

Buddha

Queen Sirimahamaya
was the most beautiful of women.
No pedestal was ever placed higher,

no purity deemed whiter
than hers. One summer night by the light
of the full moon, she dreamed

she was transported to a palace
on the peak of the Himalayas.
There, she had a dream in which

a silvery-white elephant descended
from the mountains, entered
her room and bowed down before her.

In its trunk it bore a lotus.
Impregnated, the Queen gave birth
to the fruit of the divine phallus

under a tree in the tranquility
of the Lumbini Garden.
Such was Buddha's reincarnation.

I tell you this for no reason other than
that it's delightful. I've stolen it.
I envy her. The zipless fuck. The man

and not the God, the sex and not
the birth. Speechlessness. Though
in real life it was precisely that

I objected to, oh where were the words?
How many deaths I died in silence.
In God it is meet, in man, violence.

Literature

is one of the saddest roads remember?
that leads to everything, so Breton said:
el camino where a traveller,

slumped in his saddle, wanders;
a motorway in Sophia where a cyclist's scarf
flutters; by a stream you hear laughing

and catching a glimpse of, wonder
how a stream so small and dry
could dream itself a river:

all the roads you have ever sung to,
fought back tears in, helped a blind man
cross and crossed again,

all our sad processions, down to the very
smallest, on some dry
and dusty shelf.

Mothers dip their nose to a baby's scalp
like animals at water. Come up for air.
I smelt a sweetness in your hair,

close to the scalp, something like
stale cake. I smelt blossom on the landing
and thought of Louise Glück

– mock orange – asking how could she
rest with that odour in the world?
I fed the lemon tree you gave me

summer food for citrus then the clocks changed.
Through the barking of the dog
I sensed the length of its chain.

Darling

Darling was a word I used to throw
casually downstairs. Catch! a ball
big as a child's head bouncing lower

step by step. Down in the dank
of the cellar, under the jut of planks
and legs, lies something warm and friendly,

approachable as fur.
Whose is the voice of poetry,
the animal's or the keeper's?

There I am, small, dark, wordless
but something bright and shining
in me wanting to be heard.

The world is full of infrasound –
sudden flight, a meal abandoned.
Crossing a ford at sundown, the herd,

each mother with her calf shielded
from the arrow, a hide
too thick for arrows, a field

of tenderness, pit of spears.
What will you make of it, keeper?
Catch these tears.

This is where I am
in the smoke of a cigarette.
Darling, sweetheart, angel, poppet,

I wreathed them in, children, husbands.
Protect me! I demanded
and they disappeared.

The Wedding

I dream I am to be married.
A big affair. I search the grounds
for the groom – there are flowers, garlands,

stepped lawns, strangers everywhere.
Down some steps, a room dark as a mausoleum.
The doors are open. They sit prepared.

The family dead. Undead.
My favourite aunt who has broken off
relations, great-aunts, grandmother, stiff

as statues, old as Methuselah.
And where were you at the wedding?
Groom, husband, the only male.

Entombed in your own nightmares:
a mammoth once on the family
roof and you saving us; once, an animal

you said was the most beautiful thing
you had ever seen, rising
from a lake. And someone knifed it,

knifed it in the eye, a boy
you saw running in the distance, but all
I saw was moonlight, lake, animal,

a unicorn rising like a lady,
a knife, a flash, someone running and you
were that someone, yours was the beauty

you couldn't bear. We are who we dream of,
we are who we dream of, I tell myself over
and over when I am plagued by nightmares.

Mahout

We trust each our own elephant
till our own elephant kills us.
The attendants holding the silk umbrellas,

the one who plies the fan
of peacock feathers, the man
with the flyswatter of yaktails.

You cannot cheat on the amount of oil
poured in the lamps for an elephant
will always honour the pace of the ritual.

Nor is the elephant's love less manifest.
He will insert his trunk, like a hand,
inside your garments and caress your breast.

He will follow, with his mate,
the undulations in B minor of *Iphigenia in Tauris*
or, on solo bassoon, *Oh, my Tender Musette.*

And the cow will stroke him with her long
and flexible member before bringing
it back upon herself, pressing its finger

first in her mouth, then in his ear.
While over their transports, whistling fire,
the harmony of two human voices

falls like summer rain.
Meat that walks like a mountain
among giant flowers, huge nettles and lobelia.

Child, don't be afraid.
The circle of nine precious stones
is never absent from his forehead.

VILLANELLE

No one is there for you. Don't call, don't cry.
No one is in. No flurry in the air.
Outside your room are floors and doors and sky.

Clocks speeded, slowed, not for you to question why,
tick on. Trust them. Be good, behave. Don't stare.
No one is there for you. Don't call, don't cry.

Cries have their echoes, echoes only fly
back to their pillows, flocking back from where
outside your room are floors and doors and sky.

Imagine daylight. Daylight doesn't lie.
Fool with your shadows. Tell you nothing's there,
no one is there for you. Don't call, don't cry.

But daylight doesn't last. Today's came by
to teach you the dimensions of despair.
Outside your room are floors and doors and sky.

Learn, when in turn they turn to you, to sigh
and say: You're right, I know, life isn't fair.
No one is there for you. Don't call, don't cry.
Outside your room are floors and doors and sky.

THE PIANO

You have found your digital metronome.
Where, you didn't say. I have never said,
or always said in so many words, how a piano
is nothing to the weight I bear. Your throat
so soft, feet bare, where you played the violin
in pyjamas, and the black and white cat whose instinct
for camouflage would draw him to the stool
when we weren't there – you didn't find it there.

Downstairs. On the ground floor of our lives.
Nor, in a flat whose floors walk into trees,
was it anywhere near the old metronome,
broken, mechanical, you'd repositioned;
flung aside with your oval clock I rescued,
reassembled, dismissed the missing sliver
of glass no one'll notice. The piano tuner
didn't steal it then. – Just as well.

A body is a thing of dread. A thing
of guilt. Desire and dream. Something
to purge with percussion. How rare it is
to merge with, to have your own organs sing
through another's. See, it has taken blindness
from your touch, the grime you took from newsprint,
down escalator rails. Milk will revive
its ivory. It must be cared for in silence.

And even a piano must have water.
Be tempered to the precise pitch of health.
How it hurts you. Hurts where you have already
hurt yourself. It is in step. I will take
the shawl it has worn so long only washing,
ruining will remove its folds and dents.
I don't want to remove them. Such a worn-in
fit is rare. I am cold. I'm cold, Tom, play.

WINTER DAWN

Winter dawn has more doom than dawn in it.
Words on your lips. Dream words that made you wake.
That you must now translate. And born in it,
in winter dawn, out of a language like
the one you can't remember, like a lamb
being licked into shape, a child-self, the child
you spoke those dream words to, will say 'I am
what you said I am, though I'm not the child
you thought to comfort in your dream, small boy,
your boy, but you, you as a child, as lost,
and just as brave.' But it's hard to enjoy
your own voice sounding like a therapist
and not at all like telling a child you love,
a child who's wracked, *I think you're very brave.*

TERRAPIN

My daughter's fish are fine, she says,
three so small they haven't yet
changed colour; two fantails.

In shortening light our days
will be nosed through glass,
an afterglow of holiday.

She's got two tanks now.
One for fish, one
for a terrapin she's rescued.

They take up all her
living room, what with
friends crashing out, a father

for a lodger. They're thinking
of buying a boat, *don't*
I'm dying to say. Boats sink.

One I heard of left no trace
but a teddy bear floating on the canal –
true or not, boatpeople are always

saving cats, scraping hulls
and sooner or later moving into flats
they take months to redecorate.

Time my son moved out. Where to?
Where'll he put his piano? Who'd
put up with it? Round and round we go

swapping rooms, beds. September's
my own aquarium I was going to say.
My memory's getting short as a fantail's.

THE EVENT

Draw a floor plan of your childhood house,
place a cross in one room, write the event.

If the cross were a single star – for stars
these nights come singly – on a paper flower
I could fish out of black waters, if water
didn't wash out ink, ink was magic ink
forgotten languages were written in
and memory the floor where I could kneel,
unfold and smooth the crumpled sheet, decipher
over a flame the starword, codeword, godword,
I would. Believe you me I would. I'd pore
with all the strength my eyes, wits, left half, right half
of my brain could muster over that crease,
cross, whatever the sign, could be a sound,
bell, cry, to lead me backwards to a street,
house, this one not that one, this with the trellis,
through its door with that same brass knocker, up
those worn blue treads. Floor plans would be no problem.
Never mind the event. I know what that is,
it's the poem. This one and every other,
happening, sprouting, coming up like nettles
in a rash of words. I've lost heart in them.
Today is my daughter's birthday. My pregnant
daughter, sleeping daughter. I'll let her sleep
her sickness off. I feel sleepy myself.
(When she wakes, your baby wakes, lift her
up to the windowsill, to her red giraffe
and watch her widen eyes of pure grey slate.)

BABIES

There ought to be another word for babies.
Painters should paint them like women, the size
of continents, cloud formations, whales, Bacon
should have been their high priestess, specialised
in mounds of pink, primal soup of pink, muscled,
boned, straining away from buckles and braces;
dropped on all fours, teetering at odd angles
to exit from canvas, howling in cages.
There ought to be a God, capable of
metamorphosing into every hurdle
of a dream: a heel on the rung above
your hand, a Lucifer under your heel.
There ought to be a word, a God, for us:
us mothers, protectors, dreamers, creators.

IL BACIO DELI

for Sara

A baby, brown as its mother is blonde,
sits gurgling at the table next to me
under the yellow awning of the new
lilac café. It must be statutory.
The last time I was here a mother sat
with her newborn, her husband, a pregnant friend
and hers. Soon, Sara, you will be among them.
Young mothers smiling in the shade of cafés.

I liked the day we sat in the pub garden
– under an apple tree I think it was –
with a wasp Brian said liked Branston pickle.
The way you asked sharp questions at the printer's.
And how you smile, dimpled. Whenever I sit
in a café or park I've always said
– and did perhaps that day at High Wycombe –
babies swarm round me like wasps, noisy, sticky,

with their noisier but not so sticky mothers.
I came here to write, in peace and quiet; despite
the traffic, to rest my eyes tired from reading
poems to e-mail at the Royal Mail
and hundreds more for competitions. A bus
draws up, almost at my feet but I still hear
that mother and her baby going bye bye
bye bye, call and response, jingling a rattle.

They're staying though, while she bounces a foot,
clean as only a child's can be who has yet
to flip-flop pavements, know what bye bye means
and not to smile at strangers. Sara, I wish you
many cafés, and may strangers smile on you
and your child, as they will, and you smile back
as you will, knowing a grandmother's smile
when you see one, knowing we're never strangers.

THE SUZUKI METHOD

When I was nine they gave me
a half-sized violin and half-sized feelings.
When you were seven we gave you
a Cornflakes packet sellotaped
to a ruler. We gave you footsteps,
placed them in a boat and asked you
to stand in them. You stood.

You rowed your boat lightly,
jerkily, according to the numbers.
All the mothers in the class
were charged with the same numbers.
You stood in a fleet
of boats. You learned
to find your balance.

The fleet sailed.
Some boats capsized.
Some are sailing still in all weathers.
In the meantime, the mothers
forgot the numbers. Sometimes
at the bottom of an escalator
they heard them played by buskers.

Your feet are calloused now
with white callouses. Perhaps
they're fungal. And your
lips are white with foam.
No one wipes them.
They have given you medication
to give you half-sized feelings

– Yehuda Amichai's words.
I cut the pills in half
but even half a pill's enough
to fell an elephant.
I listen for your breath.
Cot death. Now you are twenty-six.
And I am fifty-seven.

EDEN

In this country, nature is green on green.
In mine, green grows out of ochre, fawn, dun –
what are the colours of dust? Caught between
fruit trees what are they but shifts of the sun?

In this country, grass and tree are implicit
in each other, as in water. In mine,
dust and tree are awkward friends who elicit
only the same blessings at the same shrine.

But it's dust that deepens shadows, the tree
that plays on colours watermarked by shade.
When shade is deep as water, roots drink deeply,
and drinking from the same pool, friends are made.

If only we were dust and tree. My children,
grown from my poor soil. I imagined Eden.

III

LIFE IN ART

With the simplicity of frost,
the muddy depths of dream
you can't recall and yet, lost
as they are, they gleam

with the clarity of snowflakes
melting under an eye,
an ambiguity that wakes
to rain's late lullaby

with words as small as pronouns you
or I could take as ours,
a big heart and an old one, new
only in its scars

the way a thistle's colour draws
a thumb along its brush
and tells you it's not spiny wars
but softness that can crush

the way children know breath rises
like white manes in the mist
and lovers look for no surprises
on lips so often kissed

with these and other ways in mind
I might seduce a verse
to wake to, speak with, touch and find
that poetry's no worse

for frost and mud, snow and rain,
the languages of war,
of love that fears to hear again
abuse it's heard before.

I might renew acquaintance, mend
walls I never breached
or breach them now and not pretend
I practised what I preached.

I might forget my small concerns,
leaning against the jamb,
watching the world go by that turns
me into what I am.

And as for larger griefs – well, they
are the dumb stones in my heart.
They will not speak nor I betray
life in art.

SNAILS

Thousands there must have been, scaling the wall,
hanging from stems like sloths, lined under thistles.
Two were coupled. One slid along the coping
inch by endless inch, many waved their horns
as if in dream and in the undergrowth were
hosts of them, households hidden from inspection.
I stood staring, horrified, fascinated,
horror dissolving into something close
to tenderness. I walked to the Post Office
on the watch for them. Other gardens, driveways,
clumps of weed by railings, everything, even
the people, seemed peculiarly bare. As if
there were too few of us, too much space,
as if Stoke Newington were a new country
and I should be glad to be living here.

THE FABERGÉ EGG

Lilies of the Valley Easter Egg, 1898

It is born as a shape, the shape of birth.
    Always the same shape but no sooner born
than form, the buried form spring must unearth,
    must make new, however timeless or timeworn,
calls to its maker: 'What am I, what am I
    beyond my shell? Am I fish or fowl, flower
        or fruit, whose roots are these, whose clay? What lies
            in my white mortuary,
rocking, crowning through slippages that shower
    stones on my head?' And its maker replies:

'These are the hands I have trained for you, these
    their veins. Running across the grain, so thin
not one runs straight. Let them run with the ease
    of grasses, tendrils, stems, over the skin
I stretch for you, look, against the light, fine
    as pink enamel, how the sun's glow steals
        through each soft web, soft as a fontanelle.
            See how my fingers shine?'
Form nods its head. And each nod breaks, peals
    into a lily of the valley bell.

Bells so true to life, life's put in the shade.
    'In these fonts I'll christen you in ablutions
of gold rivers, turn you through ruby, jade,
    diamond, pearl, rockcrystal revolutions.
And under the crown that will spread your fame
    with three Easter kisses, a "Christ is risen",
        "Yes Christ is truly risen", I'll install
            heads in a threefold frame.
Who but a goldsmith would think to imprison
    their likenesses in such a small cathedral!

The Czarina, she'll thank me for it. Olga,
    Tatiana, their father Nicholas…
As for these hands that work as well in vulgar
    gunmetal, on copper pots, nickel, brass
shell casings and grenades – it's not your hoard
     or your precious stones a new world will praise
      when a mother's love has bitten the dust
       and you're banished abroad
but these, their skill.' There's no response. Buds raise
    their heads and hang them. Droop as lilies must.

THE LOVE BARN

Remember the swallows – or were they
swifts? – in the love barn where the wooden
rail we peered over might have been
the height waves tip out of over
rocky pools or the bar of a certain
Sicilian café scattering waiters
like birds or the fence of a driveway
where lupins grow tall as you were
in the barnlight where we stood, leaning
over a railing, smelling the hay.

THE COAT

I'm travelling to meet you, through a long
black tunnel with one strip of yellow light
into the New Year. A good year, this one,
I feel it in my bones. Warm in red fleece
and my fingers red with bad circulation.

How we've circled each other through the years,
travelling north to south and back again.
Waited for light at the end of the tunnel.
It flashes on my paper. Sunstrobe. Flickers,
steadies, flickers again. I lift my eyes

to red housing estates, soft greys and greens
of England. How lovely it is to travel
on a quiet Saturday. And tomorrow
I'll be on the train again, heading home,
missing you and most likely knocked off-centre.

We must have reached an impasse. Lovely to
stop, draw breath, lift eyes to the russet golds
of embankments, purples of winter branches
and only on ploughed fields the dearth of colour
I take for granted travelling on trains.

How small the houses are. How sweet it is
vanishing out of a weekend. I see
too many colours to name. How quietly
they talk me down, gainsay my view of England.
Do the same. Quietly so I don't notice.

Wear me down, my view of you. As you meet me
at the other end. In your new warm coat
that doesn't fit. What colour? Not brown again.
Not black, not grey, I'll leave a space I'll fill in
later. Here _____. (We've just arrived at Luton.)

JUST TO SAY

I miss you – let me count the ways –
morning, noon and night;
I miss you on my darkest days
and when things for once go right.

I miss you in the inbetweens,
in shades of grey and gaps,
like bowling-alleys miss their greens,
lost mariners their maps.

I miss you like the tide its mark,
a church its congregation,
Londoners a place to park,
refugees their nation.

My old mistrust gives up the ghost,
my new misfortunes don't,
I miss the boat, the bank, the last post,
the film, the joke, the point.

I'm a misfit in my own skin,
a fist without a glove,
a bow without a violin,
an amoeba in love.

Counting pebbles on the shore,
I'm splitting hairs much finer
to mount up ways I miss you more
than all the tea in China.

I'm Christmas without mistletoe,
a firework missing fire,
so lost without my Romeo
I'd settle for the friar.

Yes, a misbegotten mismatch,
a score without a song
for a good-time girl in a bad patch,
a ding without a dong.

I missed my chance, I threw away
the line and missed my cue
the day you rang me just to say
miss you, miss you, miss you…

MOVING THE BUREAU

for The Philatelic Bureau, Edinburgh

I've never owned a bureau. If I had,
I'm sure I'd move it. I move everything.
Compulsively. I'm not sure I even know
what a bureau is. But what furniture
I do have, moves and I move with it. Dance
with it really, left, right, left right left, up
to the skirting board, back into the chimney.

And then admire it. See who else to dance with.
I'm sure a bureau would be admirable
in its tact and adaptability.
All those cubbyholes. And drawers and flaps.
I could keep my stamps in it. First day covers,
Millennium issues, letters, cards, catalogues,
bulletins, bills, then move the whole shebang

again if necessary. Which it would be.
Size is never what it seems at first glance.
The first dance never wholly innocent.
And once you've moved one thing, everything
shifts: that play of light on the wall, the way
your hips swerve corners, even in the dark,
and your hand unerringly finds the switch.

Even the way you think or don't think changes.
But once you've done the tango, quickstep, mastered
the paso doble with a fridge, a bureau's
nothing. A Nureyev. Baryshnikov.
Lord of the Sword Dance, of the Highland Fling.
Hermes on heels with impossible wings.
A bureau's a beau with a secret spring.

SONG

I have landed
as if on the wing
of a small plane.

It is a song I have
landed on that barely
feels my weight.

Sky is thick with wishes.
Regrets fall down
like rain.

Visit me.
I am always in
even when the place

looks empty,
even though the locks
are changed.

TENDERNESS

I washed the grapes, let clear water run through them
till my nails went numb, gave them hours to drip
lopsidedly from sieve to sink while I rinsed
the small Greek cucumbers, laid them in rows,
patted them dry, sluiced the fat vine tomatoes.

I did this for you. Took you in my mouth.
Lingered over you. Ridges rose along
your feet, ribbed them like miniature canoes.
I lay still on the shore. Not talking, smiled
as you rabbited on, your gripes, your jokes.

I aged myself as slowly as I dared,
once in a while suggested walks. Waylaid you
under the young acacia, looking up
into a word for green that was a word
for gold. Let you sleep to a silent phone.

Now you house me. Stumble on my misnomers
under the kick of language, catch my drift
in a chance remark and hurry me home.
Tenderness, ah tenderness, you observe,
on the tip of your tongue, a hint of cachou.

I am the silk page at your fingertips
running down on me, the fruit you revolve
and leave mapped in bloom, the blur of a lens
you lift a shirt hem to, rub over, breathe on,
I am the way you see the world anew.

LOVE IN AN ENGLISH AUGUST

Twice I've gone as far as the High Street phone.
For no good reason. But to rein in passion.
August in London. Making time my own.
For while sun comes and goes, love is on ration,

lying open to the weather, on heat,
on hold. And I was never one for halfway
houses, never did learn to compete
with mild-mannered sisters, cope with rebuff,

temper quarrels with jokes. Freak storms with sighs
like small rain when drought's at the door. False comfort
to borrow heat from the sun when sun lies
under leaf, heat under cold. 'Temperate'

let's call it, for it cuts both ways, this trope
to prove even a full sun brings false hope.

To prove even a full sun brings false hope,
largesse earns little thanks, recall a cot
we broke, you mended, badly, as if rope
could hold together sleep as delicate

as that, a corner cupboard, big red cushions,
yellow mugs, the colour and history
two people meeting late in life might fashion
a new life with, leftovers of a party

the other wasn't party to till later
in the kitchen, when salad's at its best,
telling it how it really was, they savour
rich pickings, scrape the trifle bowl and test

the water, breakages, take out the trash.
For no good reason. But to rein in passion.

For no good reason, but to rein in passion
or rather, give it free rein, for without it
how can I swing goodbyes, stroll from the station
late at night under trees and sing about it,

how can I not 'concentrate on you'?
Perhaps, like that letter I wrote from school
about a fancy dress party, it's true:
to win a prize all you need do is truly

'consantrait'. I never knew – I've just looked it
up – I was going as a wedding cake.
And you, marking your one Lottery ticket
do, I recall, pause, concentrate. Good luck.

And keep it. My share I mean. Strictly on loan.
August in London. Making time my own.

August in London. Making time my own.
So quick to tell me everybody steals it
and I let them, where are you thief? Don't groan.
Own up. Where's my life, what thicket conceals it,

where've you put a decade and more, my prime,
my time with the children out of my hair,
over the hill and far away, that chime
of my maligned spinsterhood? Is it there,

under those papers, books you never read
or, tired of good intentions, pitched like tents,
dropped out of diaries, left lying in bed
with clothes? Come clean thief, where? And where's the sense

in playing for time? Here, sign the confession.
For while sun comes and goes, love is on ration.

For while sun comes and goes, love is on ration?
Can paupers then imagine, when sun's nailed
to the spot, rimmed round with fire, that creation
might decree free rations at least till sun's sailed

out of sight? No chance. So don't hold a glass
up to sky. Love's chained to a rock, come rain,
come shine, and heartache's been put out to grass.
But if sun's nailed to the spot and love chained

to a rock, then each in the mirror sees
what I see: who I was, became, am now.
Double-locked. Three skylights opened to tease
my menagerie of moths. Some huge, some slow,

too slow for me. Their wingbeat for my heartbeat.
Lying open to the weather, on heat.

Lying open to the weather, on heat,
on Hackney Downs, accompanied by Dante
and Love, his 'gaze on the ground', with *La Vita
Nuova* blurred by sky, I'm near where we lay

that once… but you wilt. Sigh. Abbreviate
my name, short as it is, hitch up your glasses,
rub your eyes, gaze into space as if fate
had called from a long way off and impasses

were all you had to go by. Love, so at ease
with bluffs, why don't you revisit a side road,
from a whole lawn pick one of poetry's
old standbys: dandelion clocks I showed you

how to tell time by. Blow. There's still a half-puff
on hold. And I was never one for half.

On hold. And I was never one for half-
etched outlines, loose holds on reality,
but with wingtips skimming grass and its rough
nap pricking shins, wind in my hair, with every

circle they describe, head-high, birds go through me.
Weave passages through flesh and blood, a rush
and throb of beat and swoop, a brush to groom me.
Groom me for vanishing in the clear plush

of air, flesh and fell, absorbed by the sheer
drive of it. And I, my own drives on hold,
who thought I could always steer on course, veer,
take leave of my senses, give in. To cold

winds from your halfway, your 'when-can-we-meet?' –
way, houses. Never did learn to compete.

…way, houses. Never did learn to compete…
might be a fragment unscrabbled from sand,
torn and stained, heeled in from untrammelled feet,
from a stone where an ode, elastic band

were once balled around it; a message sea
spewed, a bad dog chewed and salt or saliva
made the first word run, the last bleed and me
mad about it. For I'm no deepsea diver

to fish unfathomable meanings nor
a mermaid wed to their beds where old seadogs
get wrecked, snore an eternity and more
and she too dumb to kick them, stick those hogs,

make no bones about it. I just get tough
with mild-mannered sisters, cope with rebuff.

With mild-mannered sisters, cope with rebuff,
With sweet serenity, keep your mouth shut
And when charity moans 'nothing's enough
For love, true love', give up those fags, you slut.

Called you a slut once, remember? Of course
you do. Wouldn't even bother to answer
the question. So why is it such a source
of embarrassment to me, yours? Mine never

was to you, was it? Of course it was? Oh.
Forcing me to kiss with a mouth rinsed out
with ashes, was that lust? Hardly think so.
Don't like to think what that was all about.

Thought I'd sing a song. Try it on for size.
Temper quarrels with jokes. Freak storms with sighs…

Temper quarrels with jokes. Freak storms with sighs.
That's no song. That's a dirge, mirthless and dour,
'defeated' you'd prefer. And I, loath to rise
to the bait of your defeat being ours,

ours mine, would give nothing away. No use
crying 'when's my turn to be given to,
given to first?' when someone who'll refuse
you nothing, nothing spare, is driven to

give in the ways he can, and can't, and won't
deny he's failed. I wish you had. Wish I
had allowed you to, asked for less, said 'don't
feel that way'. But you did. I didn't. Why

bolt the stable door? Feed self-pity? Covet,
like small rain when drought's at the door, false comfort?

Like small rain when drought's at the door, false comfort
pocks my sleep and I ache, dowsed with the feel
of you, you and you and you, to stay anchored,
moored to black rivers, grounded on the keel

of dream rows unresolved. Dream men, you motley
crew, shape-shifters who slip the hold of nightmare,
shiver in a shaft of motes, ghosts, I'll shortly
have you. But daylight brooks no see-through nightwear,

limbs in limbo. Daylight melts you. Like smells
you could swear you've scrubbed of all trace and can't
understand why they're still in your face, bells
that keep ringing after they've stopped, you'll rant

and rave, finally cave in. Dumb disguise
to borrow heat from the sun when sun lies.

To borrow heat from the sun when sun lies
in your voice, spring from the air when larks sing
at your approach, blush from a peach when fruitflies
buzz as you unload, shyly, everything

money could buy, I'd like, you'll cook, and one
wholenut bar I'd wish were bigger if only
I were smaller, is to belie the sun,
moon, flowers, trees, birds and bees, ads for lonely

hearts I read, secretly, and you don't. Don't
make me do all the wrong things now, like long
to love you. Don't turn my views back to front,
undo my vows, break my heart; leave it strong

enough for being, when sun's desperate
under leaf, heat under cold, 'temperate'.

Under leaf, heat – under cold, 'temperate'
skies now intemperate and glowering
with storms – takes the last of the sun, irate
with gnats, mosquitoes, chainsaws. Flowering

ramblers wilt on walls. England is at peace.
Your country, tiny island, devastated.
Mine, no news. Darling, we are refugees
from love, nurture, nature. And implicated

is our own, so unable to sustain
what is alien, intractable, fuse
colours of a flag into alltime rainbows.
Why not raise the white then? Let's call a truce.

Hand out blessings. Play archbishops and popes.
Let's call it, for it cuts both ways, this trope.

Let's call it, for it cuts both ways, this trope,
this bluff, this marriage of true minds, sly two-way
mirror, bending-the-truth-twice telescope.
Star to ships that pass in the night, a blue bay

that sparkles, green havens, earth's heavens, scrub
them all out, redraw, rewrite them. But this time,
each to his own, don't share them. Only trouble
is, won't they look the same, find the same rhyme

for thee and thine, rivers of wine and maidens'
veils so fine you can see not only limbs move
but marrow through them? For how many heavens
make one, which is the one on earth but love?

And love's not one to – oh grope for it, grope –
to prove even a full sun brings false hope.

To prove even a full sun brings false hope
how many times, when it blazed, did we cling
to shade, pronounce its grey, slippery slope
as safe and flames, homespun, poor candled things

the merest breath can snuff, as passions breath
inflames. Hatred, revulsion, rage. How many
flares did we scorn, each spark a shibboleth?
Prove me wrong. Show me an ear of corn, any

golden thing that grows, any vine tomato
religiously watered, courageously
staked on a windowsill and swear that no
fire, no faith inspired it. Outrageously

prove me wrong. This once. But go it alone.
Twice I've gone as far as the High Street phone.

GHAZAL: WHO'D ARGUE?

If I said every tear, each sob, each sigh
quietens, stops and all our tears soon dry,
                          who'd argue?

If I said every voice stung to the cry
'What is the point?' doesn't want a reply,
                          who'd argue?

If I said time will tell, heal, steal, fly –
take it, give it, do with it as you're done by,
                          who'd argue?

But if hopelessness did, who would deny
its right to be heard, if hope were to try,
                          who'd argue?

Who'd argue over love? Who'd follow my
example? You, my love? Then who am I
                          to argue?

DON'T ASK ME, LOVE, FOR THAT FIRST LOVE

after Faiz Ahmed Faiz

Don't think I haven't changed. Who said
absence makes the heart grow fonder?
Though I watch the sunset redden
every day, days don't grow longer.

There are many kinds of silence,
none more radiant than the sun's.
Sun is silent in our presence,
unlike love, silent when it's gone.

I thought that every spring was you,
every blossom, every bud;
that summer had little to do
but follow, singing in my blood.

How wrong I was. What had summer
to do with sorrow in full spate?
Every rosebush, every flower
I passed, stood at a stranger's gate.

Weaving through our towns, centuries
of raw silk, brocade and velvet
have swilled the streets in blood. Bodies,
ripe with sores in lanes and markets,

are paying with their lives. But I
had little time for the world's wars,
love was war enough. In your sky,
your eyes, were all my falling stars.

Don't ask me, though I wish you would
and I know you won't, for more tears.
Why build a dam at Sefid Rud
if not to water land for years?

Though we'll never see the olives,
ricefields, shelter in an alcove
from the sun, in our time, our lives
have more to answer to than love.

THE MEANEST FLOWER (2007)

I

THE MEANEST FLOWER

i

April opens the year with the first vowel,
opens it this year for my sixtieth.
Truth to tell, I'm ashamed what a child I am,
still so ignorant, so immune to facts.

There's nothing I love more than childhood, childhood
in viyella, scarved in a white babushka,
frowning and impenetrable. Childhood,
swing your little bandy legs, take no notice

of worldliness. Courtiers mass around you –
old women all. This is your fat kingdom. The world
has given you rosebuds, painted on your headboard.

Measure the space between, a finger-span,
an open hand among roses, tip to tip,
a walking hand between them. None is open.

ii

Cup your face as the sepals cup the flower.
Squarely perched, on the last ridge of a ploughed field,
burn your knuckles into your cheeks to leave
two rosy welts, just as your elbows leave

two round red roses on your knees through gingham.
How pale the corn is, how black your eyes, white
the whites of them. This is a gesture of safety,
of happiness. This is a way of sitting

your body will remember: every time
you lean forward into the heart of chatter,
feeling the space behind your back, the furrow

where the cushions are, on your right, your mother,
on your left, your daughter; feeling your fists
push up your cheeks, your thighs, like a man's, wide open.

iii

The nursery chair is pink and yellow, the table
is pink and yellow, the bed, the walls, the curtains.
The fascia, a child's hand-breadth, is guava pink,
glossy and lickable. It forms a band

like the equator round the table. The equator
runs down the chair-arm under your arm, the equator
is also vertical. The yellow's not yellow
but cream, buttery, there's too much of it

for hands as small as yours, arms as short,
to encompass. Let tables not defeat me,
surfaces I can't keep clean, tracts of yellow

that isn't yellow but something in between
mother and me be assimilable.
Colours keep the line to memory open.

iv

Here where they're head-high, as tall as you, will do.
This is the garden in the garden. Here
where they're wild and thin and scraggy but profuse
such as those ones there, these ones here, no one

looking, no one within a mile, you'll find
flowers to pick and to press but before their death
at your hands, such small deaths they make of death
a nonsense and so many who would notice?

with the best ones, flat ones, left till last, take time
to take in the garden, the distance from the paths,
the steps and the terrace crunching underfoot.

Soon you'll hear a whistle. The garden is timeless.
Time is in the refuse, recent, delinquent.
Go as you came, leaving it out in the open.

v

As if they were family, flowers surround you.
As if they were a story-book, they speak.
They speak through eyes and strange configurations
on their faces, markings on petals, whiskers,

mouth-holes and pointed teeth. They are related
to wind. Wind is a kind of godfather, high up
in the branches. They're willing you to listen
to them, not him. Even now you're too old

– though too young in reality for most things –
to understand their language. Once, you could.
You can feel the burn in the back of your mind,

as you hold their gaze, where the meanings are,
too far away to reach. What creature is it
that can stand its ground, keep its mind so open?

vi

There are stars to accompany you by day.
After you've gone to bed, they fall to earth
like dew but, to accommodate that dew,
presumably fall first. You've seen the fluff

from your blanket, a blue cloud in the air;
hooded in your cloak with its scarlet lining,
walking between the pine trees late at night
seen stardust so fine you took it for granted

or took it for vapour, mist, a kind of mistake –
the way a sleeve rubs chalk along the blackboard
and the numbers smudge, x's disappear.

Well then – you've only to turn a midnight sky
upside down to show, when they close above,
the stars below of chickweed, speedwell, open.

vii

The pink primrose flower's an aberration,
a nail discoloured, blood clot on a yolk,
a cuckoo in the nest. How did it get there?
You'd like to pull it out, out from the clump,

beak it like a worm. This time it's an odd one
but sometimes the whole clump goes red as if
some shadow had passed over and instead of
letting it pass, the blooms had taken on

the stain themselves. The yellow ones are true
registers of light and shade but the pink ones,
no matter how bright the sunshine, far away

an overhanging hedge, can never change.
They carry the shade inside them, their veins are blue
and your blood runs cold to see they too can open.

viii

Because you are a child, the earth's dimensions,
of which you know so little, rise to greet you.
Walls, albeit with peepholes into orchards
long abandoned, may be too high to scale

but who would want to scale them when scale itself
and a wall risen up like earth at eye-level
have appointed you like Gulliver to dwarf
the already miniature: ivy-leaved toadflax

mimicking waterfalls, curtaining caves?
The same insect cities you'd see in grass
you now see in stone without bending, stooping,

and your spine is a wall itself. For this,
you are thankful: earth's horizontal shelves
standing, like a glass museum case, open.

ix

These are the things you have made or have yet to make:
six knitted egg-cosies, a sailboat in cross-stitch,
the coronation coach replete with its team
of horses painstakingly cut out and glued,

an apron, a book of miserably pressed flowers,
countless milk bottle-top pompoms, embroidered
handkerchiefs and one darned for Janet Blue,
all of them neatly and the last passionately.

But materials are intractable
whereas spelling, grammar, punctuation,
bend to the curve of your thought and your thought,

brighter than any needle, magnetised
to their rule, kneels to their rule: a knight errant,
lifting his visor as the Queen's casements open.

x

You're not the centre of the universe
nor do you wish to be. The very thought
fuels your fear of fire, of Joan of Arc
terrifyingly bald, burnt at the stake.

You'd prefer death by invisibility
and diminution, death by camouflage
in florals. You don't think of dying, however,
hovering on the edge of being noticed,

organdie sleeves perked like butterfly wings,
your antennae alert. In later life
you will home in on fields of tiny flowers,

an infant's fading kaftan pinned to the wall,
Annette in an orange shawl, linings, borders,
bindings and trims, each dot, each floweret open.

There was always that familiar ache:
finding your own spot under the trees to read,
the heart always gravitating to love,
still smarting from the last humiliation.

There was coconut ice in pink and white,
between sugar and spice, time to apportion.
You were always fair. When it came to tears,
however, you were mean, a veritable

Scrooge, a Shylock crying out for his jewels
while all the monkeys in the wilderness
scattered and scrambled, gesticulating wildly,

until the savannah, the whole plain, was bare.
What *were* the thoughts that lay too deep for tears?
Oh monkey-child, it's time to lay them open.

I think of Wordsworth's hermit in the woods,
that shrivelling in the heart that leads one deep
into solitude, the longing for it,
as if life were not already too lonely

and a grandchild learning to shred a catkin,
as you once did, no more to be cherished
than her catkin stems. I am entrusted with them:
in one hand, balled, a nest of rusted tails,

in the other, stripped stalks I'll gratefully
chuck from the train. Poetry's on the run.
From exhaustion, the inability

to imagine a larger world and one
too sick to be hurt into words. Be kind,
sweet April, you with your mouth, first vowel, open.

GHAZAL: IT'S HEARTACHE

When you wake to jitters every day, it's heartache.
Ignore it, explore it, either way it's heartache.

Youth's a map you can never refold,
from Yokohama to Hudson Bay, it's heartache.

Follow the piper, lost on the road,
whistle the tune that led him astray: it's heartache.

Stop at the roadside, name each flower,
the loveliness that will always stay: it's heartache.

Why do nightingales sing in the dark?
Ask the *radif*, it will only say 'it's heartache'.

Let *khalvati*, 'a quiet retreat',
close my ghazal and heal as it may its heartache.

GHAZAL: LILIES OF THE VALLEY

Everywhere we walked we saw lilies of the valley.
Every time we stopped were more lilies of the valley.

Umbrellas passed – fathers, sons,
holding out a hand that bore lilies of the valley.

Every citizen of France
bearing through his own front door lilies of the valley.

But we were out of the know,
though reluctant to ignore lilies of the valley.

Our first May Day in Paris,
knowing nothing of folklore lilies of the valley.

Of Jenny Cook and Chabrol's
buttonhole the night he wore lilies of the valley.

He who sang *Viens poupoule, viens!*
and started the fashion for lilies of the valley.

How fashion then conferred, free
on *les ouvriers* at Dior, lilies of the valley.

Mais nous, sacré bleu, who knew
of charmed *muguets des bois* or lilies of the valley?

And though I wore the perfume
I have always worn before – lilies of the valley

– Diorissimo that is,
no one whispered, 'Meem, *j'adore* lilies of the valley'.

No one made false promises.
And if France did, who blames poor lilies of the valley?

GHAZAL: THE CANDLES OF THE CHESTNUT TREES

I pictured them in the dark at night –
                the candles of the chestnut trees.
Their name alone made them self-ignite –
                the candles of the chestnut trees.

I pictured them in the pouring rain
as they really are, pink-tinged on white –
                the candles of the chestnut trees.

How many there are and each the same!
same shape and colour, angle, height –
                the candles of the chestnut trees.

Seen from below, most unseen,
they throw no shadow, cast no light –
                the candles of the chestnut trees.

I saw how distance matters more
than nearness, clearness, to see upright
                the candles of the chestnut trees.

Inspired by 'Christ the apple tree',
I looked for a figure to recite
                the candles of the chestnut trees.

Lacking faith, I could do no more
than find a refrain to underwrite
                the candles of the chestnut trees.

As May drew on, the more I saw,
the more they lost that first delight –
                the candles of the chestnut trees.

I've searched for sameness all my life
but Mimi, nothing's the same despite
                the candles of the chestnut trees.

GHAZAL AFTER HAFEZ

However large earth's garden, mine's enough.
One rose and the shade of a vine's enough.

I don't want more wealth, I don't need more dross.
The grape has its bloom and it shines enough.

Why ask for the moon? The moon's in your cup,
a beggar, a tramp, for whom wine's enough.

Look at the stream as it winds out of sight.
One glance, one glimpse of a chine's enough.

Like the sun in bazaars, streaming in shafts,
any slant on the grand design's enough.

When you're here, my love, what more could I want?
Just mentioning love in a line's enough.

Heaven can wait. To have found, heaven knows,
a bed and a roof so divine's enough.

I've no grounds for complaint. As Hafez says,
isn't a ghazal that he signs enough?

GHAZAL: TO HOLD ME

I want to be held. I want somebody near
                                        to hold me
when the axe falls, time is called, strangers appear
                                        to hold me.

I want all that has been denied me. And more.
Much more than God in some lonely stratosphere
                                        to hold me.

I want hand and eye, sweet roving things, and land
for grazing, praising, and the last pioneer
                                        to hold me.

I want my ship to come in, crossing the bar,
before my back's so bowed even children fear
                                        to hold me.

I want to die being held, hearing my name
thrown, thrown like a rope from a very old pier
                                        to hold me.

I want to catch the last echoes, reel them in
like a curing-song in the creel of my ear
                                        to hold me.

I want Rodolfo to sing, flooding the gods,
Ah, Mimi! as if I were her and he, here,
                                        to hold me.

GHAZAL: OF GHAZALS

Ah sweetheart, you have sent me a book of ghazals.
You have sent me a bough and a brook of ghazals.

I have even become tears to live
in your eyes. Let me live in their look of ghazals.

Shahid is dead, great poets dying,
but his swansong is hung on the hook of ghazals.

May the rarest editions of love
bring us both to a shop with a nook of ghazals.

If love's too dear, Mimi, then wander,
penniless, in a long empty souk of ghazals.

II

THE MEDITERRANEAN OF THE MIND

i.m. Michael Donaghy

It's not just the heat and sunlight
I love so much in this landscape
as the whiteness of the ground,

glare of limestone, occasional
shells among stone and rubble,
ground feeling lighter than sky

as though heaven were already
here, and real, and detailed.
White dust rims my toenails.

The peaks of the far mountains
are so thick in mist one can't tell
if they are flat-topped or belled.

Villagers, in their mind's eye, supply
the missing crowns, their true shapes,
and cockerels points of the compass.

Everywhere else, death is an end.
Death comes, and they draw the curtains.
Not in Spain. In Spain they open them.

Many Spaniards live indoors until the day
they die and are taken out into the sunlight.
The duende does not come at all

unless he sees that death is possible.
The duende must know beforehand
that he can serenade death's house

and rock those branches we all wear,
branches that do not have,
will never have, any consolation.

★

Playing at house is divine.
What would one do with handfuls
of lavender picked on the hill?

I like the mixture of frugality
and generosity both of the village
and landscape. Lemons have spilled

to circle their trunks and wild
pomegranates silhouette crags.
Small and profuse, white figs,

ripe when they're splitting their skin,
are there for the reaching and
almonds galore that refuse to crack.

Fresh limes too and persimmons,
green on the tree, with the callow bloom
that will still be on them when they're red

and people ill-informed in the ways
of persimmons will eat them,
thinking they're ripe, and pull a face.

They are vessels for jam and properly
eaten only when the vessel's skin
is thin as glass and as clear.

The local delicacy is *turrón*,
'a blending of sugar, almonds,
orange blossom, eggwhite and honey

from bees that have dined solely
on rosemary'. Though how they
police the bees I've no idea.

★

As you'd expect, the morning
was quiet as a church, the doors
and windows shuttered, not a dog barked,

cock crowed, nor did the earth-shaking
tractors (usually one man and his dog
sitting on the hood), trundling

up the Carrer de la Mare del Miracle
under my window, pass. Even
the weather knew it was Sunday,

being chilly and overcast. Then,
as though someone had turned on
a radio at full blast but even more

immediate and loud (I thought
it was upstairs in the little apartment),
a brass band burst into full song.

I rushed to the window in time
to see a small group of followers
vanish round a corner and shortly after

they came again, on the other side,
this time preceded by a band of stout
women in turquoise shirts who handed out

leaflets to the women in doorways,
stopping to chat and laugh. Meanwhile
the musicians stayed tantalisingly out of sight.

Later, I saw a thin girl in red Lycra
with her clarinet and clip-on score
going, I assumed, home for lunch.

★

How joyful the sudden music was.
The whole village sprang to life.
Here, on the quiet mountainside,

I feel like a child, dependent on doors
and windows – or in this case, pines –
for a glimpse of shining brass.

Like flying above a hometown,
knowing your own house is somewhere
down there or passing it by train

behind all the familiar landmarks.
Seaside music without the sea.
Seaside music in a small Catholic

mountain village down in the heart
of the valley and the sound
rising to the very mountaintops.

Earlier in the week, I was listening
to the builders just behind the villa.
For every blow of the hammer,

an echo, more sound than echo
so clear it was, answered back
and where the echo struck

behind the sierra, I imagined
an invisible pueblo growing nail
by nail as the hammer fell

and the echoes nailed them flat.
But the fancy is never as inventive
as reality with its brass bands.

★

Tonight, a gecko is silhouetted
inside the glass of a streetlamp,
every small alternate stepping

magnified as he patrols the pane,
the bulb so fierce and close
it's a wonder he doesn't burn

while outside, circling the lamp,
a bat caught in the light. Today
a *langosta*, camouflaged in greys

on the cane of a lounger, so still
even its antennae were visible,
yet alive. Now crickets are trilling

the seconds, the pulses of night.
Chris talks about Michael
as we sit at the kitchen table.

Michael reciting 'Ode to Melancholy'
and Yeats. Michael and Ruairi
going down to the almond grove,

their voices drifting up from below.
Michael crossing the room, strangely
often, to hug Maddy on the sofa,

how patient he was with Ruairi,
how steeped he was in Lorca.
On the last night, during supper

on the terrace, fetching his flute,
how he played and when everyone
stopped talking, urged them to carry on.

★

Constantly struck by the abundance
of fruit rotten on the branch
or ground: figs trodden underfoot,

kumquats blackened to tar,
whole verges heaped with carob.
The trees themselves sapped of life.

You wouldn't starve here, living
in the wild. But you might die
of thirst, so dry is everything

on the outside but inside, nurturing
juice – thousands of prickly pears
tumbling in swags down hillsides.

You seldom see anyone working
in the fields, save for the little
fearsomely noisy tractors winding

along the terraces. Black lemons,
shrivelled to the size of walnuts,
smell twice as lemony, caramelised.

Occasionally you see a newly planted
rose looking false and out of place
but the fields are covered in a host

of rusted flowerheads and the butterflies
too are rust, orange and brown.
The great burnout happens in June

but in April and May, there's
always the almond blossom
and as early as January, wildflowers.

★

My eyes find it hard to focus –
is it the light? The dramatic rise
and fall of mountains, *barranca*,

the near and far? And my ears
assailed with buzzings and dronings –
even the trees, with barely a breeze,

rattle their pods. I have umpteen
bites. Bites, sunburn, a surface of
innumerable itches and underneath

a sadness for the land and its people,
many of them old and disabled,
leaning on the arms of daughters

who sing as they crawl, arm in arm,
up and down the one street
every day at the same time.

I move quietly through my rooms,
wash fruit and hardly talk
to anyone. *Hola!* I say quickly

to everyone I pass, sometimes
so synchronised with their replies
or mine to their greeting, it sounds like

the same voice, without overlap
or counterpoint, just the one
Hola! between two strangers,

I being usually the younger,
though the children too playing
on doorsteps say hello as I pass.

★

I was mentally tracing the path:
follow the wall – a strange
butter-yellow painted balustrade –

to reach Carrer del Calvari
where the wall gives way to a sudden
very steep flight of steps in sandstone,

on one side planted – and drip-fed
through thin black plastic tubing –
with indigenous and imported shrubs.

The Carrer del Calvari is a white
zig-zag path laid along the cut
of terraces, bordered with pines

and, at intervals, wayside shrines.
Inset, on glazed tiles, the soldiers'
faces often obliterated and gouged,

are the XIV stations of the cross.
My 'study', as I call it, lies beyond
this path in the yard of an abandoned

café under the old Arab fortress
where the children's pool is hidden
by ivy, padlocked, and corrugated iron

makes ticking noises in the heat
like rain; where Spanish fir, Aleppo pines
smell sweet and aromatic, cones

on the topmost branches still fierce
and clinging on, even on those trees
whose spurs are blown away and dead.

★

Everything is quickened by knowing
how short my time is here,
how easily I'll forget it, how

different it will be should I return.
I struggle with the names for things
and even were I to learn them,

whatever the language might be,
they wouldn't evoke – except for me
perhaps – themselves. Today

I have a visitor to my 'study',
an old gentleman in shirtsleeves
who asks how it goes and tells me,

in Valenciano and mime, bunching
his fingers and motioning them
in his mouth, it's time for lunch.

Very Cézanne the whole landscape –
you sense the presence of brushstrokes,
round-headed and flat, almost

the palette knife. But I'd place my words
behind the surface, weaving through nouns,
the undifferentiated but various pines,

into a Mediterranean of the mind
where, like the white *ermita*
culminating in open ground,

some white and holy destination
hoves into view and at the foot of it
one looks, not up, but out.

★

Ermita Sant Albert
is always locked, its tarnished
bell chained and silent.

I look through a small dark pane
like a porthole set in the doors
and cup hands round my eyes

to telescope the dark. A plain,
spartan interior: cloistered arches;
a niche with stucco cherubs, a lace

tablecloth and at Christ's left foot,
a large bunch of dried flowers
jutting out from the shelf; in front,

a table also with a cloth, a picture
and other devotional paraphernalia.
Nothing else. But the big church

in the village square, forever
clanging its bells – heard in London
if you use the public phone –

is fronted by benches and orange trees
where groups of old men sit and,
on market days, middle-aged women.

The padre has been renamed Juan.
He's a refugee from Rwanda
and much loved by everyone.

The side doors are currently a gruesome
shade of brown. It's the undercoat,
we overhear him say at Pepe's.

★

Sitting in the last strip of sun
setting behind the Moorish ruin
I am, having spent all day at the pool,

glad of the breeze and shade.
This is the time I normally leave.
Now, I come to take my leave

of my 'study', the sun, this week
outside my life and the last heat
before the dreaded winter.

Smoke's rising from a bonfire
and through it, the olive terraces
look charred, trunks black and leafless.

The surface I'm beginning to penetrate
seems prickly and sour, despite
a generator's hum, jasmine at the gate,

the old tragic pines with young ones
at their feet, newly planted in rows
with rather unpromising oleanders.

Sounds are isolated in the quiet
much as the trees are in barren soil.
It's not they that grow naturally

out of the soil but the ochre
houses, tile-roofed, earth colour.
I could weep for the flies and the dog

who seems to be barking at his own
bewilderment. But to weep
is to own, is an act of presumption.

★

I do not think any great artist
works in a fever. One returns
from inspiration as from a foreign country.

Every artist climbs each step
in the tower of his perfection
by fighting his duende, not his angel

nor his muse. This distinction
is fundamental. The angel dazzles,
but he flies high over a man's head.

The muse dictates and sometimes
prompts. The muse and angel
come from without; the angel

gives lights, and the muse gives forms.
But one must awaken the duende
in the remotest mansions of the blood.

I'd like to be here in the dark
and look down on the lights of Relleu
rather than up at the floodlit chapel.

Even the stars last night were suspect.
Stars where no stars are, and lightless.
But the moon was bright and legitimate.

I'd like to write with my eyes closed,
blurred as they are with oil.
Behind my lids today at the pool,

I saw the sun as one green light
like a green persimmon. Angel fruit.
A green sun like a green apple.

Almàssera Vella, September 2004

THE MIDDLE TONE

Seldom do we Andalusians notice the 'middle tone'.
An Andalusian either shouts at the stars or
kisses the red dust of the road. The middle tone
does not exist for him; he sleeps right through it.
                                  – Federico García Lorca

Just so I spend my life asleep.
Stars, if there are, might shine above
and dust, dust that I've always loved's
now dirt at most I lightly sweep.

But *cantaor*, I too exist.
My middle tone of dung and nectar,
flower and carrion, is a star
that fell, dust I too once kissed.

AL FRESCO

Look – there's the thrip on the daisy
too small to see, the spangle galls
on oak, the noonday-fly on walls
basking in my insectary!

And what are these – millipedes? –
strewing the ground like broken springs
while cicadas whistle, crickets sing,
harvester ants sit husking seeds.

Horsefly, housefly, scorpion, bee,
wasps that drowned in the pool but flew,
rosemary flowers I forgot were blue,
I salute you, hesitantly.

Here's ham for you, melon and cheese,
tortillas, tarts, to your heart's content
and for you, mosquito, bent
on blood, gallons to drink as you please.

Summer's on the wing. So, earwig,
locust, beetle and bug, spoil yourselves,
don't stint. Once we've flown you can delve
in dung, in rubble topped with figs.

But when night falls on the floodlit hill,
lacewing, chafer, beware that glass!
Not every window will let you pass.
One light is all it takes to kill.

SCORPION-GRASS

I travel with groundsel, ragwort, poppy,
seed anywhere and don't look back.
Let any wind sow me, any rough patch be
my home between the cracks.

Forget-me-not call me – if only, if only
memory grew in my tracks.
I blow at a window, away on a balcony,
kick my heels down a cul-de-sac.

The child who stoops to examine me
– my cymes, my sign of the zodiac –
will see, for every star in the galaxy,
there's one in the broken tarmac.

Give me a bombsite, wasteground, masonry,
history I'd otherwise lack.
Shallow my roots but how instinctively
I live without rooting for facts.

Facts are a bind and biography
a woodsman wielding an axe.
Don't give me a plot or a family tree
but a garden swing, a throwback.

I travel with groundsel, ragwort, poppy,
seed anywhere and don't look back.
Let any wind sow me, any rough patch be
my home between the cracks.

WATER BLINKS

From the height of a child, the shortened height
of a child stooping, massed along wet banks,
opening only when the light grows bright,
all the infinitesimal eyes of blinks
in water seem, not as you might think larger
by proximity, but more like shrinking funnels
a child might feel herself sucked into, emerging
into a fiery wheel of suns until

she knows in a flash how the whole world spins,
stars have their origin in gravity,
just as the budding scientist, impatient
to know how voltage works, becomes – imagines
himself – the transformer and as the current
runs through him, understands electricity.

THE VALLEY

Through a thin spray of flowers from the valley
(and frailer for the shyness you gave them with),
through sprigs of blue, their minute suns, many
and angled to many corners of the earth,
I saw, not the valley or even the hill
that rose in front of me, but half-imagined
plateaux that lay beyond these disused mills:
meadows waist-high, horizons mountain-rimmed.

Wildflowers grow there in abundance, so many
you could reap armfuls of them, cauldrons
of colour stoked with their dyes, cornflowers, teasels
snarling your hair and on your headscarf, apron,
skirt and shawl, the whole sky would spill a pinny
studded with seeds. But thank you, thank you for these.

OVERBLOWN ROSES

She held one up, twirling it in her hand
as if to show me how the world began
and ended in perfection. I was stunned.
How could she make a rose so woebegone,
couldn't silk stand stiff? And how could a child,
otherwise convinced of her mother's taste,
know what to think? *It's overblown*, she smiled,
I love roses when they're past their best.

'Overblown roses', the words rang in my head,
making sense as I suddenly saw afresh
the rose now, the rose ahead: where a petal
clings to a last breath; where my mother's flesh
and mine, going the same way, may still
be seen as beautiful, if these words are said.

COME CLOSE

'Come close', the flower says and we come close,
close enough to lift, cup and smell the rose,
breathe in a perfume deep enough to find
language for it but, words having grown unkind,

think back instead to a time before we knew
what we know now. When every word was true
and roses smelt divine. What went wrong?
Long before the breath of a cradle song.

Some lives fall, some flower. And some are granted
birthrights – a verandah, a sunken quadrant
of old rose trees, a fountain dry as ground
but still a fountain, in sense if not in sound.

Like a rose she slept in the morning sun.
Each vein a small blue river, each eyelash shone.

SOAPSTONE CREEK

The creek sings all night long and all night long
we listen in our sleep, waking from dreams
we recognise as our own undersong
to grief, a gabble of diverted streams

under the paths our lives took, our children's lives
we listened to so avidly but missed
the earliest signs where the ground first gives,
tracks to the water in our own tracks twist,

thinking how blessed we were, wise our choices,
skirting the treacherous silt. Yet all the while
those streams, under the cover of animal voices,
were making a mockery of free will.

Nothing's as constant as the creek. The silence
of the forest depends on it. Our deeds,
misdeeds, omissions too, make no more sense
than rattle-cries, flung where the kingfisher breeds.

Under the alders' canopy that steals
their share of sunlight, understory trees,
spread their leaves as they may, can only feel
sun sideways. And some grow accordingly.

SOAPSTONE RETREAT

Late summer sun is falling through the forest.
As if the forest knew it would soon turn yellow,
it shifts a little, stars in the creek below
signalling to the sunlight on its crest.

In the centre it is still. Still late August.
On the periphery, branches, leaves, follow
the scent of autumn. Like a woodfire slow
to get going after the stove's long rest,

the forest stirs with ambivalent longings
for movement, stillness, as if its life were elsewhere
but its heart were here. And as cold nights near,

these last sweet sips at the cusp of the year
hang suspended in the balance as the flask swings,
hummingbird feeds and the sun sinks, stair by stair.

ON A LINE FROM FOROUGH FARROKHZAD

It had rained that day. It had primed a world
with gold, pure gold, wheatfield, stubble and hill.
It had limned the hills as a painter would,
an amateur painter, but the hills were real.

It had painted a village lemon and straw,
all shadow and angles, cockerel, goats and sheep.
It had scattered their noises, bleats and blahs,
raising a cloud, a white dog chasing a jeep.

It had travelled through amber, ochre, dust
and dust the premise of everything gold,
dust the promise of green. Green there was
but in the face of a sun no leaf could shield.

It had rained that day. It was previous,
previous as wind to seed. O wild seed,
as these words proved. 'The wind will carry us'
– *bad ma ra khahad bord* – and it did.

III

IMPENDING WHITENESS

i

It was only in retrospect we knew
it was coming. We weren't thinking in colour,
we were thinking in animal, a new
category of thought and feeling. Dull
as the plates of encyclopedias are,
they were imprinted on our memories.
Comparison was called for and erasure,
and greeting the continents' emissaries:

Bennett's wallaby, Reeves' muntjac, red marmot,
Chinese water deer (solitary things),
mara and peafowl by the dozen roaming
freely through the carparks and cafés, spotted
from the steam train and waved to, then forgotten
underfoot, so fickle are human beings.

ii

It was only in retrospect we knew
how close we were to birth and to the spirit.
Whiteness came as a chick. At first it grew
as a question without our asking it.
Why is it white? we wondered, staring at mud
and the cesspool where the black rhino pissed,
is it male? Does the peacock's tail that floods
more colour than we can bear grow out of this?

We didn't ask, entranced by size and scale
as we were and the picture of a peahen
ushering two plain daughters and the male
heir to her husband's looks into a pen
where the poor rhino, never one to threaten
small children, backed off as they strode in gaily.

iii

It was only in retrospect we knew
how a paintbrush slides from the zebra's flank
down to the shin; how it drops from the blue
to swirl in the depths of a mottled tank
three layers of dapple: cloud, water, seal.
How often have we thought, looking at art,
what is that creature, mythical or real?
Equally, seeing life imitate art,

marvelled at evolution's artifice.
But if the model were extinct, as this
white donkey from north Iran almost is,
we would never have found in Bedfordshire,
from the heart of a Persian miniature,
a half-horse, half-mule, we thought legendary.

iv

It was only in retrospect we knew
white animals, like stones, had laid a trail
behind us: runes from which we might construe
something magical, lodestars that would pale
into nothing. Weather was part of it,
light weakening. And the end of the summer.
And distance, too, that made white tusks hit us
in the eye but the bull elephant dimmer,

a greyish blur round butts of ivory.
The strange became familiar and domestic
cows, ponies, grazing with camels, exotic.
White rhino, no more white than the black are black,
walled a line of oaks and – Rabbit! a cry
shot out while yak announced prehistory.

v

It was only in retrospect we knew,
passing a pygmy goat so white it shone
like a ghost and the silence fell, wind blew
and the trees and grass, with everyone gone,
came into their own, that this place never closed.
We could come in the dark by moonlight, torchlight,
recapture, in the smell of dung that rose
like a flood in the dusk, worlds without sight.

We would be the ones at a disadvantage,
seen but not seeing. We would be as men
and the animals behind bars veiled women,
watching. Matriarchs cornered in a cage,
waiting, waiting for the patriarch's rage.
We would be perpetrators, if and when.

It was only in retrospect we knew
it broke our hearts to hear the howling, see them
moving, an older cub among them, and through
the wire fencing, feel the desire to *be* them,
like them, even the lone wolf wandering,
nose to the ground, in the wood. They seemed at home,
content to congregate on the hill with nothing
to call them further afield, nowhere to roam.

In this country, they died out long ago.
But past the wolf wood, in an open meadow
that took us by surprise as if our worst fears
seen in broad daylight or here, by the glow
of a moon, really were to disappear,
white wolves have lived among us all these years.

vii

It was only in retrospect we knew
it was whiteness we were heading toward.
None of the animals minded us; few
held our gaze but with a tacit accord,
as though we too had a natural place
in the scheme of things, as indeed we had,
allowed us to observe them. But the grace
of lowered necks, lofty horns and ears glad

to obey command words more readily
than children, created an aching barrier,
an invisible veil nothing could tear.
As we headed for the car, solitary
in the carpark, a safari bus roared by
with a bride, waving, throned in the open air...

Whipsnade Wild Animal Park

AMY'S HORSE

Amy's horse looked doleful. More pony
than horse, he looked lugubriously
out of his fingerprint eyes at me

from the huge front pane of night.
Outside it was snowing, inside,
orange then green then golden light

flashed through Amy's horse as if
electricity could grant him life.
He had two tails: one short and stiff,

one, superimposed by Amy's friend,
cursive and corrective. Diamonds
glittered in his outline, rainbeads

mapped him like a constellation.
He was a Christmas decoration,
the donkey of our childhoods risen

like a saint on a stained-glass pane.
His eyes were mean and close-set, his mane
a stumpy fringe, his face as lean

as any Christ's but what with the cold,
the crowded bus, the sudden gold
that flooded him, he seemed to hold

not only our eyes but all our anguish,
the terrible burdens of our flesh
and blood, for he had none, no flesh,

no body, nothing but an outline
a finger traced on glass, a sign
for the very naught we can't imagine.

And when Amy's friend erased
what body he had, it recomposed
that naught, ghosting it through the glaze.

THE YEAR OF THE DISH

It has been the year of the dish.
Like the man who found a button
and had a suit made to match,
for every dish I've been given,

I must re-arrange my kitchen
and, fine as a meridian ring
round a brass celestial globe
as their band shall be, bring

sheikhs to dine on my dishes:
dish with leaves and blossoms,
dish with ewer, grapes,
dish with portrait of Italian,

dish with clouds and lotuses,
dish with ducks, leopards,
dish with fish-scale ground,
dish with two fish, birds

(small birds perched in a grapevine
painted under the glaze),
dish with ship in fritware,
ranged on which my crudités

will hide ship, birds, fish,
leopards, ducks, lotuses
and clouds, portrait of Italian,
grapes, ewer, blossoms

and leaves from their greedy gaze.
It has been, as I said, the year
of the dish. Next year shall be,
I decree, the year of the cafetière.

MOTHERHOOD

Suppose I emptied my flat of everything,
everything but my books? The elephants
would have to go. They'd be the first to go
– being the youngest – and the last, the plants
perhaps, relics of early motherhood.
I'd keep the piano, all my files and photos.

I'd keep my grandmother's chest to keep my photos
in, in and not on top of, everything
swept absolutely clear of motherhood.
Nothing shall move: no herd of elephants
proceed down my mantelpiece, spider-plants
produce babies, carpets moths, moths shall go

into the ether where all bad spells go.
I'm sick of the good. Of drooling over photos
that lie, lie, lie, breaking my back over plants
for whom – *Oh! for whom?* Not everything
I thought green greened. Not even elephants
consoled me for the bane of motherhood.

Therefore motherhood must go. Motherhood
must go as quietly as prisoners go
and all her things go with her, elephants
troop behind her, tapestries drown her, photos –
OK photos can stay but everything
dust-collecting goes the way of the plants.

Everything shall live in name only. Plants
now extinct shall be extolled, motherhood
shall be blessed but not mothers, everything

everywhere being their fault though they go
to the dock protesting, producing photos
of happy toddlers, citing elephants,

rashly, as preceptors since elephants,
however vicious they may be to plants
or photographers with blinding flash photos,
are the very model of motherhood.
Such are the myths of nature. They shall go.
There shall be room, time, space, for everything:

room in the wild for elephants and plants,
time to go rummaging a chest for photos,
space for everything cleared of motherhood.

THE ROBIN AND THE EGGCUP

A robin flew into my room today,
into the sun of it, the wood, the plants.

A robin flew into my sleep today,
once for mischief, twice for very good luck.

A robin flew into my soul today,
queried it, rose and flumped against its glass.

So I opened it and the cold came in,
I levered it wide and the bird flew out.

Not for the first time. I let it out too,
my son said, out of the kitchen window.

No! When? Earlier, when you were asleep.
It broke an eggcup. Eggcup! What eggcup?

Not one of those nice blue and white eggcups.
Yes, he said joyfully, I swept it up.

SONG FOR SPRINGFIELD PARK

Because this park is a musical park
and I'm here alone,

because yesterday we found by mistake
any three notes

like all roads led to the very same tune
(Rome in this case

being *All of Me*) and because I said
I like this park,

it's a musical park, I mean the trees
and the curve of the slopes

and you said melodic, I said melodious,
another song

must have stuck in my head. Crookedly, what with
the kids and the crows.

ON LINES FROM PAUL GAUGUIN

How do you see this tree? Is it really green?
Use green then, the most beautiful green on your palette.
And the gold of their bodies God made to be seen?
Make love to that gold and make it a habit.

Use green then, the most beautiful green on your palette
to shadow the world always chained to your feet.
Make love to that gold and make it a habit
to leave love eternally incomplete.

To shadow the world always chained to your feet,
don't be afraid of your most brilliant blues.
To leave love eternally incomplete,
nothing shines more than the love you will lose.

Don't be afraid of your most brilliant blues.
At night phosphorescences bloom like flowers.
Nothing shines more than the love you will lose –
these are lovers' bouquets with miraculous powers.

At night phosphorescences bloom like flowers,
like spirits of the dead in a Maori sky.
These are lovers' bouquets with miraculous powers
where all the colours of the spectrum die.

Like spirits of the dead in a Maori sky
with one eye on lust, one on disease
where all the colours of the spectrum die,
paint, blind Paul, your flowers and trees.

With one eye on lust, one on disease
and the gold of their bodies God made to be seen,
paint, blind Paul, your flowers and trees.
How do you see this tree? Is it really green?

MAGPIES

I have one tree in my garden
and two magpies in it;
two magpies in a yard
growing greener by the minute.

I have two kids by one father,
three husbands I regret;
the tree that was my grandmother
is dying in my head.

Everywhere is shrinkage
but we've heard it all before;
still trying to count the damage
on old battlegrounds of war.

In black and white, the magpies come,
two heralds in a tree;
in tailcoats and as handsome
as black and white can be.

The first sign of spring is children
yelling in the street;
by *Eid* we will have killed them
before the killing heat.

What season shall we pray for now
when we know what March will bring?
In a mass of green on every bough,
the weapon that is spring.

I have one tree in my garden,
two magpies in it;
two magpies in a yard
growing greener by the minute.

GHAZAL: THE SERVANT

Ma'mad, hurry, water the rose.
Blessed is the English one that grows
               out in the rain.

Water is scarce, blood not so.
Blood is the open drain that flows
               out in the rain.

Bring in the lamp, the olive's flame.
Pity the crippled flame that blows
               out in the rain.

Where are the children? What is the time?
Time is the terror curfew throws
               out in the rain.

Hurry, Ma'mad, home to your child.
Wherever my namesake, Maryam, goes
               out in the rain.

GHAZAL: THE CHILDREN

The children are not ours
but the child they might have been
    is in their eyes.
The children live in camps
but the freedom they have seen
    is in their eyes.

The children wear boleros,
beads and kaftans, tribal
    paint and feathers,
sandals in the snow and *hejab*
as white as snow whose sheen
    is in their eyes.

The children stand with younger
children on their hips,
    in their arms.
Like animals at grass,
stopping in a day's routine
    is in their eyes.

The children hold belongings –
pens and notebooks, blankets,
    shoes and saucepans;
their fingers tell us stories
and what these stories mean
    is in their eyes.

The children are not ours
but you, Salgado, have brought them
    this close, this far.
I stand within a hand's-breadth
and the world that lies between
    is in their eyes.

GHAZAL: MY SON

He's wearing a red silk shirt, my son.
He's done me a dreadful hurt, my son.

Now that the devil has shown his face,
he's hiding under my skirt, my son.

A mother is earth, but earth is sick.
A mother's nothing but dirt, my son.

The floor of the gym is strewn with limbs.
Children are lying inert, my son.

I see lights, he says, *hear voices too!*
Obscenities to pervert my son.

Don't look at the lights, the voice is yours.
What can I say to alert my son –

Don't look at the world, a beast that kills,
a savage you can't convert, my son?

What's happened to trust? Don't screen your eyes,
green eyes you always avert, my son.

White roses have buried Beslan's dead.
Mother, don't let me desert my son.

SIGNAL

You'd think that in all this open space,
nothing but fields for miles around
and some cows and trees, you'd get a signal.

Only behind the goosehouse, the roses,
in one of those patches of grass that make
no sense, too small to cross or lie on,

with a sheltering wall at your back, beanrow
on your left, on a triangle of grass
doing nothing and going nowhere,

can you stand and even then, only
with somebody else behind you, wind
blowing their hair and their own mobile

fisted against the rain, with two
or three others besides to bulwark you
– you a child stripping down on a beach,

they a towel or windbreak – do you stand
a hope in heaven or hell of reaching
somebody out there sometime, somewhere.

SUNDAYS

for Tom

i

Together, we have made sour cherry rice,
rolled minced lamb into meatballs and listened
to the radio while eating, him to stall
hallucinations and me to respect his silence,

the time he takes to eat. We've strolled slowly
in the park together, our favourite park,
lapsing into pauses with the falling light –
tennis in the distance – as we slowly climbed

the hill. I've left my shoes at the door, him
reminding me, to scrub off the dogshit later
and now he's at the piano in the nowhere hour
before TV. These are the things that make him

well – company, old and easy, recipes
old but new to him. His playing brings
the night in. Turns the streetlamps on, makes
the kitchen clock tick. Softly a chord falls

and out of the ground grow snowdrops, fat
and waxy, with green hearts stamped upside down
on aprons, poking their heads through railings.
Between his fingers things grow, little demons,

fountains, crocuses. Spring is announced and enters,
one long green glove unfingering the other,
icicles melt and rivers run, bluetits
hop and trill. Everything talks to everything.

ii

How it poured with rain today. My gutter,
blocked and inaccessible to anyone bar
the man with the longest ladder in London,
waterfalled down the window alarmingly.

No, the waterfall is here, under his fingers,
steady wrists, the years of training paying off
in instinctual music; and the fat raindrops, spraying
up like diamanté; and the tailing off

of rain, all the languages of rain, rivers,
gutters, waterfalls, the treble runs
of rain and the bass's percussive beat;
all the liquidity of youth, youth gone

to rack and ruin. How little he ate today
and how much there was to eat – stuffed pepper,
salmon, apple and blackberry tart, coffee.
He can't even swallow his own saliva,

holding it in his mouth minutes at a time,
without hearing them, the voices, seeing
babies streaming towards his mouth, limbs
trigger words command him: that, there, take, eat.

iii

He ate all of it. All of the rice
and all of the *khoreshté bademjan*
– the aubergine dish – I carefully filled
his plate with, not overfilled. He liked it.

He was always sweet about my cooking.
We ate while watching *West Side Story*.
How easy it was to sorrow for Maria
and Tony. Easy to cry and grieve.

Now he's at the piano, today
so tentative but gaining in assurance,
like someone 'learning to live with disability'.
Is he? Or is that someone me?

all of us, all of us who love him.
Joey rings. He's free tomorrow,
Tom's saying – he hasn't decided yet
whether to stay with me a while,

I hope he will. And suddenly
there's sunshine, brightness and a bounce
and his fingers are dancing. Voices
might bedevil him but voices also

save him – Moss's, Joey's, Sara's –
or let him down without meaning to,
without knowing, after they've finished
a call, the music stops again

as suddenly as it started. But now
he's into it – and what's that tune?
coming and going. Tom, what's that tune?
'All the Things You Are' he tells me.

TINTINNABULI

How sad he was, Arvo Pärt,
not to have thanked his teacher
for the parting thought she gave him:

that the biggest mystery in music
is something about – he couldn't
remember her exact words –

something about how to enter
a single sound, just as his janitor,
when asked how should a composer

compose, replied: he has to love
each sound, each sound – so that
every blade of grass would be,

Pärt adds, as important as the flower
(and the bent man on the bent road
picking raspberries, the soprano

holding a green pencil to mark
on her score where to breathe)
and the soul yearn to sing it endlessly.

This one note, or a silent beat, or a moment of silence,
comforts me. I build with primitive materials –
with the triad, with one specific tonality.

The three notes of a triad are like bells
and that is why I call it tintinnabulation.
Tintinnabuli – itself the sound of grass,

blades moving like bells, harebells say,
though there are no flowers but stems alone
and a breath of wind to give the grass direction.

from CHILD: NEW AND SELECTED POEMS
1991-2011

IOWA DAYBOOK

Two men are rolling tables,
round tables like golden discs,
one golden arc of circles

on the amphitheatre's strip.
Now they wait, the tables,
the round golden masks

and the sky says nothing.
Now the white canoes
and the three white geese.

Now they peck in tandem
while an insect calls from among
the trees. Where are the gods

of Iowa? The 'drowsy ones',
'he who paints pictures',
'dust-in-the faces'?

A day so grey. I did my laundry.
There was nowhere I wished to go.
Whatever pain I had left behind

was better left. I switched on
all the lights in my room, all
the reading lamps and ceiling lights

and still the day was grey.
I will go quietly to the bookshop
and hear what the poets say.

★

The river feels the rain before we do,
rain-rings quickening to signal it.
All the many trees of Iowa

– Norway Spruce and White Pine,
Cottonwood and Maple,
Linden and Sycamore –

are as nothing to this tree of light,
rainlight, shimmering
an arrow across the river

and the sky leans down to say,
'I am the tree their shadows create,
fallen that you may see me,

shining that you may float,
oars still, moving me in your wake
as the wind moves spruce and cedar.'

How lovely to lie flat on the ground,
trees overhead and birds I can only see
because I'm underneath them.

Like fish, their bellies are pale
to camouflage them against the sky
and their backs dark to mimic earth.

Last night we saw a praying mantis
scaling a wall, a plain thing,
inches long, more stick than insect.

★

This is a landscape made for
woodcuts, carvings, patchwork quilts,
cornfields thrown like doormats

on distant hills. Fields and roads follow
the old grid pattern for homesteading.
Let the home-hunting immigrant

be informed that a free home awaits him
in Iowa, the Waterloo Courier proclaimed
two decades after a troupe of 14 Iowa

had sailed to Europe to perform
tableaux vivants in George Catlin's
Indian Gallery, the venture ending

when Little Wolf's wife and child died,
and a decade after the Republican Party
was founded in Iowa City in 1856.

England, London, I am
homesick for you. My little
local streets, messy and human,

cafés where I can sit and smoke,
each so close to the other.
Homesick for the small-scale,

the crooked, the left-alone.
I sit among trees, old and young,
in the lobby of a landscape.

★

Every road is made for dapple.
Shadow can be as shadow
was meant to be – lovelier

for being grey. The precinct
is a flood of dapple that lends
itself to smells – kerosene, coffee –

in every city of the world.
We walk in the cast of mind
that dapple gives us. Nothing,

not even the bright acacia,
is lovelier than the ground itself.
And now that our lovemaking

has accepted failure and limitation,
how gently we lie together, asking
for nothing, giving sleep permission.

Why have I never been in love?
Singing in the shower, washing
my voice in water, spray.

And the woods – I miss the woods,
someone says, and hearing him
we see him as if he *were*

the woods he has vanished in
and love is like that too,
a wood we cannot search.

★

The Amish, like the Mennonites,
are pacifists but, unlike them,
they practice shunning. We pass

the water tower, schoolhouse,
the windmill and cider press,
a birdhouse for purple martens,

the chicken house for 8,500 hens,
clothing centre that fixes buttons, zips,
sends bales to third world countries,

the Sunday School where services
are held in German, the silo,
Jo's welding shop, brother-in-law

Simon T's quality horses,
grandpa houses, the coffinmaker's
yard and the new Kalona library.

The cardigan was in blue, wool shades
of blue like a Fair Isle knit but
so finely done I knew I couldn't afford it.

Bizarrely, the names of America's ten
most dangerous men were woven in it,
men who had murdered somebody

close to me in my dream. I buy the rainhat
I've been looking for. *I see unknown places,*
I let myself slide down the slope of dreams.

★

Emily Dickinson sat in her room
and the galaxy unrolled beneath her feet...
She sat in her room and the garden

and the orchard outside her windows
took on the ghostly garments of infinity...
There are poets of the dark and deep.

Not all of us can go there.
Depths were never truths I reached.
More, the quiet monotony I never

thought of as monotony
but peace. Nothing I loved more
than making torn things whole.

I never looked to be healed.
Torn rather, torn open,
to prove I too could feel.

Oh to be a better reader,
a patient one, steadfast
and young enough to know

years of reading lie in wait.
To live with Dante, say,
months at a time, to live,

tracing a finger from side to side
across the trough of an open book,
bilingually with Hafez!

★

The song must come from elsewhere,
from some other organ. The word
'organic' was first used by Aristotle

to refer to parts of warships – parts
of a whole that made the whole thing work.
(Suspended between the giant spokes

of the wooden starboard paddlewheel
as it turned on display were two spiderwebs,
one a perfect diagram, one half-rent.)

Why am I awake? I have climbed
out of the pit of sleep, out of the river
itself. Foghorns call over Iowa.

'Here is the place', 'beautiful land',
in all its spellings: Ay-u-vois, Ayavois,
Ay-u-ou-ez, Aiaoua, Ayoüs, Ayoës, Ioway.

These were never journeys
that we planned, travelling
on boats that tipped us in the wind

though the lake was calm
and fish, if fish there were,
yes there were, those three or four

you pointed out, calling, fish,
there are fish here! had faded
out of fish and into memory's hair.

★

It was when I learned as a child
the word for 'yesterday' in English
– and what an odd word it was –

that the underside of all my words
was suddenly revealed. Nouns
I had secured with gravity and string

levitated; furniture grew wings;
every chair I had sat on, bridge
I had crossed, called me to account:

where were you, who were you with?
(An Iowa student changing my sheets
is an art teacher at the local Montessori

where the kids have a globe covered
with sandpaper so all the continents
feel rough, he says, smoothing the slip.)

*Yes. The earth is flat, like a lost
floating board…* and I remember
little tasks of pleasure, how the world

lies flat on my ironing-board, warm
to my palm, while my children
sleep upstairs. What have we sacrificed

to come here? Jamby, whose mother
died only weeks ago, whose mother
became transparent in a sunset.

★

People cling to each other
but no one has the strength
to be the branch – we are leaves

now, nothing but leaves.
Choi, from South Korea, who says
her language is useless, useless,

who has spent her time translating it;
Genti, struggling out of Albania's
fifty years of isolation; 'Doc',

Ashur from Libya, who tells me
my poems are all the same; Srijato,
sad to have his young wife leave;

and Choi again, stepping off
the path, saying in her useless
language she likes the sound of leaves.

Dusk and everything comes closer.
Iowa's first Baptist Church,
its gabled roof under the maple,

four flights of shallow steps,
moving with small blind windows
towards poetry it can hear

in another language, another age,
in fly-over country as Emmanuel
reads at Shambaugh House, comes closer.

★

'It is what bears our name'
Chief No Heart said when he
and Moving Rain presented it,

a map to back their land claims,
before the Indian Commissioner
in Washington D.C.

Big Sioux and Little Sioux,
Niobrara and Rock, Raccoon
and Skunk, Cedar and Turkey,

once rivers that were torrents,
run-offs from glaciers piling land
at our feet – here they are in charcoal

like a forked branch outside
my window, meeting at the junction
of the Mississippi and Missouri.

A false fire alarm in the night.
We stand, shipwrecked on the grass,
islanded without our things.

To say island is to invoke
bells ringing, people missing,
to name, like Adam, all your things.

And since the island is ageless,
time is told, if told at all, only
when the lyric spreads her wings.

★

I move bench, following the sun.
The candle of the sun is enclosed
in a copper cylinder casting

shadows along the ground
much like the filigree of trees.
But the filigree is that of letters,

each perforated scroll of which,
illuminated at night, projects
headlines on the Adler Building

in an indecipherable script.
'They will be able to read
what I wrote, but what I wrote

is a mystery itself' the chandler
said to the CIA who cracked the code
of a light sculpture similar to this.

I too have been a candle
filtering languages. Why else
would I sit, on the first morning

of wintertime, in a courtyard
outside the School of Journalism
& Mass Communication building,

if not to escape the cacophony,
the babel of other languages
I can't hear silence in?

International Writing Program,
Shambaugh House, University of Iowa.

THE STREETS OF LA ROUE

From the red house on the fish quays
where the old harbour was, the plane trees
and the cobbles, in Wednesday drizzle
when thought travels on diagonals, colour
is pure and unlascivious, take the metro
from Sainte Catherine, via Jacques Brel
and Saint Guidon on the Erasmus Line
to Anderlecht – Anderlecht being, myth says,
a rough translation of 'the love of Erasmus' –
to find yourself between places, languages,
on the outer ring between city and countryside
where roads abruptly give way to fields, cows,
in a garden city whose streets commemorate
the aspirations of its founders and its people.

La Roue is on the outer ring. La Roue
could have been a blacksmith's wheel,
La Roue could have been a torturer's wheel:
spin it – *roue, roue, roue,* in a backstreet,
a hoop and a stick and here come the twenties,
a little bruiser in his grey shorts, grey shirt.
Here come the pavements, double crocodile
of nuns with their charges, the tramlines, river,
the lake where the children bathed. Here
come the houses, big ones, little ones, four
small wooden ones in a block that in fire
would burn. Here come the Belgian, French,
the Spanish and Portuguese and here come
the old who were born and still live here.

Like an old film star, the lone magnolia
is in flower but this is not Sunset Boulevard,
this is *Droits de l'Homme*, boasting mailboxes
in metal, wood, tin, most like birdhouses
with two tiny dormer windows looking out,
perplexed. Where is the postman? Where
are the addressees? *Attention au Chien!*
C'est moi qui monte la garde ici! But
what does he guard? The cherub urns,
barbecues, slides and trikes, basketball posts,
looking up and barking, the number plaques?
What need for number when each doorway
is marked by its own carefully chosen tree tile,
wall bracket, weathervane, carriage lamp?

On Rue de l'Émancipation, parked in a white van,
Façade Express undertakes the cleaning of facades.
But nothing is what it seems. Under the asphalt
run the old tramlines, under the tramlines, damned
for all its sewage to run eternally underground,
what might have been a tourists' caféside river.
But for all the builders' rubble, plastic bags,
piping, wires, breeze-blocks, tiling, planks
and paving stones, there are giant brussel sprouts
vying with camellias, geraniums and compost
sitting beside the pebbledash, japonica flowering,
rhododendron and broom and in a window,
behind the yellow primulas, a black and white cat,
black-nosed with a soot mark, looking anxious.

From No. 4, particularly pretty with an espaliered
peach tree, climbing rose on a three-way arch,
the sound of running water, a windchime
and an awning still bearing traces of artificial
Christmas snow, a lady opens her window to ask,
Vous cherchez quelqu'un? I am looking
for La Roue, I am looking for its guiding spirit,
where will I find it, *chez vous, chez vous,
chez eux?* Look, here is a bench for poets
and the elderly, a crescent where daisies grow
freely on the verge, *Place Ernest S'Jonghers*
overlooked by an orange crane and tremendous
sudden drumming from some den or loft
where a teenager drives them all berserk.

But let us praise folly, for 'He who loves
vehemently no longer lives in himself
but in what he loves…', Erasmus says,
and no more so than on *Rue du Symbole*,
where a young girl in a tracksuit is pulling
on a pink string a toddler on a trike, sucking
a dummy, surveying the world; a grandma
in a long brown robe and hejab accompanies
a gaggle of Moroccan schoolkids; an old spruce
wears a wild afro of ivy; a baby stone rabbit
nibbles at weeds and on net curtains, embroidered,
spreads an idyll of ponies, pastures, windmills
and turtledoves flying out of their cages to flirt.

'The more perfect the love, the greater
the madness', Erasmus concludes in his praise
of folly. And folly it is, surely, to come upon
an open space in the *Rue des Colombophiles*
where, beyond a fence of corrugated iron strips,
car panels, wire fencing, is a flat area of allotments,
well dug but empty of produce save for a few
yellow mustard flowers and some far greenery.
Back gardens flaunt chickens and daffodils,
a fine cedar fronting a row of poplars, the chimneys
of the concrete factory, the railway bridge, trains
going to Ghent and, over the fence at the bottom end
of the allotments, helmeted cyclists gliding past
on the canalside like ducks in a shooting gallery.

Doves cooing on the *Rue des Huit Heures*
bring you to the *Plaine des Loisirs*. Pleasure,
more folly. Sun sets above the black plane trees
and on a bench this time, *ALO MAMAN*,
Je t'aime Valentin, are messages from Kelly.
A young one in her mother's arms, stretching out
a baby arm, is calling repeatedly like the dove,
'da-ddy, da-ddy'. Grass is littered with daisies
and the long thin diagonal shadows of the trees
underline the white lines the daisies scribble
like shadow-writing. A blade of a boy in a black suit
with a black dog yanks on the lead, making the dog
snarl and twist and half-leap as if on circus training.
The glittering of the grass swells like waves at sea.

'…and his joy is in proportion to his withdrawal
from self and his preoccupation with what is
outside himself' our guiding spirit, for I believe
Erasmus himself has been invoked, continues,
'When the soul meditates on travelling without
this use of its limbs, this is certainly insanity.'
And suddenly Soul arrives at a basketball ground
and, not wishing to travel unfingered, unlimbed,
straddles a bench to carve a soulful message:
pour la vie mon bb, invoking the names
of Christel, Souliman, Ismael. Soul kicks
at broken sidelight glass, plastic fork tines
scattered in the dust of *Place Ministre Wauters*
and asks, 'Who once ate here under the elms?'

On the corner of *Rue de l'Énergie*,
you will find the boulangerie/fromagerie
of Tonton Garby. In a French beret
and moustache, Monsieur Tonton
(whose less energetic brother serves
alternate days in a seven-day week)
holds forth in English, in French.
He has lived here for forty-three years,
travelled all over – Oxford Street,
Piccadilly Circus, America (here
he bursts into an American accent)
and once, with his family, to Sri Lanka.
'Come on', he cried, 'let's do the elephant tour!
Everything, everything!' And so they did.

We've come full circle back to *Place de la Roue*
but this time behind the church, once too small,
now, rebuilt, too big. After all, it's only a moderate
garden city, swelling with immigrants' kids:
these two girls, one with bad eyesight and glasses,
both with long brown ringlets, bright blue rollerblades,
legs splayed like young deer finding their legs;
this tubby boy, pushing his sister, *Vite, vite!*
Two boys bending to their mothers' headscarved
brows with kisses. And the young Moslem women,
laughing, handling the baby in the pram as lightly,
with as little concern as their mothers before them did.
This little girl in plum, standing a foot away, swinging
her arms violently from side to side like a windmill.

'A glutton for letters', Erasmus said of himself,
his humanism trying to unite, above the confusion
of beliefs and races, all the clerics who desired
not to betray the cause of the spirit. In his house
lie a cast of his cranium, fragments of his coffin.
In the Room of Rhetoric, a statue of him stands,
the saint holding back his torn entrails, armed with
carpenter's tools and hoe, square and compass.
In profile, sharpened quill in hand, studied hands
on an open book, fingers ringed, he sits writing.
He wears three coats, so cold were the winters,
and the black hat from which he was never parted.
Outside, leaf ponds float his adages – UBI BENE,
IBI PATRIA, brass letters half-submerged, rusting.

AFTERWORD

for Archie

Today I adjust
the favourite wall
of a lover.

The vine it supports
won't arbour us
as promised.

The old arrangement
looks odd to others,
to us;

looks like another
country
we must have known.

> – E.A. Markham, 'A Life'

Not in my heart do I carry you
with me everywhere
since your death, but in my mind

have you accompany me –
pedestrian and passenger,
side by side on the top deck

or standing while I sit
when there's only a seat
for one of us on trains.

Not in my heart but in my mind
beside me, talking, while I
gaze out through a mist of green

as I have always sat with your absence.
Even the rain is green in London,
so much green in May.

★

I have but recently arrived, am,
in fact, arriving. I look to the right
to see if the tide is coming in or out,

to the left to see the mountains
disappearing. I have settled in
but the horizon is departing.

How can one imagine a person
in death without his lifelong feelings:
the shame, the pride, the lifelong

cover-ups and disguises, sudden
jolt of eyes without their glasses?
No one was here to meet me.

I can come and go like the cats
under the tables with only
the odd face turned toward me.

★

At the depth of my shins and calves,
a pale green filter, deepening
to the height of the pelvis, creates

a bridge to the deepening blue
of L'Outro bay, at first aquamarine,
then turquoise, then pewter blue,

then way out there where the hills
become like Chinese hills, hardly real,
the rulered royal blue of the horizon.

The green filter creates an aquarium
for stones, the large ones green as if
a layer of algae were swaying over them.

There are zigzag lightning lights in the water
and then, where the cold will hit my belly
and breasts, the lightnings disappear.

★

Of your body what is left
but ash and a single hair?
A perfect ring, one coiled spring

of microscopic wire.
Archie, you are gone now.
Gone, gone, gone. Gone utterly,

irrevocably, yes, you are.
Look how solid our buildings are,
how material the sky.

Paris is where you left it,
so am I.
I, small as a single hair,

the infinite divisible.
You the indivisible nowhere,
whole, entire.

★

Mid-afternoon when snorkellers,
knowing the sea has warmed sufficiently
for their old age, take to the waves,

so the waves too, for those who lie
listening with their eyes closed,
come like dolphins out to play –

their swishes and flurries creating
fish-shaped sounds to play across
our ears. Beside mine I place a shell,

a glint of mother of pearl on its whorl,
and think of that one last stray black curl
clinging to a tile back home for weeks,

months maybe, after your death.
The last bath I took, cleaning
the bath beforehand, washed it away.

★

There was a wall or kind of cupboard
and, caught between the louvres,
the elbow of a shirt I recognised

in the language of dream-recognitions
as my son's and I leapt on it as I would
a drowning child and, grasping some corner

of the shirt or sleeve, dragged it out
in one great slash from between the slats.
Last night a small boy slipped perilously near

the edge of the quay and his young mother
leapt from her chair to yell at him, pointing
at the dark night water, and I wondered

at anger and the fearsome tenderness
it springs from, the fear and helplessness
despite all our warnings and harangues.

★

Was it twice or three times
I woke from a nightmare?
Each nightmare twinned

to the one before, one
brother to the other.
Nothing is yet forgiven.

A sickness rises in me.
I will take it with me
on the long drive home

for I have nothing else to take –
no ring box, no sarong.
When I think of the word 'sickness'

childhood calls to be born again,
this time in the open air
with an open mouth.

★

However long I listen to birdsong,
I distinguish neither vowel nor consonant
and therefore can't describe it in words

though the rhythm does persist
like the rhythm of persistence itself.
And so you, being dead, are like birdsong

and the rhythm that persists is the afterword,
he's dead, he's dead, he's dead.
On one side of me at the beach today

were Italians, on the other, French.
And I revised my opinion of the French,
both the people and the language, finding them

charming, the fat women and the thin men.
(Only because you, who loved the French,
are dead.) Death has altered me too late.

★

There is a step up to the shower-closet –
the showerhead is blocked and I wash,
sluice myself half-squatting under the tap.

Through the shutters I see the back
of the chair on the balcony spread
like a fan. There is a ceiling fan.

My blanket is very soft at night, even
against my face. In the fridge are
half a melon, seeded, some apricots,

the last of a small pot of honey
and a knife. Wind bangs the door
at night even though it is locked.

I light a last cigarette. The nights
are black. Everything in my room
is white, including my pencil.

★

I'm surrounded by the wild furniture
of Crete – boulders, light tan and grey,
cushions of sage, trees, chandeliered,

forming a pool of shadow beside the church,
a window on a choppy turquoise sea.
Yet I'm drawn to the long bare stone table,

speckled where the whitewash has eroded,
a bench for the solitary and arthritic.
A poem should be a makeshift thing,

Bishop said, and the spirit too needs
furniture to invite it in – otherwise
where would it be, lost on a headland

of heat and wind, nothing in its hands
to carry home, no home but a windy church
with a banging door, a music of wind and tin?

★

Imagine a corpse laid out on a hill.
Imagine a hillside with a goat
grazing halfway up it; the bell;

the wind; the difficulty, when a wind
blows really hard, of seeing.
But the sound rises; at one point,

almost sounds like singing.
There'd be birds circling, surely.
Here there are no birds – the odd seagull,

tilting in and out of visibility.
There'd be wolves, hyenas, jackals.
A quiet, concentrated tearing.

And a loping away to their young,
a red around the mouth like her sheep,
Louie was telling us, who love beet.

★

Yiorgos, you haven't fixed my shower yet
but every morning you glide to my table soundlessly
to bring me coffee with a deference I don't deserve.

If I thank you in Greek, you smile. After a year
you have cut your beard. Now you bring us brandy and cakes,
wheat, nuts and honey, for it's the one year anniversary

of your brother's death. Your mother, old now and heavy,
helped me carry my case up the steps. It was heavy
with paper and books and too many clothes to wear.

I was here last year as you remembered, clasping
my hand in yours, warmly in greeting. During the year,
now and then I thought of you sitting in your chair,

the long sea-gaze in your eyes. Man of few words,
here are a few for you: *efkaristo, kalimera, kalispera,*
and the silence that lies between them of a long sad year.

NIGHT SOUNDS

I can hear myself moving around
                in the dark. My footsteps
      lagging up the stairs. Now
I am quiet, listening to the light
          that strikes the plant in
    leaves of light at the turn.

An animal in the brush, large
              enough to encompass a shuffle
    here, a footfall there. Ooh.
I am lovely in my sounds.
          I am moonlight and darkness,
    death and habitation.

I thrill to the sounds my memory hears.
            Sounds I have made in my life
    through all my life – a child's hand reaching
for water, chink of the glass
          replaced. They moon about
    the house, free to help themselves.

They do. How bright it is
          in the fridge! You can hardly
    bear such brightness. But where am I
between this soft thud
          and the next? I am in all rooms,
    on all stairs, lumbering and animal,

enough to make you worry
           when a door clicks and I, on this side
    or on that, forget myself. Hear that?
What? Nothing, I hear nothing.
          Only the pillow crackling,
    a rasp, a whistle of breath.

RIVER SOUNDING

after Bill Fontana's sound installation, Somerset House.

For six weeks the river has been brought
into dry dock – like the ark with its animals
on board – six weeks to tell its story.

Live feeds, hydrophones, accelerometers,
have cast a spell to subdue, to set adream,
bring audiences to listen, languages

in young mouths aflame with travel.
Our eyelids droop. We long for sleep, to lie
like Gulliver in long grass, eyes like pools

for rainclouds to traverse. The whistle buoys
are probes in our ears. Their story doesn't reach us,
drowsy in the white noise of the fountains.

We are all eyes, not ears. We like to watch
the pigeons, iridescence on their ruffs,
going about their business; the fat lady,

lifting her sari, paddling in the fountains.
We are impatient, too impatient to hear stories,
too sceptical of history, too eager to connect.

★

There might have been music from the barn,
animal grunts on the other side of the fence
or a barely discernible suck as I drew on a cigarette.

I could hear nothing from the goosehouse and the silence
that lay over the fields, distant copse, and far away
over the sea itself, was a silence you could smell.

It smelt of frost and dung, nicotine in my hair.
A young couple, sitting on stools outside a cottage
in Connemara, would remember it for years.

My own partner, dead now, more than two years dead,
had no inkling of it, tapping ferociously on his old
manual typewriter and I, leaning on the fence,

hearing the silence but without an inkling
of the years, painful, diminishing, that lay ahead,
would hear it doubled, trebled, one silence

crouched within another, whenever I lay in bed,
the radio on like conversation under the sea,
as I pulled the duvet up and over my ears.

★

Through it all, the drone, the whine.
Foghorns, whistle buoys, bells that clang together
from the four points of the compass,

sink into silence as you raise your head
to listen: that one note, mechanical
and lonely, orphaned from the river.

The fountains become meadow, become grass.
Kneel to their own feet, lift and rise like
glass jellyfish on stems. Sounds at my back –

call and response, chatter, consolation.
Untethered sounds with nowhere to go
but into the void, calling out their –

'I am bull, I am horn, I am herd.'
The animals are lowing in their stalls.
The lonely buoy, the long-necked bell.

'Wish-wish' the fountains go. 'Over here,
over here' go the bells. 'John!'
the big clock strikes. 'Jim, Jim!'

the little ones say. 'The experience
being out of control' a voice butts in,
signing off to a darling on the other end.

★

Without my love, there is no song.
Without my love, no silence.
A carousel without a pole,
two apple halves without a whole,
no centre, no circumference.

Without him, the idea of him,
desire draws up its blanket.
Stars come out and look about,
a halfway moon gives way to doubt
with no one here to thank it.

Ears grow deaf, eyes grow dim,
and why is the street so long?

The best is over, you know it is,
for he took your best and made it his
inimitable song.

Without my love, there is no song, etc.

★

The shadow of Seamen's Hall, crowned
by five gilded urns, guards sunlight
from the lightwells. Who would forego

the light of the courtyard, jet grove
of fountains, for the dungeon damp,
cobbled dark of the passageways?

My dead would never come here.
People of sand and sunlight, people
of snow and mountains. Who are these dead,

collective dead, poets so love to write of?
My dead were never collective, were
as singular as they were in life, touching

all four points of the compass, homeless
as these bells. Their names won't thread
on a string, and too few of them for chains.

Down in the catacombs, the walls are made
of water, but not sweet domestic water
to cup in palms, sluice in public baths –

no, underworld water, rivers of dream
and nightmare, rivers of sons and daughters.
My living dead cling to their curtained rooms,

dim corridors, wedged open doors to parlours.
But the dead come one by one: each has
a stanza in the heart, each an echo chamber.

★

I have heard two voices in the river,
one of the singer, one of the listener
and both were the voices of poetry.

One was a daughter and one a son,
one would listen as the other ran on
and both could do either equally.

Where one was blind, the other was dumb,
when one of them wept, the other grew numb,
changing place simultaneously.

I have felt two terrors in my heart.
If one fell silent, the other would start
but it was the silent one that broke me.

Time stepped in to heal the breach
till both of my terrors were out of reach
and I returned to normality.

But the river ran on, I knew it was there
in the either/or, the when and where,
hiding, dividing, mercilessly.

★

Enter the warmth of the Dead House,
green subaqueous light, soft planking
underfoot, piped rumblings overhead.

Turbines, beam engines, flex their muscle,
lagged iron, steel, lift ten-ton weights.
The coal bunkers are utterly silent,

blacked in, set back in brick pilasters.
What do they know of water, ambient
memories of river? Steel cables

are all they know of sky, slow roar
of the city, trundling above on giant rails.
We ourselves are the drums, arteries,

hollows through which the sounds vibrate.
There is nothing inside the Dead House.
What is inside, inside the rust-stained walls,

trapped, enormous, are the unfathomable
languages of water. Nothing to do here
but feel. Listen. Choose to forget.

★

I never remember my dreams.
I wake exhausted from them.

And when I do it feels like
I'm wearing a skin inches thick –

glutinous and alien. I never remember
my dreams for I'm not who I am in them,

what bred them. God forbid
I should write, then read them

through the glass of a vivarium
when I could be out in the sun!

I'm not answerable to the dark.
Let others sing the snake.

★

For a tidy soul, one who relishes balance
and, above all, symmetry, to be pencilled in
at a corner of this courtyard is to inhabit

nothing so much as an architectural drawing.
Shadows under arches cross-hatched, banded
masonry, pediments, lintels, balustraded

parapets punctuating rooflines, become
two-dimensional, perfect in perspective.
But into the frame, like a princess in a story,

runs a young girl through the fountains, sparkles
on her dress and sash, pink, silver, green.
She squeals, she streams; her father in city clothes

holding ready a large white handkerchief,
her grandfather in the shade reading a leaflet
in his quiet greys and signet rings.

Not the bells, whistle buoy in the distance,
fountains sparkling in the sun, but an Indian
lunchtime outing has served to make us real.

★

I barely cried. When my father died,
and my grandfather before him,
when I heard the news, I smiled.

Some force pulling up the corners
of my mouth so irresistibly
it was all I could do not to laugh.

Some people cry for months, even if
they live abroad, the more so for not
being there, for the guilt, anger, love.

As far as death goes, I'm a child.
With a child's curiosity, I wonder
what they look like. 'Like an angel',

they said of him who was no angel,
'clean as a baby, not a mark.'
I remember the soles of his feet, my Dad,

pumiced and soft. The safety pin
he pinned to the lower end of his sheet
for fear it would touch his mouth.

★

Today sympathy is our watchword. Sympathy
and symmetry, a line of sun and shadow cutting us
into perfect halves at 5pm the clock confirms.

And dividing the blue above, a vapour trail,
long as the courtyard's wide, driving its parallels.
Granite glints, silver water throws clouds of spray –

great silver fans of diamond. Pigeons burble
contentedly, sun warms the wool of our coats,
settles on a cheek or two to burn. Strawberry red,

red as cherry pulp are the pigeon's three spread talons.
Up and over it climbs the iron strut of the chair.
Could it be drums at play, softly in the lightwells?

The river winding up for the day, packing away
its instruments? And the bell calls, lucidly in silence.
A woman is wearing a rose, two of them in her hair.

CRETAN CURES

As well as blue eyes to ward off the evil eye,
you may also find *filahta* pinned to the back
of a small child's coat or discreetly tucked away

in a grandmother's layers. *Filahta* are most commonly
gold medals of the saints, sachets filled with basil,
pieces of olive branch, candle shavings from an altar.

As for me, I've crossed the water under a starlit sky,
stars falling around me like jangling charms on a bracelet.
I've looked up at the stars, seen sevens and eights

– wishbones, tents – a sky of Arabic numerals.
I've searched for blue, blue of the bay, among pebbles.
Green I find, muted, and every possible shade of grey.

I hold a handful of the cool ones that have slept
in shade. They're like skin, I think, so we lie
on the beach holding hands, me and the pebbles.

During the power cut, I step out on the terrace
to check on the stars, now shorn of light pollution.
The tavernas have never been so noisy, so excited,

like children playing hide and seek in the dark.
But when the lights come back on at 3am,
while we lie thick and drugged with seaside sleep,

still the tables have to be cleared. A silent army
in the night collecting cutlery, bottles, glasses,
threading braziers where coals grow cold and ashen.

Should you be suffering from a summer cold or sniffles,
grate onions for a poultice on your chest, grind them
with Ouzo into a paste for swollen wrists or ankles.

Garlic is also good. Dangle a braid above your door,
carry a clove of it somewhere on your person.
A single clove grown into a head is best, but rare.

In the narrow shade of the seawall, cats, lined up
like china ornaments, sit gazing seaward. It's not sea
they're gazing at, it's Nikos on his fishing boat,

untangling fish from his heap of nets piled up
like yellow seaweed beside a white plastic bucket
into which he plops the good ones, throws cast-offs

to the cats on the quay who eat, one eye open.
Fish are wise and knowledgeable. Revere them
for their silence. And never throw bread away.

Instead, throw it to the chickens, pigs, dogs even.
Bread must be consumed by some living creature,
it would be a sin to throw it away. 'Verona' lists:

still the gunny sack on deck is full. Nikos
scratches his head, sets to, slipping his hand
through a hole, braceletted for a moment in gold net.

Among us, Hazel is a nurse – luckily for Jean
who slipped in the shower and gashed her arm
to the ulna. Jean's eyes are round blue cornflowers.

I use perfume on mosquito bites, hoping to quieten them.
The fridge is empty of cherries now – I've washed
the plastic tray. How soothing plastic is, and melamine,

on holiday. I provide my own room service, stand
on a chair to slip the curtain rod back into the finial
(to see my skirt-length I have to stand on the bed).

If someone pays you a compliment, remember to say
Skorda (garlic) under your breath and spit three times;
ask them to spit on you too. Garlic doesn't smell

till peeled, so you can stick a clove of it in your bra.
Bat bones are also lucky (though killing bats is not),
so if you find one, slip a fragment into your purse.

Hazel is wearing a straw bonnet, Macmillan daffodils
and a blue enamelled butterfly clustering at the back.
Henry's hat sports an orange bandanna, two butterfly pins

in two shades of blue, but essentially they are dressed
in beige. Are they married? How well they sleep!
Well, together. Well-travelled as people steeped

in their own roots often are – 'We survived', she says.
Their breakfast table is a small cluttered island and they
two kindly weather fronts holding it between them.

Hazel, don't hand him a knife. Let him pick it up himself
or there'll be crosswinds later. And never, on any account,
empty your account. Money begets money, remember.

And when the crow caws, say *Sto kalo, sto kalo,*
kala nea na me feris – go well into the day, crow,
bring me good news! Crows anywhere spell disaster.

The cat sleeps soundly as a carpet. Flies don't wake her.
She sleeps like a crescent moon, horned moon, tabby moon
under the taverna's awning. Slip off your sandals now

and lay them down the right way up, upturned shoes
spell death. If the soles by chance fall facing up,
turn them over immediately, side by side, say *Skorda*

and a spit or two won't hurt. Now that you've taken
so many precautions, you're bound to be safe and well.
Now that you're closing your eyes, you still see light,

an eyelid edged with it, and your cheeks rising up
like a rock of shadow, double-humped, below them.
And when you open them, how doubly bright the water!

Ellie, with her sight restored thanks to laser surgery –
after a lifetime of seeing in a blur, how doubly bright the sea
for her! (and Marmite helps with her loss of taste and smell).

THE POET'S HOUSE

for Robert vas Dias

The poet's house gestures towards a roof
and a chimney aslant the lemon grove
raised on the first of the bancales which climb
the mountainside towards a daylight moon.
It's like Waller's dark cottage of the soul,
dark inside but facing the rising sun
blind-eyed and its rusted ironwork balcony
with room enough for the old poet to stand,
early mornings, sipping coffee, hoping,
hoping today for a visit from the muse.

Pigeons roost in the rafters and the night wind
would bang the door, hanging on its hinges,
were it not wedged by long grasses and rubble.
The poet's house is for viewing across a valley
where it guards the view. Barely a love nest,
set square against a landscape – harsh maybe,
but softened by olives, pomegranate trees,
scrub dotting the lower terraces and the walls
weathered, bleached, remembering in their plaster
gouges and pocks the soft pale colour of frescoes.

No smoke from the chimney, no floor for a bed,
but something cosy as a cottage loaf
the way it nests: a square with a sense of rondure.
Does it hear the quietness of the morning
or is it, being centuries old, stone deaf?
A poet's house that was never built for song,
not for talk or companionship, for wine
or laughter. And its balcony too small
to sit there reading as the sun moves over.
Set at the foot of a slope, commands no vista.

Negatives, absences, withdrawals, withholdings,
under its red-tiled roof, hold conference.
For the soul is nothing if not negative –
look how its furniture has been abstracted,
it is all shell, shell, shell, the seed of a dwelling,
husk of an old migration. We long to possess it.
We dream of bright conversions, enough to make it
habitable: a floor, a stair, a shower;
a garden but no fence, for the goats, the dogs,
would be welcome; a riot of tumbling flowers.

But when night descends, the poet's house
is illumined by a borrowed moon, by floodlight
from the castle. Inside, nothing is illumined.
Remove its shell and it would stand, a Mecca,
Kaaba, for the soul to circle, but not
with the eye, the ear, a groping hand
or tentative step, only with the passage
of the whole body, being, the self's dissolve,
for without dissolve, there is no emergence.
Were it in my gift, Robert, I'd ask you to stay.

Come and sit here with me on the old stone wall,
half wall, half rubble. Let the sun beat down
with the sound of running water way down
below in the gulley and a visible breeze
blowing the oat grass, the very thought of breeze,
to cool us. We should have sat by the pool but no,
here we are, ringed with the sound of cicadas
in a central well of silence. Insects hum,
nose-dive past, leaving a nervousness behind them.
Come, let's brave the door. Or at least its shade.

Slip into the cool now. Sit quietly
on a blue rush seat chair, framed by cobwebs,
a timber plank with a row of rusted nailheads
and two wooden poles to prop the splintered
roof beam overhead. Once, the house was painted
in pastels, Edwardian pastels, childlike patterns
on the walls in faded greens, blues, ochres.
A staircase leads out of sight and plaster, brickwork,
stripped bare, reveal an ocean underneath
of shell striations, fish eyes, land mass shapes.

I've left the door ajar, dragged vines in, greening
at their tips, it's so cool and quiet in here,
tiles underfoot covered in leaves, stalks, dirt.
Don't worry, nobody will ever come.
Even the animals, strewing droppings
along the path, know to keep away.
There's nowhere to move to, only the eye
can travel, seeing nothing but ruin, naming
nothing but ruin and the ear that listens,
through the door, for unfamiliar birds.

Look back on where you were, across the valley,
the middle distance arid, melancholy,
drawing the heart towards it, straight on a sightline
towards this buckling roof, red gentle slope,
the balcony door half-open like a mind
in two minds whether to penetrate or drift
around an elevation like a face.
The poet's house looks steadily beyond,
towards the object of its own desire,
knowing its own mind which is also gentle.

And so it stares in stasis, blank and immune
to interruption, a stand against forgetting,
the loss of where we were. A hermit's dwelling.
And in place of electricity, plumbing,
there's the steady hum of cicadas, sawings,
whirrings and buzzings, a whistling stream of sound
like gas jets hissing: its mechanical life
is without, not within. Within, on diagonals
spiders walk, spins a gaping hole of thought,
waiting for a poet to come and think it.

A Tree of Heaven, *Ailanthus altissima*,
grows near the house, its canopy bowed down
with clusters of samaras turning pink.
Sun longs to enter. Making little forays
across the grass, hanging little flags
of light along the trees. Shadows are misty
now and the face of 'Casa Fenollar'
watchful as if to call the shadows in
from where they hang precipitously by handholds
down the ravine or in the depths of branches.

But it does not call. It trusts to the campo
till, in time, of their own accord the shadows
thicken at the door and the fingers of sun
let go, sliding off the guttering.
Vast the vistas are but the casa looks
only to its own patch for it's enough
to be so wakeful and so solid. Backlit,
the Tree of Heaven flutters, edged with gold,
but why talk of heaven? Right here on earth,
Trees of Heaven grow everywhere like weeds.

THE WEATHER WHEEL (2014)

I EARTHSHINE

HOUSE MOUSE

Even the mist was daffodil yellow in the morning sun,
a slant of April sun that glowed on my banana skin.

And in the shadow of my arm a mouse lay, white belly up
like a lemur sunbathing. Begging she was, paws curled,

miniature paws like nail clippings, hind legs crossed
in a rather elegant fashion, tail a lollipop stick.

Pricked on her shadow, her ear and fur stood sharp as grass
but her real ear was soft, thin, pliable, faint as a sweetpea petal

and her shut eye a tiny arc like the hilum of a broad bean.
Yesterday she was plump. Today she's thin. Sit her up, she'll sit.

You can see how Lennie would have 'broke' his, petting it –
mine weighs no more than a hairball, nestling in my palm

as though it were wood pulp, crawlspace, a 'wee-bit housie'
and she, the pup, the living thing. The baby look's still on her.

And the depth of her sleep. I tuck her into the finger
of my banana skin – a ferryboat to carry her over the Styx.

MADAME BERTHE'S MOUSE LEMUR

We should have been lemurs, lowering our metabolism
to suit, going into torpor in the cool dry winter months

to save on water and energy. We too should have sailed
on a raft of matted leaves out of poor Africa, out to Madagascar

into a forest of mangrove and thorn scrub, feeding off gum,
honeydew larvae, bedding down in tree holes *en famille*.

The very smallest of us, the veriest Tom Thumb, the most
minute pygmy, *tsitsidy, mausmaki*, itsy bitsy portmanteau,

little living furry torch, eyes two headlamp luminaries, front
a bib of chamois, tip to tail – and mostly tail – barely as long

as the line I write in, despite illegal logging, slash and burn,
would survive longer than many folk, especially in captivity.

Only the barn owl, goshawk, to watch for in the dark – raptors
with their own big beauty. But Madame Berthe's Mouse Lemur

is caught in the act – a chameleon clasped in her hands,
a geisha lowering her fan: the smallest primate on our planet.

SUN SPARROW

Sun, like a sparrow in the house, seeks dustgrounds
small as a handkerchief to play in. Sun sparrow, house sparrow,

I give you landing strips of dust on wood, runways
between photo frames, wood grain and wood knot roses,

nests of cane and cloth for you to steal, netherlands I never clean
for you to bathe in. Here's a dust bath, look, under the bed,

large enough for you and all your family. Why, even
the numbered hairs of my head, fallen, have lined a nest,

innumerable nests and silver they are, the better for you
to shine in. Come, sun, roost. And here is my skin. Warm it.

Sun sparrow, didn't Sappho herself have sparrows,
fair fleet sparrows, draw Aphrodite's chariot to wing her plea?

I ask no such thing. But I see you land, on wood, on wall,
take flight again and you who have your own warmth,

who need no streetlight, neon sign to roost in – why flee?
Be sociable, stay awhile on my flaking sill, hop right in.

KNIFEFISH

Lit, lit, lit, lit are the estates at dawn:
honeycomb stairwells, corridors, landing lights,

flare paths for passengers flying home.
Three jets like electric fish streak the sky with rose.

Black ghost, ghost knifefish, how many days
since you went abroad, lurking in your murky pools,

locating dawn by sonar, by electric fields alone?
To image your world in darkness – driftwood

casting distortion shadows – no matter how weak
your receptor organ, faint its discharge, barely a volt,

through tail-bend, waveform, you fire, you feel,
sensing lightning, earthquake, your own kind

turning their dimmer switch up and down,
for this is how you talk. Old Aba Aba, grandpa,

with your one room lit at a time, feeling for walls,
navigating as surely as in the brightest, highest dawn!

SNAIL

Close the trapdoor. Let no light in. No,
not the luminous apricot cloud or whale cloud,

fat peach cloud or the isthmus of blue,
the sky lanes in between. Close the chink.

Sea slug, land snail, one head and one foot,
draw the one foot in. You are all head now,

helmet, foetus and dome, oceans under,
trapdoor sealed. Safe, safe, safe.

Snail-deep, slug-dark, shu-shu-shush.
Waves roll in. But here you are landed,

relic on the sand. The moon has carried you
on his back but what do you know of love?

Its arrow, smear of silk. And of hatred?
Salt, drawing your love juice into its grains,

giving you age, old age and its snail-slow shrivelling.
Be lazy, snail, be slow. Savour every inch.

SCIURUS CAROLINENSIS

Sun rivers on glass, threatens to mount, blaze
into my eyeline so that, heat-struck, I headlong

down to hump squirrelled in the shade below, leaves
moving as I move, as grass moves with the snake.

I am the grey. Born helpless, blind and deaf.
My mother lays me across her forepaws, fetches me

out of a cave, weans me once my teeth appear.
Sciurus names only my *skia*, shadow, *oura*, tail.

I displace the red. Acorn-bred, carrier of the pox,
I infect it with lesions, ulcers, scabs, weeping crusts,

it shivers, shivers, *skia*, *oura*, and then it's dead.
I mean no harm. I'm no image seared on your brain

only seen side on, tail up, ears tufted like conifer spurs;
no nutkin on a branch, jug on a wall, graphic loop,

no ampersand between presentiment and trace.
Skia, *oura*, I flicker on the walls of the cave.

THE CONSERVATORY

If you keep two blinds down and one blind up
and sit under the one that's up under the skylight

and the Sunday morning rain, you create –
at absolutely no expense – the kind of conservatory

you've always wanted but without the wicker
and kelims, the view onto the dripping garden

and the cat, all soaking, hidden under a hedge.
You are elevated instead. You are a bird in a nest.

Rick as a small boy sold birds for pocket money.
He made his own trap out of a wire washing basket,

a stick, some fishing line, some bread, catching
sparrows, dunnocks and, if he was lucky, a finch,

before progressing to proper trap cages with a call bird
that would sing and attract more birds he'd extricate,

sell, then start over again. Now he's a mouse-catcher
with no pension. 'You're not illegible', he said they said.

THE LITTLE GLOSTER

With such icy winds, facing the rising sun in the garden
makes no difference so I take shelter on the terrace,

comforted by two black sheepskins, one under me,
one over, kindly provided by the establishment.

Seagulls, seen from below, their red feet neatly stowed,
beaks and eyes painted like wooden toys, hang

immobile long enough to be scrutinised in flight
before they swerve away. Propped against a fence,

a reindeer is spotted with fairy lights you expect to see
vanish like daylight stars and everything that loomed

last night on a smuggler's night black with storm
– the distillation tower's disembodied four red eyes –

retreats into its rightful place. Young waiters, chefs,
preparing for the fair, are lining up white deckchairs

close enough to the seafront to feel spray. Sandwiched
in these sheepskins, I am half man, half sheep, myself.

MICROCHIROPTERA

Only human noises populate the night. No owl, pheasant,
wailing fox, only stars that have buried their heads in cloud.

Listening becomes a momentous task. The eye as always
fights for supremacy and the ear, fazed as a bat in rain,

imagining it hears a rush of water, hears 'all things hushed'.
O *chauve-souris*, flying mouse, leather mouse, flittermouse,

jealous naked microbat, winged seed of sycamore,
umbrella man, acrobat hanging in your own skin parachute,

flying patagium carpet, O bat-being in fairy wings,
string purse, anus face, where are your echoes now

– dry flutter of a mothwing, rustle of a centipede –
where is your pulsing cry, your lovesong in the dark?

In the vast homelessness of a country night – dear country,
left behind – we come back into our moral being, back

into the animal ground of our being under the absent stars.
Under their roofs and rafters, we navigate that ground.

THE LANDING STAGE

How slippery the path just at the end where the indigo stutters
of dragonflies rain against glass water! Where everything is flower –

the air, its scent, cabbage whites, single, paired; pines, cedars,
carpet dew; where old age flowers in its slow walk to the water;

where the left brain flowers and the right, the lawnmower
sprays grass fountains; where sadness settles for the pine cones,

not knowing if they are really pine cones at this distance;
where Anne flowers in an orange shawl and our lungs

are grey wildflowers, minds a mindless garden; where,
in the event of fire, we are to collect at the bottom of the lawn.

We are to collect our belongings, blankets, iPads, medicines.
We are to collect sunlight silvering on our shoulders.

Our shoulders are thin. We collect our thinness, our boniness,
in a huddle of silver water down by the river. Be careful!

they warn me, those who are, going down to the landing stage
raised high enough to dangle younger legs over the water.

EARTHSHINE

Under the giant planes beside the gate where we said goodbye,
the one bare trunk where squirrels flatten themselves on bark

side by side with a voluminous plane whose ivy outraces branch,
under the two great planes where we stood vaguely looking round

since it was a clear night, the street empty and we, small gaggle,
newly intimate but standing a yard apart, keeping our voices low

though they carried bright as bells as we counted the evening out,
gestured towards the cars, deciding who would go with whom

and gradually splitting off, under the planes with the squirrel dreys
hidden in all that ivy, but hanging low directly above the station,

there, where we looked pointing, like an Oriental illustration
of Arabian Nights, lay the old moon in the new moon's arms:

earthshine on the moon's night side, on the moon's dark limb,
earthlight, our light, our gift to the moon reflected back to us.

And the duty we owe our elders as the Romans owed their gods
– duties they called pietàs, we call pity – shone in the moon's pietà.

PRUNUS AVIUM

We buried my mother's ashes in the holes, the four
we dug to plant four cherry trees for her, *Prunus avium*:

wild cherry, sweet cherry, bird cherry, gean or mazzard,
each name carrying something of *Prunus avium* on the wind,

the wind that blew drifts of ash like bonemeal across clay.
In three years they'll be grown; in twenty, diamond woodland.

But we'll recognise our trees, set back where the path ends.
Surrounding them will be native oak, beech, alder, hazel.

One cherry tree from each of us: Tara, Bea, Kai and myself.
And on Tom's behalf, we invoked the name of Yax Tum Bak,

Mayan God of Planting, there in a desolate, bitterly windy field
in Buckinghamshire. Clay stuck to our boots in grassy clumps

and as Tara heaved her spade, worms, lustrous as white mulberries,
fled, upturned. Later, in the Garden Centre – 'Oh, how beautiful!'

my mother would have gasped on entering – I bought Tara
a peach tree for Valentine's Day, *Prunus persica*, from Persia.

II UNDER THE VINE

UNDER THE VINE

Yes, I should be living under the vine,
dapple at my feet and the bare dry dust

singing of drought, of heat. Look at the pile
of rubble round the roots, curled dried leaves,

mound of ant homes I can't see. Look at
the flower fallen in the dirt, flake yellow,

listen to the wasps, the bees. And the vine
above me, the vine that smells of nothing,

yields nothing but the music of its name,
the memory of some long-forgotten terrace.

Yes, under a flock of swallows that repeat
– because we have to believe it – the end,

the end, nearly the end of a summer
so long it knows neither month nor week.

Yes, I should keep my happiness hidden,
under the vine, from those who envy it.

STARLIGHT

Only the brightest stars were out with a half moon
centred in the sky: a ceiling to learn the names of stars by.

And in the gaps between the stars, milkcarts went to market,
pony traps crossed viaducts, oxen drove sad water-wheels,

history trundled by as birds awoke and the distant sound
of a plane winked lights. Her owl flew back to Minerva

as she flashed her shield while, on Apadana's stairways,
processions of bearded guards, Persians, Medes, marched past.

Cedar palaces were torched; frigates, night-fishing boats set out.
Passengers flew like vesper bats straight across the moon,

roofscapes listened for child lovers leaning over balconies,
geraniums grew in the dark. I had never been so happy

and historical. Happy enough to see, holding them up,
stars on the tip of each finger, countable, spread far apart,

one by one go out as day rose to pluck the first strains
of a Spanish guitar. Then the silver moon went white.

ANGELS

Updraughts lift sounds of language imperceptibly, even
the silent language of Lula as she hobbles up the steps.

Dogs Lula doesn't know bark along the terraces, cockerels,
though it isn't dawn, crow anyway. It could be any village

anywhere in the world, everything in decay. But things
retain their scent – the rubbed tomato leaf – and sound

– the bamboo river – and as if heard behind closed doors,
the angels: angel of September, of the fallen fig and dapple;

angel of perspective that staggers the terraces upward,
white steps downward; angels of the sister mountains –

the first, the second, the third. And the angels, cowled,
circle us like lepers on the hills, they unveil themselves.

And I love my angels not as they were in childhood,
angel of the crab-apple and chine, of calico and sandal,

but as they are: leprous and discharged, violent and betrayed.
Angel of the soft wind that blows across my breasts.

ORCHARD

However small, it's still an orchard –
three limes, a pomegranate and a kumquat.

Each stands in a circle of shade
and bedding plants. Sweetpeas brought

from England have died at the foot
of their canes. Above, the pepper tree

that went wild in a sudden storm,
throwing its branches all over the place,

hangs droops of coral berries against
a calendar sky. Cones, black droppings

in the dust, a fragment of rope
knotted at both ends, a fleeting shadow –

a swallow if you look up. But no,
I keep my gaze on the ground.

If the fruiters were ponies, they'd be foals
and the pepper tree their barn.

WHAT IT WAS

It was the pool and the blue umbrellas,
blue awning. It was the blue and white

lifesize chess set on the terrace, wall of jasmine.
It was the persimmon and palm side by side

like two wise prophets and the view that dipped
then rose, the swallows that turned the valley.

It was the machinery of the old olive press,
the silences and the voices in them calling.

It was the water talking. It was the woman
reading with her head propped, wearing glasses,

the logpile under the overhanging staircase,
mist and the mountains we took for granted.

It was the blue-humped hose and living wasps
swimming on the surface. It was the chimneys.

It was sleep. It was not having a mother,
neither father nor mother to comfort me.

On our last day on the roof terrace, our own 'heavenly message
of the third floor' that Matisse had in mind for *Les Marocains*,

the air's so still not even the cellophane of my cigarette packet
blows out of the ashtray. Morning sun lies on me like a blanket,

le baromètre a remonté d'un quart de cadran while down in the storeroom,
where two caged budgerigars have never seen the light of day,

il fait clair comme dans une cave. Daisy, the indoor cat, grubs around
the soil of the young olive where a few wild grasses in the tub

are all she will ever know of lawns. Fatiha has watered the palm,
oleander, succulents and a dribble of water crossing a barrier

of sun and shade gleams like oil. The cat moves soundlessly,
the sun with stealth until the shade, the chill, swallows our feet.

There's no accounting for joy, the way it bubbles in the most arid
of deserts or rains blue gold. The muezzin climbs the minaret

in leather mules not on foot but by donkey as if riding, hill by hill,
into Jerusalem. Proust's voice obeys the laws of night and honey.

MARRAKESH II

I have been looking for the famous gentleness of light
floating on the paper field in the pink city and have seen it

only in passing: as we crept into the old town, the taxi
nudging the cyclists, donkey carts, through mud-walled lanes

as if entering a bible story; in the smoky vaporous haze,
the smoky hooded figures enveloped by it, each man a Yeats

declaring 'I am a crowd, I am a lonely man, I am nothing';
in the blind walled pink of the Tombeaux Saâdiens at sunset,

set off by small red rosebeds, a tall magenta bougainvillea,
the colours proceeding by pulsation, exhaled from within;

seen it in the mosaic of light falling through the reed roof
in the Berber souk or down thin alleys of keyhole arches.

Travelling on a paddleboat to Corazón, battling a channel
of reeds and branches, Paul Bowles wrote that it was like

being in the bloodstream of a giant and so it is, immersed
in a memory of sundown, at any hour, in all one's arteries.

MARRAKESH III

To see him at his easel, *H. Matisse par lui-même*, black hat,
tailcoat, beard, glasses, on a camp stool facing a marabout

in pen and ink is to feel a small breeze coming off the pages.
A horseman, acanthus, basket of oranges, a smoker at the window,

another, another, the medina, the portal of the Casbah mosque,
Seated Moroccan, Standing Moroccan, a calla lily and bindweed,

riffle like water through my palms while I sit surrounded,
three floors up, by the same raised, lowered, false perspectives.

But Arcadia is not something to project into deep space
but onto the surface of memory. *Ah! que le monde est grand*

à la clarté des lampes! Aux yeux du souvenir que le monde est petit!
In Jemaa El Fna, the lanterns are lit. They congregate like stars,

tin palaces of fire and flame, a sultanate of miniature cities.
But at cruising altitude, above streaks of indigo and purple clouds,

a blood continent broods on black estuaries, archipelagos, reefs,
for black is the simplifying force of memory. It is a form of elegy.

'These recumbent figures, all in the same gray nuance,
such a soothing gray, whose faces are represented by

a yellow-ocher oval, you know that they were not always
painted like that. Look! At the top, the man on the left,

he was red! The other, next to him, was blue; the other
was yellow. Their faces had lines, eyes, a mouth.

The one at the top smoked a pipe… The slippers, the pipe,
the lines of the face, the varied colour of the burnooses,

why have they all melted away?' *C'est que je vais
vers mon sentiment; vers l'extase… et puis, j'y trouve le calme.*

*J'ai mon bol de poissons et ma fleur rose. C'est ce qui m'avait frappé!
ces grands diables qui restent des heures, contemplatifs, devant*

*une fleur et des poissons rouges. Eh bien! Si je les fais rouges,
ce vermillon va rendre ma fleur violette! Alors? je la veux rose,*

*ma fleur! autrement elle n'est plus! Au lieu que mes poissons,
ils pourraient être jaunes, cela ne me fait rien: ils seront jaunes!*

MARRAKESH V

The floral motif is the initial cell from which the pattern
spreads to the edges of the cloth, canvas, the material world

which is drained of meaning and hierarchy. In its place
the underlying void, aerated, animated, expands like gas

until cloth, rug, garden, agave, succulents, yukka, cacti
and sky-high bamboo forest revert to dreamlike pentimenti.

Jemaa El Fna, once a bus station, has been recognised as
a Masterpiece of the Oral and Intangible Heritage of Humanity

but Berber water-sellers, snake-charmers, storytellers, scribes,
shoeblacks, tooth-pullers, mendicants, fortune-tellers, masseurs,

are more than oral, intangible, in a plaza where no building
should rise higher than a palm tree. Near the Koutoubia,

the booksellers' mosque, Lalla Zohra, the children's saint,
entombed in a castellated, icing-white cube, makes her escape

and visits us regularly. A woman by day, a dove by night,
she sits against the skyline silently, as if transfixed by chanting.

MARRAKESH VI

More megaphone than bird, his whole body pulsing,
the Sahari House Bunting, stringing himself along

the riad's parapet, repeats himself ad infinitum
with a second's pause to catch breath. In that pause,

his mate replies but with a different call, a yes, a maybe,
or occasionally interrupts without disturbing his rhythm.

On his ledge, he rotates to the north, south, east, west,
calling out to the four corners of Marrakesh while she,

catching the sun in flight, fans this way and that before
flitting back to her perch. Now he's on the corner outpost

of his sentry walk, faithfully plugging away and finally
stunned into silence as the braying starts – a most marvellous

cacophony of muezzins from Ben Youssef, Sidi Ishak,
Mouassine, Ben Salah, Koutoubia, Berrima, crowning noon

until, with a lone *Allahu Akba-a-r*, the last muezzin's *adhan*,
melting distance into song and song into the distance, dies away.

LE CAFÉ MAROCAIN

after Henri Matisse

This is the soul. In aqua and gold.
It rhymes with the body as burquas do,

as birdsong with arches, nine to a wall.
The goldfish are spoonfuls of honey,

spoonfuls that dissolve in the bowl.
Glass is the ground of contemplation,

this and a flower, the three-pronged rose.
The gold of men's calves, feet, hands

– lower limbs the body in broadcloth
set loose as it burned off in smoke –

was the first idea, as the soul is, before
the image, the afterthought was formed.

This is the last we shall see of the fathers
in grey burnooses, meadowsweet turbans,

faceless in ovals, forgetful in youth:
this ore, this residue in the alchemical bowl.

III THE SOUL TRAVELS ON HORSEBACK

NEW YEAR'S EVE

Night is a rush of noise, an Indian hilltown train
steaming up gradients through Himalayan tunnels,

morning the destination, quiet as a mountain top
after the snow has melted, celebrants have left:

a Shimla of the mind, its local aspirations – work,
money, kinship, health; a time to think things over,

let them settle in the recesses of imagination.
They'll raise their heads of their own accord, lean

out of carriages to wave. For now is the time
of watering the splendid platform displays, of

gathering at The Ridge, the Scandal Point in the mall,
fingering oak and rosewood souvenirs. In Shimla,

mashkis will be carrying goatskin bags of water,
sluicing down the tarmac while I, at the last

hill station of the year, will bring the silence in,
fold it like a three-flower Kullu shawl on my table.

THE PEAR TREE

And when there's no poetry in it, the hour, the sky,
only cumulus and the first faint ossicles of rain

pattering on glass like a bone bundle thrown
for a shaman to divine, when no answer comes,

faith gives up, brain slackens, skin sloughs off
like a turtle shedding old scutes from its shell,

when the same dread incubus squats on the heart,
hiding a breathing hole on the top of his head

for all breath, desire, have long fled his mouth,
when friends disappear – and were they friends? –

and your head on its single stem weighed down
heavy as a baby pear tree not with pome or pear

but with time's three globes, what then,
little pear tree, bletted by frost? A rootstock

has dwarfed you the better to bear but quince,
pear, whose bridal kiss will you perfume now?

RAIN STORIES

Huddling under an umbrella like two old lovers
arm in arm under the pouring rain, we took up

where we had left off, catching up on the years,
their stories common knowledge now – rain

audible and visible. (Affection returned although
before we share such rain it will be years again.)

But mine at home, and only mine, is secretive,
soundless and so fine, it's only against darker leaves

it reveals itself. Winter, it tells me, means
'the time of water'; raindrops, it shows me,

are spheres and only tear-shaped when they fall –
though in Oaxaca the Church of Santa Teresita

had a glorious rain of roses; more instances,
it gives me, from its own backstory as in –

a r. of kisses, 1893, of calm moonbeams, 1821,
melody, 1820, frogs, 1593, of sparks, tears, 1541.

AUNT MOON

Aunt Moon, Old Glamour Moon in a haze of smoke
puffing behind your folding screen, Old Barren Moon

with your round pig belly, what lies, what lies!
I love you for the lies you've told! Lies with a belly

of milk, lies to call the children in, gather them
round your mirror fogged, Old Moon, with death.

No lying now, is there? No creeping round the houses,
sly Jokester Moon with your pearly teeth, implants

that went wrong, aren't they? One look at the truth
and you vanish. O what a clear clear sky, clear as day!

But I saw you, Moon, in the doorway. Spliced in two
as the glass revolved, in purdah with your back turned.

Who were you whispering to, Aunt Moon? No one,
was there? No one ever to lisp to, bribe, stab in the back,

no one to avenge. No, the best lies are told with a bevy
of innocent stars in your eyes, not in a revolution's doorway.

STATHAM GROVE SURGERY

Seen in disbelief through fug in the workmen's caff
with its canisters of snow, in the panoramic distance

of Clissold Park wearing its hood of grey wool, chef's hat
in the snow, behind a fallen tree trunk languid as a nude,

a human hare, grey on grey, white gloves, white hind paws,
is shadowboxing while their trainer, red on grey, holds up

focus mitts for a second sparring jackrabbit, black on grey,
like the hare on the moon. Amber eyes glide down the road;

horse chestnuts waltz in whalebone, braceletted with crows;
my cappuccino breathes out smoke. Ruled on park railings,

black is a marriage of scissors and snow. In Statham Grove,
among red pillar-box hills, gold corridor woods, we turn into

house plants, umbrella plants, gum trees, rubber leaf hands
still charged with snow, deaf to a story a young dragon tree

hears, enthralled. Dr West wears a bright red stethoscope.
Homeward bound, we leave footprints in a black leaf fall.

THE WARDROBE

How secluded we are under a sun we should be out in.
Cupboarded in shadow, one foot in twilight, we tilt.

Childhood snuffs its master light, light we need to love
and be loved by, to write, to read. Else all is dusk,

dusk in the heart, in all our finer feelings. Had I
a wardrobe of my mother's furs, mink, fox, Persian lamb,

how my heart would sink. I'd slide my fingers along the rail,
feel the carcass weight of coats, shoulders zipped in plastic,

how the metal hook of the hanger sticks, see the bridge,
German bridge, where I wore my own grey astrakhan,

a yellow patch of impetigo on my chin. A dirty disease.
From masturbation, unclean hands, some kind of lonely shit.

It has to be foetal or under three days old, a Karakul lamb,
barely able to stand on the kill floor where dozens more

are bleating, or its pelt will lose colour, curl, lustre,
and its meat is simply tossed, too meagre even to eat.

FOG

World is headless, cut off at the waist and we, bundled,
seeing snowflakes only as they pass across a face,

we earth dwellers who know heaven's a cloud, a bank,
an upperwhere, otherwhere, whose cloud deck homes

lure our spirits with lights in the fog, paraffin stoves,
our Bethlehems, our backyards become Bethlehems,

we whose hearts race the blinder we grow, we moles,
we dirt-tossers, we mouldywarps with no eyes or ears

with a mouth at one end, anus at the other, we pipes,
we cylinders, who have stockpiled our subterranean hell,

our mole runs, underground galleries, larders for a clew
of earthworms, we labour of moles with paws like rakes –

what have we left but these hands now, we boars, we sows
with four limbs, one nose, a body plan and a taupe pelt?

World is headless and we, who have only touch and smell,
must touch and smell gas, smoke bombs, blood meal, bait.

SNOW IS

Snow is a rubbing of sorts, a wax heelball on ground,
an impress of ribs – exoskeletons in high and low relief.

Each snowflake is witness to the cloud-womb that formed it,
how wet, how warm, the union of crystals, how powdery.

Trapped in firn, air will evidence ash from Krakatoa,
deposits from lead smelters, pollen and greenhouse gases.

Snow is adjectival. On foliage particularly, discriminates
between the feathery and lobed, the linear and pointilliste.

In itself is silent, but on contact, creaks. Acquires an air
of sanctity in repose but in action earns oaths and profanities.

Snow is a friend to children, those who have scarves, mittens,
snowboards and wooden sledges. To others, it is the devil's own,

akin to the djinn who frequent sinkholes, wherever mud rejoices.
To the children housed in sheep sheds, chicken coops, tents,

dressed in cut-up blankets, seeing things that aren't there in forests,
snow is the devil they know. Better him than the live bombing.

THE BLANKET

Cold, yes, under a sodium sky at three o'clock in the morning.
But there's this shawl to wear and tea with Manuka honey

and across the only gap in the border, a thousand refugees an hour
pouring through Ras al-Jedir. An hour? By morning, my morning,

another five thousand, by lunchtime, another five and how many
have even a striped hemp blanket? Fifteen thousand blankets!

Imagine one. The way it folds stiffly as a tent around the head
bent back, the shoulders jutting, knees drawn up, wrists free,

the lone triangular edifice. Feel the weave. Hairy, ridged.
Smell it. Determine the sightlines either side of the hollowed cheeks.

Imagine the scene in silence, not as it would be. The blanket
as a block, a wood carving. The tools: straight gouge, spoon gouge,

back bent, dog leg, fishtail chisels, V-tools, punches, vices;
hook knives, drawknives, rasps and rifflers, mallets, saws, abrasives;

slip waterstones – how quiet they sound – and strops for sharpening.
Figure in a blanket. In acacia, sycamore or, most likely, olive.

THE SWARM

Snow was literally swarming round the streetlamp like gnats.
The closer they came, the larger they grew, snow gnats, snow bees,

and in my snood, smoking in the snow, I watched them.
Everyone else was behind the door, I could hear their noise

which made the snow, the swarm, more silent. More welcome.
I could have watched for hours and seen nothing more than specks

against the light interrupting light and away from it, flying blind
but carrying light, specks becoming atoms. They flew too fast

to become snow itself, flying in a random panic, looming close
but disappearing, like flakes on the tongue, at the point of recognition.

They died as they landed, riding on their own melting as poems do
and in the morning there was nothing to be seen of them.

Instead, a streak of lemon, lemon honey, rimmed the sky
but the cloud lid never lifted, the weekend promised a blizzard.

I could have watched for hours and seen nothing more than I do now,
an image, metaphor, but not the blind imperative that drove them.

MODEL FOR A TIMELESS GARDEN

after Olafur Oliasson's light installation, Hayward Gallery

You are the shadows who have miniaturised the cryosphere
into a garden of paradise, yours the silhouettes facing fire.

Yours the skeletons, crystal wasps in the long black coffin,
spiders with egg sacs and glass intestines, stalagmites, goblins,

vertebrae and antlers, melting candles, yours the serpents
swallowing mice; infinite, interminable, your Lazarus dance.

Have you seen aerial fossils, spiculae, birdwings frozen in flight?
Kittens iced to branches, glazed drops, objects crystallised by light?

Yours the glass apple, glass core, that ballooning missing bite;
the wedding arch of crossed swords, apertures jagged as kites.

Go home and imagine them, you can't. Even as they're here,
now, they're gone. And everything outdoors, buildings by the river,

boats, buses on the bridge, everything that runs in lines will run
into fountain, the beauty of the arc against the formality of line.

Yours this catwalk, ghastly, spectacular, and all the faery forms
of fungus, plankton, Venus's girdle, that have swum through time.

THE SOUL TRAVELS ON HORSEBACK

and the road is beset with obstacles and thorns.
But let it take its time for I have hours and hours to wait

here, snowbound in Lisbon, glad of this sunlit café
outside Departures, for an evening flight to Heathrow.

Being my soul's steed, I should like to know its name
and breed – a Marwari of India, Barb of North Africa,

the Akhal-Teke of Western Asia or a Turkoman,
now extinct? Is it the burnt chestnut colour of the ant,

grey as a Bedouin wind, the four winds that made it?
O Drinker of the Wind, I travel by air, sea, land

and wherever I am, there you are behind my back
pounding the cloud streets, trailing banners of cirrus

or as Platero once did, from fear or chill, hoofing a stream,
breaking the moon into a swarm of clear, crystal roses.

No, no matter your thirst, ride swiftly, mare, stallion,
mother, father, for without you I feel forever homesick.

IV TEARS

THE OVERMIND

Even when I was a child, tears were something
other children had – a permission I didn't understand

other people gave, I thought the children gave it
to themselves: a special treat when they'd already

had their share. My overmind, as H.D. called it,
isn't a jellyfish, a kind of swimming cap on my head.

My overmind seems to be this sadness – I nearly always
carry it and it *is* a kind of hat, skysize, skyshape.

I feel sorry for my smallness, short trunk, short legs,
sleeves rolled up, feet too large to be in proportion.

When I sit and plant them squarely, side by side like shoes
with no one in them, I feel how flat they are and firm.

If I were a pot, a round ceramic pot with a mustard glaze
on a whatnot in the guest room or on an outside table,

I'd be, like H.D.'s Delphic charioteer whose feet made
'a firm pedestal for himself', I'd be always balanced.

READING THE SATURDAY GUARDIAN

A yellow ladybird is reading the *Guardian Weekend*,
alternately reading and grooming, rubbing her hands,

slapping the sides of her face. To do so, she tilts back
on her tail, rearing up as if into a magnifying mirror.

For the time being, she's entirely forgotten about flight –
the ridgy terrain of a brown paper bag, a valley dotted

with croissant lakes, is only a ten-minute hike away.
Of course she isn't yellow yellow – more goldenrod

with many black spots, a black and white harlequin head.
I present her with a flake. Momentarily, she looks baffled,

rears again and, in the one instant I look away, disappears.
Next thing I know the ladybird and (croissant) flake –

twice her size – have toppled over the rim of the *Guardian*,
one on top of the other – a perfect landing, ladybird on flake

like man in boat, then, capsizing out of sight, she sails
over the edge of the table, the table travelling to Portslade.

MIDSUMMER SOLSTICE

Sun keeps taking its jacket off and putting it on again.
So, down here, do I. Of every shape and size and species,

wasps, flies, bees, midges, gnats, gather in this seeded
cottage garden like pilgrims to a church. The foxglove bud

hasn't yet unfurled, tug at it tug tug but there's no entry here.
So the blithe bee flies away. How busy skies once were

– as they are now – with a glut of nectar, colour, nestled
between rock walls to draw them in – fleets of giddy insects.

They land on my glasses, thigh, buzz around my hair,
whizz by, zoom in and out of vision but nothing annoys me

except my clumsy language, my laggard apprehensions.
Sleep, sleep is the only word I hear. I'd curl up in it

as a bee in a foxglove bell. And I see the blonde schoolboy
at Leeds station, left on a bench with a younger brother

and a punnet of raspberries to look after, calling out *Mum!*
holding a finger up in the air, capped with a raspberry bell.

PICKING RASPBERRIES WITH MOWGLI

It was when he leant close to me, his little naked torso,
brown and thin, reaching an arm into the row of raspberries,

that I snatched a kiss. The raspberries smelled of rosemary
and among them, like a cuckoo's egg, grew the odd sweetpea.

Do you know why they're called sweetpeas? Mowgli asked.
No, why? Because look, he said, fingering a sick pale pod,

this is the fruit and this is the flower and inside the pod are peas.
Mowgli looked inside things. Inside the sieve, a spiderling

trailing a thread his finger trailed up, over, under the pile
of fruit he prodded. Don't pick the ones with the white bits,

Mowgli ordered, they taste horrid. Sun tangled in the canes,
cobwebs blurred the berries. Mowgli progressed to the apples –

small bitter windfalls. I'm going to test them, he said, for smashes.
Mowgli, throwing apples high against the wall – and missing;

Mowgli squinting, testing the poor things now for bruises; Mowgli
balancing on a rake, first thing in the morning, grinning shyly.

SNIFF

It was Sniff who chose Kai, not the other way round, at Sharon's
Fugly Rats, by licking him all over, grooming him, virtually everything

short of saying *please choose me*. In the car, he sat quietly in his hand.
And now it's only Kai he comes to, sniffing, only Kai he's bonded with.

Sharon breeds dumbo rats, sometimes top-eared, rex and smooth
as well as hairless and double rex in a variety of colours and markings –

great pets, well handled, not 'the cowaring wrecks you can sometimes see'.
Sitting next to Kai on our deckchairs, I am finally introduced to Sniff

– 'feel his tail, it's really soft' – on my birthday. The size of him!
Sniff is a cinnamon hooded fancy rat, hooded not only by the fur

cinnamon saddle that runs the length of his spine but also, currently,
by Kai's t-shirt sleeve, whom I have presented – for his owner's birthday –

with a three-tiered rat cage complete with double hammock, straw nest,
swinging tunnel, mineral tube, cat litter tray and dog potty training pad.

I hope he knows who he is. To find out more, visit Fancy Rats Forum
whose menu includes bulletins, articles, reviews, tutorials and obituaries.

DRAWING BEA

Her voice had that dreamy quality that made me think
she had been watching telly, so early on Sunday morning.

When it brightened as I said 'It's Granny Mimi', I did,
for a moment, feel like Granny Mimi as if she had brought me

slippers, a cup of coffee. 'What were you doing?' 'What?'
'Were you watching telly?' imagining her under a blanket,

curled on the sofa, slightly sulky. 'Mum's drawing me.'
'Drawing you?' 'Yes, Mum's doing a drawing of me.'

I saw the darkened room and, in a spotlight somewhere,
Bea keeping unbelievably still. I heard the stump of charcoal

hatching, shading, stroking her hair, her mother breathing;
felt her whole outline being transposed, lifted like a transparency.

But the reality was they were facing each other, like card players,
across the kitchen table. While Tara drew Bea, Bea drew Tara:

heads down, heads only, a shoulder, an arm maybe, no hands,
quick sketches on copy paper – Tara's to bin, Bea's to sort out later.

NOCTURNE

Parked cars are sleeping like animals in their baskets.
Sally, Bea's corn snake, coils by her rock and the mollies

who know neither night nor day keep swimming round
and round behind glass. Lucky the brain awash with sleep

flushing its toxins out. However, according to my mother,
so groggy in the mornings, she never slept a wink all night.

What did she do during those long useless hours? Worry,
endlessly worry, take more pills, eat something sweet, biskwits

as she called them, never more than one or two at a time?
The dead have taken our questions with them, leaving,

in their stead, fresh shocks: discoveries in drawers, files,
that become the significant things we remember them by:

not the memories that swim round and round behind glass
– how they were, how we knew them when they were alive –

but realisations after the fact, small sleepless leapings
and floodings, spasms, nocturnal poundings in the heart.

THE WAVES

Every day the world is beloved by me, the seagull eager
for its perch. I woke this morning to a darkened room,

my soul stabled at the gate. We grow older, quieter,
hearing degrees of movement, distance, and the dead

would listen if they could to the voices of the living
as bedrock listens to the ocean. I listen to the waves,

trying to make them go one, two, one, two, to hear
what Virginia Woolf heard. But she heard it in memory,

darling memory that delineates. One, two, one, two,
and all the variable intervals in between surrendering

to 'the very integer' Alice Oswald rhymed with water,
creating a thumb-hole through which to see the world.

Light fluctuates and my soul fluctuates like a jellyfish
underwater. My hand throws animal shadows on paper

and there, outlined, is a single goat, black and white,
standing on top of the mountain, like a tiny church.

SIMILES

The yacht lies like an elegant equation in the mind.
Last night it lay on black velvet like a glasswing butterfly,

wings folded, two tall masts. The straightness of the horizon
never ceases to be astonishing, putting one in a daze –

only a slight swell in the water to prove that we are not
in a painted vestibule, that this is not an annunciation.

And here's the yellow ferry which reminds me of
Elizabeth Bishop's desk; my table, metallic, sunflecked,

of Hockney's swimming pools. Everything is always
like something else. Each makes love to the other.

You are like me, they say. Blue paint has spattered
the whitewash, speckled the flagstones – the eye jumps

from blue to blue, island to island, raisin to raisin in a cake.
Archie hated raisins in cake, peas in rice. His beard

was salt and pepper, white at the time of death. To have
one terrible disease gives you no immunity against another.

CHERRIES AND GRAPES

He stood up in my dream, very tall, and said: Mum,
I've got — Syndrome. The missing word's a dream word,

a bottom-of-the-sea, a carried-on-the-wind word.
Being so tall, my son has eyes like fruit in a tree, glassy,

Rainier cherries very high up. One cannot reach them.
The worse the news, the further they recede on the branch.

Talking of Richard who had an epileptic fit this morning,
Giorgos, who has seen it all, with that warm faraway look

in his eyes, stands shaking his head, 'So young…'
while his father, still spry, turns aside, shaking out nets –

but what's the fishing like these days? No one says.
This is how the world is today. And this is how I am in it,

rising from a siesta. My granny would have brought me
grape juice, white *asgari* she had crushed and sieved herself

and I would have drunk it slowly, ruckling, then smoothing,
the green chenille at her table. This is how the world was then.

KUSA-HIBARI

It was June and every barnacled brick of the sea wall
was drying out as we were. Had it been October,

had I been Hearn, I too would have kept a grass lark,
a Kusa-Hibari. Why? Not only because he sings,

not only because he is also called Autumn Wind,
Morning Bell, Little Bell of the Bamboo Grove,

or because he's worth more than his weight in gold,
being half the size of a barley grain, or even because

his antennae, longer than his body, are so very fine
they can only be seen when held against the light

as they will be held since to find him, you must turn
his cage round and round to discover his whereabouts,

but because, as his guardian tells me, his tiny song,
song of love and longing, 'is unconsciously retrospective:

he cries to the dust of the past – he calls to the silence
and the gods for the return of time' is why I'd want him.

TEARS

In the first weeks after my mother's death,
I curled up like a foetus on the side of my heart.

My tears were like fresh water, warm and clear.
They flowed of their own accord, soundlessly,

while my body, my mouth and even my eyelids
lay as peacefully as in sleep and the more tears flowed,

the more I wanted them. World was foetal then.
But in the months that followed, tears dried up

and world took up its stick and walked blindly
through the riverbeds. Had they been floodplains,

had there been no dams to render them obsolete,
nilometers would have measured the overflow

from faraway monsoons on stairs, pillars, wells.
Too high and there'd be famine, too low, the same.

I measured distances by her. My mother my compass,
my almanac and sundial, drawing me arcs in space.

V HER ANNIVERSARY

THE GOAT

The goat, the earliest known ruminant in the world
and hence, one might say, our first poet-philosopher,

is not ruminating now but, nose against purple plastic,
is dribbling a ball among pigeons. When he rears

against the wire fencing, towering above us, he displays,
dangling on his neck, his two wattles or toggles or tassles –

a dimorphic trait maybe, caruncles with no known function.
We cannot touch the goat or feed him. But children do,

they want to feel the fearful thrill of his tongue, his lips,
they want to console, thank him for being among us.

Does he miss his mountains? The properties of spheres
in motion are no compensation for limestone gorges,

healing dittany and sage. The pigeons peck peck peck.
The old buck ruminates. And a toddler stoops to grass,

tugs at a handful she thrusts into the air above her head
and lets fall on her father's shoes, like Newton's apple.

ON THE OCCASION OF HIS 150TH ANNIVERSARY

Let's fling down a cloak of gold leaf on wove paper,
let's do the pavement like Klimt. Like his father

before him, Ernst Klimt the Elder, gold engraver,
and his brother who took up engraving later –

whose deaths in one year were the fount of his vision –
let's do acacia in a shower of coins, engrave each face

with *The Kiss*. Semen is flowing like golden rain,
double yellow lines meander in gold metallic ink

and the streetlamps are on – *O spark of the Gods!* –
it's snowing gold flake, sweeping mosaics along the kerb,

spandrels of gold between car wheels. Werewolves,
gorgons, are sauntering out of their lairs, trick-or-treaters

with quince-red cheeks and my beautiful girl in a tent
of yellow roses twines her corn snake round her wrist.

As a night fox trots through a gold-barred gate, trapping
gold-dust in his fleece – quick, hammer him into the frieze.

IN SEARCH OF THE ANIMALS

It's not that I went in search of the animals
though occasionally one crossed my path

or stole out of Wikipedia as if it were a wood
in an English shire but looking, for example,

at a daylight moon steadfast behind drifts
of cloud I'd follow my own drift of thought

and who's to say I wouldn't trip up –
moon not moon at all but a platinum sun,

a frieze of haunches, heads, ears and mouths
evening out, dissolving back to cloud?

And look how morning becomes evening
accidentally, heuristically, in the miracle

of language leading us up the garden path
a white rabbit crosses, a badger, our local fox

who is the last commuter padding home
apart from me, lagging behind on a crutch.

MARTINA'S RADIANCE

Martina – you are in the mist now, season of mists
and mellow fruitfulness and indeed the apple tree

below my window holds reddening apples up to me
and Jude's apple tree has dropped enough fruit

for another round of *apfelstrudel*. Today the weather
suits you, dear Martina – sun's glow behind the mist,

raindrops I first mistook for petals on the pavement.
And isn't this what radiance is: the elation, the promise

before sun breaks through, the laugh behind your smile,
answers to questions you withheld – not unkindly or coyly

but because radiance and the soft veiling it demands
was your natural element? The new banisters I had built

will never feel your tread. But I feel it the way I feel
the air – more scent than air. Where would you have gone

with your stick, your crutch, had you been well today?
Where does mist go? Mist clears, Martina, clears.

MEHREGAN

She lifts the hood of the pram, attaches
a Chinesey floral scarf to the rim to cover

the opening behind which a baby sleeps
as the poem sleeps behind the page.

Wind lifts one corner. There's no heat
to speak of and the wind is only the earth

stirring as the year turns. But she covers him
as children do a table, making a house for him,

a darkened cave. What will he see but sprays,
borders thinned against the light, a chink

let in on his left? He has no left or right,
no borders, no China. Only this half-light,

the colour of his eyes, a colour bound to change.
Tomorrow is the autumn equinox, Mehregan,

a festival in honour of the Goddess Mehr
for whom my poem has been wheeled away.

SUN IN THE WINDOW

Sun has propped her bike against the skyline.
She'll write in gold today. Wear pinks and reds,

wrap up warm and enter always smiling, always
ready to be overlooked, leaning her chin on her hands,

frowning when addressed. And as for desire,
she'll reserve it for praise, be it modest as an oculus,

a round open fenestration in a wall, set high
and facing west. Terraced, she'll rest her fingertips

on wooden muntins, angle her glance through windows
splayed in Polebrook or Threekingham. And how

she loves lancets, three trefoil-headed lancets, stepped!
A quiet soul she is, an altar rail around her thoughts,

the silk cordon hooked back on its brass stave.
And shy. But look at what she writes! Outshines

the others, the noisy, vociferous others, any day.
I'd give anything for a glyph from the star nib of her pen.

BRINGING DOWN THE STARS

As a mouse sniffs for cheese, so I, reading novels,
am sniffing out scintillas. Sometimes they are few

but enough to keep me going; at other times, rare
and completely enchanting, whole pages, paragraphs,

bring starlight down to earth. Over these I dither,
snuffle back and forth, inhale, raise my nose to weather,

glue it down to sniff the spark, to take the hit again.
I am on the trail of genius whose albedo is nothing short

of fallen snow's, desert sand's, who brings me the sky
'dove-gray with stars', 'the diamond lights of Yalta'.

So what difference does it make, under such reflectivity
diffused through time and space, if I'm here at Seven Dials

where the sundial pillar boasts only six blue clock dials
since it counts itself as the seventh or here on Upper Street

where blue battery lights twine round London planes,
each trunk a princely stag, each branch a starry antler?

THE CLOUD SARCOPHAGUS

When I looked up, I was astonished at the muscularity
of clouds that were rearing up from a marble frieze

in high relief on a sarcophagus of blue. But whose?
Alexander's routing the Persians? Or Abdalonymus

the gardener king's, crowned by his very conqueror?
Now they revolved from war to peace and back again –

either way their spears were drawn, warriors, huntsmen,
lions snarling as they went, bundling up their hind legs

as if melting were a kind of leaping in slow motion.
And the cubs that littered their wake, play-fighting,

pouncing, rolling on their backs, were melting too,
panting, paws outstretched. What is to melt?

Into love, into war? Limb by limb to deliquesce,
to reaccumulate into a giant maw that swallows

a sun, a planet, like a ball in a baseball mitt,
a perfect fit, while the jaw, the hand, fragment?

THE DOE

For however long it was – it seemed an age – that I stood
leaning over the wall, looking down on the sward below,

edging closer, I couldn't discern the slightest movement.
Only the wind that moved an ear like a stalk of wheat,

a jowl that quivered. Her eyes seemed not to see. The grass,
though abundant and inches from her lips, held no temptation.

Measuring her in perspective, as a painter with a pencil,
I judged her the length of my palm, on the thin side and brown,

a perfectly ordinary rabbit but for her stillness, her patience.
Finally, her trance broken, she jerked her head up, came to life,

listened, heard and bounded off with her white scut into cover.
I couldn't help but think of my mother – that same stillness,

that same absence of intention, volition, as she lay dying;
that surrendering of a life force that turns you to stone

though the fur is fur, the hair still hair, the posture neither
sleeping nor prone but poised on the cusp of sculpture.

ABNEY PARK CEMETERY

The air in the cemetery's greener, thicker with scent.
Paths wind and twist and, whenever I come this way,

I wonder if I've lost my bearings, following tiger stripes
of sun between the graves. But here's the station café.

A patient I know from the psychiatric ward waves,
smiling his dimpled, toothless smile, rubbing his forehead.

His voice, high-pitched, accented, carries even though
he's talking to a woman at his table. I'm fond of him –

he inspires affection. The skin around his eyes, wrinkled,
rayed, has the softness of my father's. He asks after Tom,

shows me the heel of his palm badly burned from the cooker.
'It's my mind that does this – God save me from accidents!'

He knows some Iranians, Azeris, just round the corner
at the snooker club. Whenever he goes in for a drink,

a Coca-Cola – and here he gestures, shrugging, meaning
it's on the house – 'it's', as Hassan says, 'hospitable.'

MIGRATION

When I see a hand first raised, then placed
on the heart, the head tilted towards the heart,

a greeting exchanged between a pedestrian
and a passing bus driver; when I see a woman

seated at a bus stop wave to a woman passenger
sitting behind me and, picturing them still,

look straight into trees, tears spring to my eyes
even though we're stopped at Elephant & Castle.

All one way blows the wind in the trees but
which is the way to a staging post between

the Khalvatis now, scattered in the diaspora,
and our very first forebears who struck camp,

loaded their beasts, set their caravans against
a skyline, wind whipping the horses' manes,

the fringes of their saddlecloths and shawls,
and moved as a whole tribe together?

HER ANNIVERSARY

It might be grey, it might be cold, who knows
what the weather's like out there? Birds know,

so silent in the branches, animals in their lairs.
But I, my blinds drawn down, am blind to all

but my heart's November, the second anniversary
of my mother's death. Perhaps I can keep her in,

in the warmth of my rooms, fug of my flat rehung
with her paintings, her tapestried cushions strewn

on chairs and sofas, making them gardens, rosebeds.
I can sit there among them as she did, as we did,

oftentimes together. But where's the sense in that?
Their velvet backs, rusts and fawns she kept face up

to stop the flowers fading, are already grimed from
propping my back, my head. I can become her instead.

Willingly become her in every meaning of the word.
Daughters who betray mothers are in turn betrayed.

VI THE AVENUE

GRANADILLA DE ABONA I

Even this garden, a veritable Eden with a keyhole pool,
a white cockatoo glimpsed behind the bars of a cage,

a trailing orange lotus swaying shadows against a wall
and sun beginning to cast its warmth on rattan chairs,

is an orchard of sorts but with nothing wild about it
or left to chance, the body without the soul of an orchard.

An orchard's soul should be ragged, ramshackle, dapple
throwing honeycombs of shade on soil, weather interstitial.

But every view's an artwork. Trees laden with oranges
like Christmas trees with glass baubles, paired parakeets

as yellow and green as the orange trees, banana palms
sculptural, fronds sheared and scored, *cardones*, Magritte-like

– not cacti but as penile – black avocados in the background,
arbours within arbours, round every path another, offer

a series of small warm breaths: seclusion without solitude,
arrival without homecoming, a silence that rings in the ears.

GRANADILLA DE ABONA II

We are illicit. We creep around shaded paths, spit pips
into flowering shrubs at the root, leave wet handprints

on poolside tiles where we crouch to rinse our fingers,
talk in the most inaudible of murmurs. A scruffy old hen

crows triumphantly as she lays, a great tit flits into view
and, on being glimpsed, scares; we are here and welcome

only if we whisper without voice, move without noise,
leave pipettes of blossom to float by on stagnant currents.

Even our thoughts intrude, being the wiliest of burglars.
Sleep too is a violation or so the parrots would have you think,

screeching warnings enough to wake the dead. Don't breathe,
don't listen, walk if you can on air. Every path is a dead end.

Under the arch, the wrought-iron gates are not only padlocked
but so entangled with lotus – an explosion of orange fireworks –

they seem locked in perpetuity while, passing in a street, blaring
through loudspeakers, gospel singers belt out 'Oh Happy Day...'

GRANADILLA DE ABONA III

Well, no wonder. This is the site of the Garden of the Hesperides.
These the Islands of the Blessed, the Fortunate Isles where,

Sertorius waxed, 'the air was never extreme, which for rain
had a little silver dew, which of itself and without labour,

bore all pleasant fruit to their happy dwellers.' Pleasant fruit
was had in plenty – reach up and twist the golden apple

which will drop into your hand, the banana from its own hand,
the *madroño* from its cluster. Oranges will rain down like

starlight through a telescope, a green and golden galaxy.
Near enough to spy cobwebs between their nodes, leaves,

drained of their sap, crack and burn at the tip – the more
brittle they grow, the weightier grow the oranges. By their song,

imagine the size of canaries, goldcrests, lovebirds, lorikeets,
their invisible throats and beaks smaller than pumpkin seeds.

The length of life remaining to be lived can feel infinitesimal
and interminable too. Not every poet longs for immortality.

GRANADILLA DE ABONA IV

Periquito and I have the garden to ourselves.
Periquito has the shade and I the rising sun,

fierce as Periquito's fierce. 'Dominion' as in
'Multiply and have dominion over all the creatures

of the earth' has, in Hebrew, another meaning:
'understanding'. But Periquito talks Canarian,

a parrot dialect thereof which, all ears though I am,
signifies nothing but sound and fury. Periquito

has the aviary birds to chorus him. They twitter
like background water, he on one end and I

on the other of a diagonal across the morning.
Released from his cage he teeters along a parapet,

a white quiff, a waddle and limp. Nothing to say
for himself now that he's free. Later they'll call,

'*Periquito, hola hola*' and '*Hola*' he'll answer
as clearly as a boy, albino, hiding in the bushes.

GRANADILLA DE ABONA V

He whistles once, crosses from one citrus tree
to another along a hammock bridge, raises his quiff,

tests a twig with his beak, one foot held quivering.
In a sleek white tailcoat, his dress shirt ruffled,

he skids up a rope, waving a hand, claws curled,
attentive as a child in a playpen to the movements

of all and sundry. *Diario de Avisos*, freshly laid,
collects his droppings. Lord of the green canopy,

he swings below the hammock ties, perches in a cleft
to peer towards the sound of a generator whirring,

taps his left hand on the branch excitedly and twice
raises two white wings, once to declare himself an angel

and once for balance as he grows ever more excited,
hanging by his beak alone, doing chin-ups, sipping water,

shaking diamonds in a spray around him, at the approach
of Señora coming and going about her daily bustlings.

GRANADILLA DE ABONA VI

Here they come, the insects, feasting off the money plant
under the drago tree whose bloodsap and attendant cures

gave the Guanches health and longevity. My mother was
ninety-two when she died, last and oldest of three siblings.

Her family history died with her, none of it lives in my
or my children's memory. We are yesterday's people,

provisional, adaptable, borrowing and assimilating.
The Guanches were said to have been exiled by Trajan

whose captains cut off their tongues, put them in ships
laden with animals and seed and forcibly settled them

in the Canaries. Silbo Gomero, their whistling language,
has survived to this day along with municipal place names,

gofio, their staple bread, and mummies – light as scrolls
with skin thinner and softer than our best kid gloves –

that lined their burial caves. But the Guanches themselves,
decimated, enslaved, were erased from memory and texts.

GRANADILLA DE ABONA VII

On three dry pumpkins, some little white pebbles,
timples, a very small drago tambourine, a blonde flute

with a hollow reed and four pipes with green stems
and knobbly joints of barley, how sweetly they played

endechas: 'What does it matter if they take and bring
milk, water and bread, if Agarfa will not look at me?'

And while they played and sang songs of love and death,
the old Gomera people, bearers of wisdom and knowledge,

who kept their mysteries to themselves and never divulged
the sacred site of their necropolis, the mysterious words

pronounced when sowing seed or how their ancestors,
the indigenous people of these islands, came to be here,

saying only that a higher being had brought them, left them,
then wiped them from memory, while the old native songs

played on, the elders wept and rocked, leaning on their sticks
with the same, same veined hands as the mummy of Madrid's.

PLAZA DE LOS REMEDIOS

It's the childlike geometry of the square –
the octagonal bandstand in the centre, the ring

of café tables and chairs around it, the outer ring
of bifurcating trunks, their packed suitcases of leaves,

benches, balconies, windows that ask to be counted –
that calls to mind set squares, rulers, compasses

and a head bent over a see-through protractor,
an angle of time arrested in the impalpable air.

The scene is as mild as a nativity and beyond this
simple geometry, immense, immeasurable mountains,

a stormy Atlantic you can hear at night, snoring
like a sleeping leviathan. I would like a small life.

I would like a son who takes both my hands in his
and, walking backwards, inches me towards the end

of a cobbled street where a door opens and a daughter,
taking my hands from his, helps me over the doorstep.

THE WHEELHOUSE

Sun sinks behind the massif before it blazes, fires off
shadow through the balustrade. The square is a great ship

floating, rising and sinking on sun and shadow, a ship
in harbour. We stroll the decks, let wind rest in our sails.

But I know nothing of ships, wanting my feet on earth.
My mother's ashes under the cherry trees, her house

occupied by someone else. I never go there, just as she
will never sit in a café, holding her handbag close on her lap,

her scarf, her hair in place. Memory would fill her smile
as she swayed her head from side to side and breathed

sweet exhalations of regret. Peremptorily, she'd ask
for an ashtray, offer me cake. I loved forever being a child

at my mother's side, the captain of my ship whose railings
I peered over. All her absences are final now. Like wind

they've run in together. Now they form a wake; a house
I am more than welcome in, a wheel I must learn to steer.

FINCA EL TEJADO

The juniper glistens with rain. Plumes, shadowed on the urn,
waver indistinctly. The fountain gushes, gushes, wind moans

and tugs at the palm fronds – join me, join me. Raindrops
hang two by two from railings. Everything has the shine

of black on it. Marina turns the music on and the room fills
with candlelight and yearning. Lamps throw umbrellas of light

against the walls, the red check tablecloth, a bottle of wine,
its candleglints, wait for company and we must stay with them,

listening to the fountain, gutters and the plucking of guitars
before the song begins. I have slung a quilt with violet roses

over the curtain rail to keep out the light in the morning.
Now I long for it, to see the sky, the golden stars of hamlets

high in the hills. I long to see the rain in massive drifts
open its fan, lay fan upon fan above the road to Buenavista

so that even the petrol station's blinded. Rose/leaf/rose/leaf
and through the open door a closed door, a shining lock and key.

THE AVENUE

I always knew my mother's funeral would be unseemly.
I never had the wherewithal. To have the wherewithal

is to inhabit a frame of mind that stands one in good stead.
In my dream a long avenue, pale with spindly poplars,

descended from the mountain – a peak like El Teide –
and along it walked on hind legs, but as naturally as men,

polar bears and among them my mother walked towards me.
Then I knew that all the separations I had suffered, all

the anguish they had caused me were but one separation,
one ball of anguish. And when I woke, I still could see

the avenue stretching to the mountains in mountain light,
the polar bears in file, solemn and steadily walking,

at intervals the silvery poplars on either side of the road
and in the middle my mother drawing slowly ever nearer

as if the avenue were a travelator moving in both directions,
carrying me forward towards her, carrying her forward towards me.

GHAZAL: IN SILENCE

Let them be, the battles you fought in silence.
Bury your shame, the worst you thought in silence.

At last my beloved has haggled with death.
'One more day' was the pearl she bought in silence.

At night she heard the blacksmith hammering chains,
at dawn the saw, the fretwork wrought in silence.

'The only wrong I've done is to live too long',
my beloved's eyes tell the court in silence.

The bell on her wrist was silent, her fingers
ice cold as the julep she brought in silence.

My beloved, under the shade of a palm,
was the girl, the mother I sought in silence.

'Mimijune! Mimijune!' My beloved's voice
climbs three steep notes for tears to thwart in silence.

Three syllables of equal weight, equal stress,
dropped in a well, keep falling short in silence.

AFTERWARDNESS (2019)

QUESTIONS

You're smaller than you were or so you think.
You don't remember sinking quite so low
on other seats. Something has made you shrink
or else something has made the seatback grow.

You're a normal child, if a bit bewildered,
struggling to push the feelings down, the questions,
the stillborn questions never to be answered,
stretching to see a sky that simply darkens,

flying away from all you know with you
and someone sitting next to you, but who?
the only ones not gone or disappearing.

It's normal to feel trust. And you do, don't you?
Trust is a kind of seat belt, stretching, shrinking,
a *kammarband* you'll soon forget you're wearing.

TRANSLATION

I've heard them playing ball in Kacic Square,
children throwing languages in rotation –
their own, a new one, being made aware
as they leap, drop, pick up, catch, of translation,

the concept, long before they learn the word.
They learn translation is a kind of swap –
I'll give you *parandeh*, you give me bird.
But what if, whistling in some foreign treetop,

parandeh has long since flown out of mind
back to its own kind, never to return?
Then there are only local trees to fill

with bird, bird, bird; rows of them left behind
to chirp, chirp, chirp; sparrow, kittiwake, crossbill,
shrike and even bulbul to learn, learn, learn.

HANDWRITING

A line of c's is like a stylised sea
or seated monks obediently bowing;
cccc, line after line, spells safety,
sitting at a desk, doing joined-up writing.

This is the scaffolding – the alphabet
of posts and beams, the timber frame, the nave
of b's and d's whose pillars, if you let
the uprights slant, will topple on a wave –

the scaffolding and ark of spoken speech,
a chapel in which psalms and hymns become,
once you have learned to read the script, so clear.

There are wordings the ear alone can't reach,
strange idioms that make the mind go numb
but knowing how to write them helps you hear.

DICTATION

Like a bumblebee on a wild rampage,
stumbling against the sense that otherwise
ran as smooth as honey across my page,
one word I couldn't spell or recognise,

starting with k, or c, then double m
in the middle and holding in reserve
e r for the end, kept coming at random –
kommer? no, commer – till I lost my nerve.

Poor Deborah! Yoked to her father's muse.
And my poor daughter, darling. Who will be,
now she can't even see night stars, her hand,

her amanuensis? So let her use,
while she still can, her one good eye to see
wild bees, like commas, coming in to land.

ELOCUTION

She sat behind the door, squat as a toad
in a twinset and tweeds – my oracle.
How are the mighty fallen I intoned
as light poured in *in the midst of the battle!*

O Jonathan I moaned and through the pane
sun shone as though *O* were a sunburst window
flooding rays into my soul, *thou wast slain*
but who Jonathan was I wouldn't know –

I was Jonathan, the light and the sun
were Jonathan, my elocution mistress,
my first beloved, you were Jonathan

and *thy love to me was wonderful*, yes,
it was, it was, *passing the love of women*,
women and men. *How are the mighty fallen...*

BACKGROUND MUSIC

You may be in a café reading when,
after the intro, Billie Holliday
and *Easy Living* lure you out of Walden
and swing you in a trance out of the café.

You may be watching Shaun Evans as Morse
mostly to marvel at the mimicry
of his body language, so like John Thaw's,
when you're torn away, this time by Puccini,

away from the spires of Oxford to fall,
to fall as Tosca falls, defences fall,
that your heart breaks open a dungeon door

and griefs like prisoners crouched on the floor
bestir themselves and infant griefs like dolls
sleep through a bell that tolls and tolls and tolls.

BACKGROUND MUSIC (II)

Music, being as wordless as they are –
these frozen griefs no trauma ever thawed,
these griefs that thought goodbye was au revoir
and thought the dead were living still abroad,

these unnamed griefs forgotten in a wasteland
where who and what and why have long dissolved –
seems, once brought to the fore, to understand
griefs neither time nor rhyme nor love resolved.

It's left to dreams of dull bewilderment
when wrong and right change places without cause
while witnesses, thank god, seem not to notice

to dredge up feelings of abandonment,
the day's debris for you alone to witness
a flood of shame that out of shame withdraws.

DREAMERS

Dreamers, before they lived a life of shadows,
a short life but long years of chasing fear,
before they found a room, sunblinds on windows,
an L-shaped desk, a home they know is here,

were children young as – most commonly – three,
with fringes, hairslides, hair too soft to hold them,
two hundred words in their vocabulary
and shapes of sentences in which to mould them:

sentence shapes like cradles for dolls to dream in,
like railway tracks and bridges, tunnels, sidings,
paradigms for journeys, returns and crossings,

first languages, half-formed, dropped at a border
Dreamers crossed and were too young to remember –
these students, immigrants, young men and women.

AFTERWARDNESS

An eleven-year-old boy from Aleppo
whose eyes hold only things no longer there
– a citadel, a moat, safe rooms of shadow,
'afterwardness' in his thousand yard stare –

years later, decades even, might turn around
to see, through the long tunnel of that gaze,
a yard, a pond and pine trees that surround,
as in a *chaharbagh*, four branching pathways.

Where do memories hide? the pine trees sing.
In language, of course, the four pathways reply.
What if the words be lost? the pine trees sigh.

Lost, the echo comes, lost like me in air.
Then sing, the pathways answer, sigh and sing
for the echo, for nothing, no one, nowhere.

SCRIPTO INFERIOR

To know your story is to understand
not only who you are and where you come from
– even if some imaginary homeland
is all you know, shall ever know of home –

but is also to understand the nature
of story, how to prime a palimpsest
for all successive stories, how to ensure
reference points gain valence from the first.

Hence, a love of narrative; and a mind
with an ingrained habit – established by
the underwriting of your own life story –

of near total recall it is unkind
to foist on one whose underscript is less
determined and who might feel envious.

CAFÉS

Envy them, the lonely, there by the glass,
there in the corner, staring into space
for as long as it takes the world to pass,
close up, far off, sprinkled like stars in cafés.

Envy them their orbit: how flagstones throw
a thin horned shadow of a bicycle
they take for Rocinante; how they borrow
longed-for landscapes, the islands of Lake Baikal,

a handful of lights from the Crimean plateau,
O envy them their raised sleeping-car window!
'Habituated to the Vast', how they move,

leaving a good tip, pulling on a glove,
paying with the exact change from their purse,
through spacetime in an abstract universe.

JOLANTA

I don't live here, according to Jolanta.
I only come here when she comes, she teases.
Between times, plants get watered, piles of paper
shrink or grow and a vase might spring sweetpeas.

But aside from a seismic shift on Wednesdays,
nothing's ever moved. Doors are door-stopped open.
Only the rooms float in and out of doorways,
plane trees in full leaf climb in from the garden

and plans to live elsewhere prove transitory.
Wagging a finger, 'See?' Jolanta scolds,
lycra-clad in citrus, her Marigolds

pumping a cloth black-grimed with nicotine
and tar from storage jars, 'You see, Mimi?'
So I do live here after all, you mean.

THE BRAG

I am known by sight in the neighbourhood
to shopkeepers, baristas, cab drivers.
There I go, there I come, in likelihood
alone, up and down the road, in all weathers.

I am on smiling terms with hosts of people.
There she blows with her silver hair, they grin,
staking out a beanrow, spouting the Bible.
Roadsweepers chat, guards greet me at the station.

Some call me lady, auntie, mammie – ask me
how I'm doing, endorse me with endearments,
watch my footing for me, rescue my bag.

Caregivers all! Small wonder if I brag
a little, graced with such acknowledgements
and such a large extended family.

HIDE AND SEEK

Truth is, there's nobody she wants to find.
The very act of finding's frightening:
the human crouching in the bush, the blind
hump of hair and shoulder, the tell-tale clothing.

And being found's no better, backed to a wall,
shrinking on a dirt floor, hugging her knees.
But what if she were never found at all?
Left to herself with sacks of grain and chickpeas?

Once there would have been pickles, purées, lard,
mountains of melons, stores for every season,
a shop, a cookhouse, bathhouse, icehouse even

and, set on four sides of the inner courtyard,
one house for each branch of the family
no one beyond the high brick walls could see.

THE INTROVERT HOUSE

At its heart the pool, the blue rug of sky.
In the middle of my room, the kilim
with its fish and fowl. My propensity
for arranging furniture, it would seem,

in lines around the walls, leaving the floor
alone as the focal point, may be due
not to some dullness in the soul but more
to workings in the bloodstream, some residue

in subliminal memory of windows
that look forever inward, galaxies
that spin on carpets, geometric rows

of turquoise tiles ablaze with symmetries
inherent in physics; eyvans, porticos
of gardens brought indoors; a Sufi's verses.

OUTPATIENTS

In Cardiology, the corridor
is a bright blue stream of lino, a river
where, lined up like fishermen on a shore,
patients face patients ranged along the other.

One old fisherman, drumming on his cane,
sings softly to himself. A farawayness
surfaces like a shoal; a swirling chain
of choruses he strums like Orpheus.

Weddings, celebrations, birthdays, now quicken,
now subside, as his voice grows louder, quieter,
drifts down 'the narrows of the Arda River'.

Ali Kemal Ali! they call. Remember
Ali Kemal – that murdered politician
who was Boris Johnson's great-grandfather?

VILLAJOYOSA

So that a fisherman far out at sea
returning home as the sun sank or rose,
straining through fog, poor visibility,
could see, rowing toward Villajoyosa,

among seafront cottages on the shore,
his own abode and by it steer his course,
each house was painted a distinctive colour:
green, ochre, terracotta, sky blue, turquoise.

Of all the blossoms that are out in May,
the lilac – Persian lilac – shares the same
lodestar quality. Never to belong

back in the wild again but to a doorway
where a stranger might hear 'death's outlet song',
it holds the past, only the past in the doorframe.

THE BOY

The boy would always wear his coat indoors,
a long black cashmere, threadbare now and fraying.
He'd prop a folding magnifying mirror,
as though to shave before he started playing,

on top of the piano, tilt its face
towards his own, then bundled on the stool
still in his hat and coat, burning to trace
his double like Narcissus at the pool,

lean and stare in the glass, just stare, deaf-mute
to 'Don't you want to take your coat off darling?',
numb to the keyboard pressed against his knee.

Time made no sense to him. Minute by minute,
silent as time without him in it would be,
the boy, who was a man, sat fiercely staring.

DYSPHAGIA

We sat facing him, our backs to the window.
He sat facing the light which filled his eyes,
green as sea glass, with yet more light as though
to wash his skull of everything but skies.

We sat, disciples at the long ward table.
He wore a ribbed off-white garment that only
exposed how thin he was, near skeletal,
yet in demeanour upright, calm and friendly.

For days no food or drink had passed his lips.
We urged on him a phial of holy water
from Sarah's pilgrimage to Medjugorje.

Once, twice, he slowly blinked. He took one sip,
replaced the cap and thanked her. 'That's okay.
I'll leave it here,' she glanced around, 'for later.'

THE ARTIST AS A CHILD

after Federico García Lorca

Everything that happens must happen here,
he thought, within the confines of the page.
Marshal your pencils then, master your fear.
Start with the sky, take the blue to the edge.

Leave no patch of white, no eye, no space.
Every block that is coloured in permits
relief and progress up the rooftop staircase,
flag by flag, to the wrought-iron parapets.

What is the void but love between two walls?
Don't fudge the corners where the angles dovetail.
Neither love nor fear can be drawn to scale.

Limbs that won't fit in if the trunk's too tall –
abbreviate. Let fortune be your draughtsman.
Look to your moon, black moon, your red half-curtain.

'THE LESSER BRETHREN'

after Margaret Tarrant

Although she barely knew at school, at seven,
what a Moslem was or what Islam meant,
she proudly wrote: 'I know I'm not a Christian',
reassuring her mother, 'but for Lent

I have given up saying Honestly.'
And the truth was she liked going to chapel,
shuffling down the aisle, the passivity
of pews, her kneeler making her feel special.

Barred from a clear view of the altar rail
by girls in serge, blue laundered veils, she'd peer
instead at the fawn, vixen, rabbit, badger,

memorise the caption in bold serif,
see how His hands were drawn and wonder if
she really had a right to wear this veil.

TORBAY

It's not the headland pine above the scree,
the cliffs, two ships in fog, the scraps of light
between the lower branches that remind me
I could have reached them even at my height,

no, not the sight of sea that takes me back,
back to the Isle of Wight, a schoolgirl image
of standing under pines, flaking the bark,
rolling resin on my thumb, but the knowledge

that, wherever I stood, however steep
an incline and whatever blocked my view,
the sea was always there at walking distance,

as palpable in absence as in presence,
making roofs, trees, a hospital feel see-through
and those across the Solent just skin deep.

MARIA

Maria someone named her, painted her
block capitals Mediterranean blue
after they berthed her by a conifer
in grass to be the sweet spot in the view.

Not an oar in sight, her name freshly minted,
listing on the lawn so that rain and rust,
studded with pine needles from overhead,
pool on her starboard side, she lies in trust

to land now, England's apples, plums and pears.
Birds settle on her prow. I haven't seen them.
Nor can Maria see, just yards away,

where the Avon flows through the Vale of Evesham,
first canoes, kayaks, streaking past in pairs,
then green gloom like the sweet spot in a Monet.

OLD STAMPING GROUNDS

Old stamping grounds are bruises to the heart.
Go visit them at dusk. Belisha beacons,
reflected in dark windows, flash and dart
like fireflies, synchronising light emissions.

Bollards at a junction, a spot for parking,
here is a nexus *entre chien et loup*.
A confluence of roads, a zebra crossing,
they synchronise the past and present too.

Bruising can effloresce like peonies,
slide down your body like a garter snake,
emerge in secret from a secret blow.

Still deeper in the tissues lies the ache
of underlying ruptures dusk alone is
discolouring in violet and yellow.

CHAMAELEONIDAE

Why did I say I minded things I didn't –
soul-making things I'd find too crude to name?
Or silently collude with heartfelt, well-meant
sympathy it seemed churlish to disclaim?

There is no childhood house that I remember,
no mother in it, merely surrogate
houses with mothers in them but no daughter,
where I would be their Alison or Kate.

In whose name can I talk of roots, of ruptures?
Melding with backgrounds, we fade into yours –
muted, cryptic, old world chameleons.

'Lions of the ground', we swivel horizons;
stalking the rainbow, we emblazon its colours.
These are our messages, these our emotions.

THE COLOURS MY MOTHER WORE

She wore the colours of these autumn trees,
carnelians, agates, grandiose and subtle.
She blended them in paintings, tapestries
of gardens, woods, perennially autumnal.

But when cataracts turned the tones too pale,
unknown to her, her flowers went fluorescent.
Then, when miniature work was bound to fail,
she took to painting liquid skies where pigment,

linseed oil, billowed of their own volition.
Skies hang silver-framed, windowed on my walls.
Live with a sunset, moon, a cloud formation

and soon they'll seem part of the furniture.
There's nothing new under the sun but palls
if we can't see its subtlety or grandeur.

MY MOTHER'S LIGHTER

From place to place, her lighter travels with me.
People admire it. Gold, faux tortoiseshell,
engraved with her initials, marked Colibri.
Vintage, cased; still not worth enough to sell.

Half-sentimental, half-dispassionate
and with no true attachment to or knowledge
of my own history, I try its weight
in my palm, run my thumb along an edge.

I flick the lid, the minuscule flint wheel,
and the same flame, its root invisible,
its calyx blue, bud gold, that she'd have seen

flares in the sunlight even as I feel
the wind hood heat up on my finger till
I snap it shut and rub my thumbprint clean.

MY MOTHER'S PORTRAIT

Should you happen, crossing the upstairs landing,
to find the door ajar and dare to spy on
her sewing room, her instruments, her veining
tools and wire cutters, her gauffering iron,

you might be freaked by the dressmaker's dummy,
headless in the corner, its torso split
top to bottom as in an autopsy.
But should you happen to rush past and see it

out of the corner of your eye, a head
levitating just above it, head-height,
nearly joined to its neck, you'd die of fright.

For years I've kept that sketch stashed in my loft.
Instead, I picture roses cut and moulded
with tools you'd think too hard for silk so soft.

THE COURTYARD

Once we'd have jostled feral goats in here,
let them graze, scatter dung under our table,
suckle on fuchsia buds, suddenly rear
by the fork of that dwarf Japanese maple,

then head off for the wild again; but now
there's just a robin flitting, spiderwebs
showing up in sun and the slatted shadow
a chairback casts, glowing before it ebbs.

Behind this courtyard other courtyards stand
the way parents, grandparents, lineages,
grand or humble, throng galleries in air.

May this backyard join their ranks anywhere
an arch we don't go through, on pilgrimages
we never take, harks back to Samarkand.

TWELVE

Twelve! Twelve! Twelve! Twelve! yells a despairing waiter.
But who is Twelve? Not the child by a river,
the Chinese child with an extra little finger
on each hand they call Shi'Er, who's four or five,

whose name means twelve, slipping out of a jungle,
out of a book, into a crowded café.
What *is* Twelve? Nominal? A numeral?
In her case, heartbreakingly both, I'd say.

Twelve. How quick the first consonantal cluster
to escape the teeth, how slow the dark *l*,
voiced *v*, to reverberate round the vowel,

an *e* that swells, that rhymes a temple bell.
Hedged by tall consonants, *e* in the centre
peals through a gap, an entrance for Shi'Er.

VERY

Very… the very first time that I heard
– or worked out what it meant since at that age
English was still a mystery – the word
'very', I thought it strange. A sudden passage

flashed through its scrollwork gate into the heart,
the very heart and all its imprecisions
hitherto silent, every distinct part
of language. Here, like steps, all the gradations

of feeling could be heightened, magnified,
for someone else to feel. Like guardian angels,
adjectives, adverbs, standing side by side

with lone words that might otherwise conceal
the very nature of their joys and troubles,
could qualify the world and make it real.

BUSH CRICKET

I picked out *What I Loved* by Siri Hustvedt
from that blue bookcase on a garden wall
under the fig tree. Having scarcely read
four pages, closing it, I see a small

bush cricket, her antennae waving, mask
What on the spine, aligning it exactly
with her lines. *What?* her body seems to ask,
threading it through a green transparency.

Now what? she asks a glass jar. Through the glass
she's slightly magnified as if through water.
She's upside down but thinks she's horizontal,

having hatched on the verticals of grass.
I think she likes diurnal roosting better
than asking questions so imponderable.

READING UNDER TREES

Never were texts less arid. Mrs Ramsay,
knitting, times her rows with the lawnmower,
seeds and thistledown float across *Swann's Way*
while grass keeps quoting 'glory in the flower'.

Insects fly on and off, streams mingle with
their sentences, wind muddles up their pages;
the sounds of carpentry, the coppersmith,
Lambrettas, punctuating passages.

And once a woman reading under trees,
bowed to her book, sitting oddly at ease
beside a statue of a woman also

bowed to her book, the one a perfect echo
of the other, summoned a double rainbow –
one arc in graphite, one in primaries.

POSTCARD FROM CRETE

I bought this one to keep. It half-recalls,
from years ago in Turkey, a verandah,
a flight of steps, flowers like waterfalls
on either side of scarlet, pink, magenta,

leading up to a tea-room in the middle
of nowhere where we once had Turkish breakfast.
The actual place seems immaterial.
What mattered were the chickens in the dust,

petrol cans potted with geraniums,
divans with rugs, an overhang of shade.
For people who like me belong nowhere,

places leave images we love to pair,
twin surfaces we've skimmed and overlaid,
cross-pollinating all our brightest vacuums.

THE STREET

So wide awake is spring now, eyes so open,
even the carpets long to fly outdoors
and lie, spread-eagled, carpeting the garden.
But is it only sun – bright visitors

from skylights, there at the top of the stairs,
braced to run down, brass stair rods at their heels;
is it only this sunless room which bears
a weight of shade so sculptural it feels

like Rachel Whiteread's *House* pumped full of concrete;
is it, not the sensation Jorie Graham
had 'how full void is', but of void itself,

only the membrane since it has no self,
the sweet tremble of void that makes the street
cast the prefatory glow of a poem?

FRIENDS HOUSE

It's civil twilight, sparkling over Euston.
On the pavement, a blind man's white stick whitens
and frosted footlights in the low walls turn
blind eyes too to the very paths they brighten.

Not as though there's anything there to see –
no homeless pile of sleeping bags and blankets,
no friendly drunks who want to be more friendly,
no smokers stubbing out last cigarettes.

In the blue hour, hobgoblin hour when fairies,
elves, 'quaint spirits' make mischief in a garden,
Friends garden, like an apron stage, stands empty.

At such an hour, Mary Shakespeare (née Arden),
under a sky still bright enough to read by,
enthralled her brood with gloaming, fireside stories.

THE OLDER READER

The more she reads, the more her own life dims.
Stranded in the outrun, under a pole star
or in a land of paper gods, she skims
contours, heartlands that grow familiar,

akin more in their wild parabolas
to lives she always thought she could assume
given her youth, precocious as Lolita's,
than to this scanty plot, this narrow room.

Is it age that makes novelists now welcome
to implicate her in their machinations,
cast her as an addict, Arctic explorer

and throw her to the winds, fling her ashore,
then fetch her, like those missionary orphans
from Shanghai staring out on deck, back home?

THE LIVING ROOM

Blinded by sun, enter this quiet room.
Roses have entered it as quietly
and strawberries whose scent pervades the gloom
with danger signs of allergens a lady,

whose sneezes still erupt through lath and stucco,
can no longer bar servants bringing in.
Who was she? Where are we? In Melikhovo
with Uncle Vanya, Nina and Trigorin,

strolling in from the wooden porch, the garden,
summoned by a bell for the noonday meal?
Are we the guests? Whose fictions are we then?

And when we go, courteously as to leave
no living trace that we were ever real,
who will author proofs we ourselves believe?

LIFE WRITING

And if you do have a book with no plot,
story, timeline, no protagonists even
and no witnesses to events, it's not
so mind-numbing a proposition given

that there are some writers who want to write
about everything and are spoilt for choice
as to starting points and those who, despite
the conundrum that inviting a voice

out of a void would void the void of meaning,
nevertheless will listen out for nothing
and hearing it, think, as yesterday's wind

drifts pink almond blossom across their mind,
what's lighter than petals and yet, what heft
the tree bore, occluding the sky itself.

EGGS

From the first egg I ever drew, brown, speckled,
and pasted on a screen in kindergarden,
through all the eggs I ever ate, fried, scrambled,
boiled, poached, etc., down to this broken

yolk on a plate under my nose, my love
of eggs, in any shape or form, has grown.
Take the form: the prolate symmetry of
a spheroid, weightless when an egg is blown;

the air sac that expands with age and grades
an egg or backlights when you candle it
a blood red embryo; the sun-yolk shades

from marigolds the hens were fed at dawn;
the albumen: water out of which spirit
and embodiment, double-yoked, are drawn.

SEPTEMBER

Everything seems too beautiful to grasp.
I don't know what to feel, other than yearning
to stay forever neutral, on the cusp
of daydream, of a summer not quite turning,

its flotsam moving me to tears almost
and dapple on the streets, the dirtier
the better, always bringing home the contrast
of vague and real, of shadow-branch and litter.

'This vague and dream like world', Virginia says,
'without love, or heart, or passion, or sex'
might sound like a world we could live without

but 'is the world I really care about',
she pleads to Madge Vaughan in 1906,
and is the way I feel about today's.

THE ICE RINK

Like skaters tracing figures on the ice,
figures of eight, circles that overlap
since no man steps in the same river twice,
on foot, by bus, we trace a mental map

of the places we pass so little changed
through all these years and of the men they link,
boyfriends, lovers, husbands, buried, estranged,
they conjure up like faces round a rink.

We are the widows, spinsters, divorcées
travelling round and round on loops and brackets,
scribbling on ice melting under our blades.

They are the phantoms, daemons, devotees
frequenting our haunts, the tutelary spirits
who, Plato wrote, conduct our souls to Hades.

IN PRAISE OF THE SESTET

If a kind of staring into your eyes,
your eyes without their glasses suddenly
meeting mine and making me realise
how nakedly you might have stared at me,

been staring all along behind thick lenses
(the sheet thrown back, the towel dropped and love
refused, withheld under your false pretences –
the sophistry, the sighs, the velvet glove),

'a kind of staring', Peter Sacks the scholar
opined 'into the eyes of the beloved',
were indeed the origin of the sonnet,

then God bless da Lentino who appended
a Sicilian folk song to such ardour
for us to dance, 'dance the undoing of it'.

NIGHT WRITING

Poetry startled me awake last night.
Stray lines, excited to be up so late,
streaked into view then melted out of sight
in light, without the lights on, grey as slate.

I listened, looked; half-blind, half-animal.
Cool air in a through-draught ruffled my fur.
I was a blind old tabby, dazed, forgetful,
letting the lines like mice race by the sofa.

Even in bed, Proust caught them by the tail,
batted them back and forth from clause to clause
till all the truth drained out of them and lay

pooled on the page. But my dim wits, my paws
were too illiterate to read their braille –
my mice would never see the light of day.

'PETITES SALISSURES'

is what Vuillard, working from memory,
called his small sketches and it intimates
the distortions, elisions and arbitrary
vanishing points that memory dictates.

And translations of *petites salissures* –
'little daubs' like the marks that dying moths
imprint with wings on dusty furniture,
'little bits of nothing' on tablecloths –

show how memory, reticent like mine,
fogged with the condensation of old age,
if squinting at a figure blurred in outline,

nameless were it not for her dress, will barely
disturb a woman steadying her passage,
reaching down an arm to a bentwood chair.

ONE SUMMER HOLIDAY

Down in an underworld that seemed to echo
my one abiding memory of chairs
placed in a ring but this time found in shadow
at the mouth of a crypt, down headlong stairs,

they came to visit me again in dream
or did I visit them? – close family
with no English but who would smile and beam,
laugh and chatter among themselves in Farsi.

What kind of monster was I and so loved?
The kind a married man with calf eyes woos
in some wild spot where all his girls have been?

Who listens to him croon, *Mara beboos,*
mara beboos – 'kiss me' – and is so moved
she falls in love, under the moon, at thirteen?

FACADES

What they both lack in beauty they make up for
in friendliness, incongruously adjacent,
the Aziziyeh Mosque sitting next door
to the Baptist Church in quiet contentment.

While the mosque gazes down on Kentish ragstone,
a slate pitched roof and gablet, neo-Gothic,
the church stares up at gold cupolas, fullblown
Ottoman tilework, columns of mosaic.

But what goes on behind facades God knows.
Witness returning exiles who might thrill,
after so long, to see their lineaments

etched on the faces of the crowd, yet still
feel all at sea and helpless to disclose
their new-found role as 'hidden immigrants'.

PHYSIOGNOMY

Not in the letters, diaries, memoirs, archives
his kin research, hoping to find the father
they never knew, absent throughout their lives,
do I find mine, but in his doppelganger,

twin stranger in the crowd – draped at the barber's,
in shirtsleeves, moccasins, playing backgammon,
caught on a newsreel among ayatollahs,
in Marks and Spencer waiting for his women.

Physiognomy's heady – lax cheeks, eyebrows
peaked like circumflexes, eyelids that sag,
traits that reach across the diaspora

of fathers to waylay an ageing daughter
checking herself in mirrors, smoked glass windows,
and smoke her out, looking like him in drag.

SMILES

These little smiles that fill my eyes with tears
mean nothing really, signals between women
who pass each other on the street as strangers,
as casual friends whose names are now forgotten

or local friends who stop to say hello
at bus stops, coughing little coughs like Lei,
Chinese Lei from Rouge, her shop, but also
English Lily who used to welcome me

by name and I'd respond in rhyme, whose sweet
manner seemed at odds with her black Goth gear.
She's gone to art school now and down the street

Bake Street café isn't the same without her.
Why tears though? I don't know – the loneliness
of women's lives, perhaps, that smiles express.

HOMA

She was an only child but like a sister.
Homa. The sort of person who could melt
your heart unless you hardened it against her.
'I've got a slug, a slug!' I'd yell and pelt

downhill, stuffing a dead leaf down her shirt.
Homa, so gullible, who never learned
how many hardened hearts there are to hurt
girls who love freely where love isn't earned.

How her eyes shone! She chattered like a bird.
She tapped out rhythms, tunes for me to guess,
used tomboy nicknames, however absurd.

Homa, so easily reduced to tears
by slights or sins she'd happily confess,
who mothered me through all my heartless years.

MY SIXTH BIRTHDAY PARTY

It was like a little wedding – the bride
in a cream crêpe dress that was miles too long,
her hair all wrong, the boy groom by her side.
But I knew why, why it had all gone wrong.

Where's Malijune? She's gone to *Suisse*, they said.
Suisse was a sword to brandish – *Aji maji*
la taraji! – and swing it round your head.
A steely blade, not a table knife, Daddy,

to cut the cake. *Suisse* was a pair of scissors,
a needle in her hand to hem my dress.
Suisse was my mother's glance, swift as a dart

to see it *did* look wrong, redo my parting,
slide a grip in and have me look like hers,
her child in *Suisse,* not here or somewhere else.

JUNIOR SCHOOL PRODUCTION

But what are all the court going to wear?
Seven sisters from Thailand, ranged in height,
each owning silk pyjamas, not one pair
but countless pairs, produced them on the night.

The Junior School, in Thai wild silk and pigtails,
filed in. The Emperor reclined. The little
kitchen-maid pointed and the nightingale
who, the Prime Minister surmised, might well

'have changed colour at the sight of so many
distinguished personages', singing hidden
in the wood, was a solo violin.

At all events, the evening was enchanting.
Death sat on the Emperor's heart but quickly
fled and the dead Emperor said 'Good morning'.

AZARINEJAD AND BEAR

Azarinejad put aside his turban
and his blue robe and squatted in the circle.
He turned to one child, then another: 'Children,
what did Bear want to do?' Was it a riddle?

One boy sat thinking, two boys picked their fingers.
One small girl smiled a big red smile while three
girls in hejab tried to smother their whispers.
They all knew the answer. They'd heard the story.

Azarinejad had opened the boot
of his old Peugeot, taken out the books
and read them *Bear Has a Story to Tell*.

So why not put their hands up? Why act mute?
Why be so bashful, sneaking little looks?
Wasn't Bear's story theirs to tell as well?

MEHRABAD AIRPORT

They came to see me off, bearing like Magi
gifts they unloaded from Chevys and taxis,
Korans in caskets, swords of gladioli,
pistachios rattling in cardboard boxes,

only to take them home again to rooms
where gladioli were returned to vases,
glass-fronted cabinets hid away heirlooms,
samovars endlessly refilled their glasses.

What if a heritage were lost en route?
In rosebud chintz, roomfuls of furniture
were stowed on board, down to a miniature

grand piano, also in Limoges porcelain,
painted with a Fragonard courting scene,
a maid and troubadour plucking his lute.

MEHRABAD AIRPORT (II)

Sometimes you hear of someone dying when
you thought they'd died already years ago.
They come to life only to die again.
Bad memory can be so cruel although

close relatives who die abroad but live
well past their 100th birthday in the mind,
move about in their younger years, as active
or dependent, can prove it also kind.

So here they crowd in jet-black fifties hairdos,
pinstripes and polka dots, swing skirts and blouses,
siblings who rode and wore chadors on donkeys,

cousins who crouched diminutive in photos
deckle-edged like Pamuk's museum mementoes
in cabinets of curiosities.

VAPOUR TRAILS

Staring up at pure blue from down on earth,
we see them shining in the firmament,
the jets, the contrails, gliding back and forth
like deep sea fish, soundless and innocent.

Their exhaust particles and frozen vapours
show us, graphically, cause and effect:
in the silver bullet-nosed jets, the cause;
in trails like spinal x-rays, the effect.

It only takes a trigger, a single flight
in childhood, for example, early trauma,
to stretch the bare bones of the aftermath

into a lyric void beyond the finite
and knowable, a via negativa
cruising at altitude on plumes of breath.

UNCOLLECTED POEMS

MALIH AT ST MARY'S

I

Women look more like men when they are dying,
I think, watching them shroud my mother's body
in a Bair Hugger. Malih's cold but breathing,
taking deep breaths as she's told, like a yogi.
Lovely it is to be looked after. 'Darling,
buy me a mobile, just a cheap one', she asks me,
smoothing my hair, banking on a short stay.
'I think they're called Pay as You Go' she says.

II

'Ask for more any time,' the surgeon tells her,
'don't be shy.' But she's flirting, she's delighted.
Every now and then her right arm wanders
by itself through space, aimless as a kite.
Pouting, her lips blow bubbles like my daughter
did in her crib while her fingernails fight
with the IV catheters, pink and green.
Stories pour out of her, unchecked by morphine.

'You know, many people commit suicide –
they can't bear it', she's mumbling, speech slurred
through the oxygen mask, a fleck of dried
foam on her lip. 'But *my* tinnitus was cured.
It was a miracle…' Don't turn aside,
I want to tell them, even though I've heard
this one God knows how many times and still
I can't remember it. Let her have the thrill.

At one point, Malih gets confused, her tongue thick,
her palms patting her bed as though to prod
her memory – 'Where're my glasses?' she panics,
'I put them here, they were here.' 'It's alright' I nod,
'they're in your bag', her old brown bag I'd quickly
raid for a fag or tissues from the wad
kept folded. 'And my combs?' Her two brown combs,
her girlie combs … 'Because I keep a good home,

they think I don't have any pain.' Still strapped
and bruised, her wrist lies by her pillow, bloodstained.
She's asleep beside the curtain I wrapped
behind the lamp. ('Where's the light?' she'd complained,
peering round the ward, as if blindly trapped
in a tunnel with no white light at the end.)
Just once, she screws up her face. Screws up her face
like a rodent, some small thing in some deep dark place.

III

She's gone to ground with all manner of creation:
mole and beaver, wren and starling, flown tenants
of earth and air; gone to ground with fern, bracken,
and all their fine and feathery constituents.
Her tribe of small-boned women, wand-like men,
they, too, lie piecemeal, pale bone china fragments.
(She had seen them in dreams as portents, omens:
forebears who healed her broken conversations.)

THE PLAYGROUND

Three yellow roses – perhaps four, not more –
among a range of shrubberies and trees
changing colour drew my eye towards

or I should say back towards them since they
stood at the end of summer, at the end of a row
of terraces fronting the playground, empty now

that all the children were back at school
except for the unlucky few self-isolated at home
with a cough that was just a cough, the usual

cold and sniffles for this time of year only
this year wasn't usual. The spring rider,
a blue elephant with a yellow handle for an ear,

stood side-on to me, glaring with one eye.
The bench was wet with rain so I patted
the latticework with kitchen towel to dry it

and perched at one end to have a cigarette.
Yellow roses, my mother's favourite.
It was a beautiful morning, not cold at all.

It was a playground for solitude and pigeons,
for a quiet smoke and self-congratulation
on surviving, and nothing to do with isolation.

THE BARGE

The tide has come in so close, climbing up
the small bank of pebbles, that my shins
are showered with icy streaks, my lounger
ambushed with a bath of froth which quickly

slides back down the slope, dowses the rocks,
pauses for breath, rushes up to my feet again.
I'd like it to carry me away like a raft, a barge,
and for a mast, my rolled-up beach umbrella –

not too far, as far as the rock with the lighthouse,
far enough for tourists to point and wave,
then drift slowly enough for sleep to claim me,

deposit me back where I am in my oldest t-shirt,
divested of crown and sceptre and no one to know
how solitary I was out there, how unafraid.

AUTUMN EQUINOX

Even near noon, the sun barely skims the tops of trees
which, landscaped and spreading as they are,
variegreen and following the course of the river,
make up for their sudden lack of height by breadth.

Between earth and sky, September flattens us.
We are stalk, we are grass the length of a knuckle.
Hold up a thumb: nothing behind is taller.
The sun, being so low, carves every face in two –

forehead, bridge of the nose, philtrum, neck.
Gods and men, lit on the right, shadowed on the left,
are stalled mid-conversation, the globe is held in balance.

Brunelleschi provides perspective, Constable still water.
And I who sit alone, distance all the people, wipe them
out of the arena, leaving you to imagine them there.

IN THE GOOSEHOUSE

During the power cut come the sounds of
teenagers singing in the barn, playing
The Moonlight Sonata; the steady rain;

the metal clink-clanking of crutches,
regular and paced, doors being closed,
the absence of birdsong in the rain;

the shuffle of soles on sisal carpet,
a hissing, a foot tread, a high open sound
that could be wind but is actually rain;

sudden birdsong, treble and reedy,
rain on the roof but not at the windows
and in the distance, the sibilance of rain;

wet rubber footsteps making a dash
for it, one bounce of a ball, a low door
slamming, the textured layers of rain;

the cistern refilling, trickling, desisting,
'Is there anybody else?' a voice asking
with a Dutch lilt; the aftersounds of rain.

Totleigh Barton, Devon

WE STOP TO FINGER THE...

and the white – reminding me of the pink –
        flowering currant's name comes back

to me only after your assays on
        berry – mulberry, lindenberry,

loganberry – no something more ordinary
        like – currant you say, and then yes,

flowering currant comes, smelling of
        catnip, catpee, damp grey flannel blazers

and the rain, the rain, back to me
        in a kind of late relief that words, names,

still within reach not on my tongue but on yours,
        things learned anew, catkins of white mulberry

I never knew were catkins too, trail into my
        mouth like star-apple we will eat together.

SPELLING KATHERINE

for Katherine Gallagher

I'm eating millefeuille in Loutro, dear Katherine.
Yesterday I was feeding the black fish cake.
The cicadas are singing if you can call it song
but real Greek music's strumming across the bay.

We've grown old I hate to say, dear Katherine,
though every time I see you, you're just the same.
I'd invite you to coffee if you were here.
You were so kind to me in our younger days –

'Fair Katharine and most fair' as Henry had it
or the Greeks before him: *Aikaterina*,
Aikaterinē – your middle e brought back,
and first recorded, after the Crusades.

Many Happy Returns, dear Katherine,
in any script or spelling of your name.

ZERESHK POLOW

One couldn't see through the glass doors,
the glass being frosted and endowed
with fruit and flowers, but the odours
of cooking seeped through and the bowed

figures of aunts bent on their task,
positioning spoons, plates, cast shadows
against the panes, humped and grotesque,
like kindly, harmless Quasimodos.

Unlikely loves! Like Stevie Smith's
lion aunt who gave her the lion's share,
my aunts, great-aunts, who always came

in twos, the way fruit and flowers pair,
since love was the dish, ladled out rice with
barberries, cumin, then called my name.

THE KURDISH MUSICIAN

She is swaddled in pink, sky-blue and veiled
in a gold hejab that with every chime
of her santoor dangles its fringe where trailed

on her cheeks hang coins that bob in time
to her nods, throb in a pause, sway to tremor
and echo. Poised on thumbs, twin hammers mime

a flurry of wings, two thin furred tongues that stammer
at strings, streaming a swarm of rising notes
not through field and hedgerow, blossom and clover,

but through space and stars to the huge black throats
of gulley and scarp where all music is stilled,
hived in a dome, as she is, rapt, remote,

impervious to the here and now, hands filled
with flightpaths winging home. Through her who knows
what trails might meet or where pollen has spilled

strange hybrids take, scrub thrive or desert rose;
groundcover prove alive, on five dark grounds
now train its greening shoots? Or who'd suppose

in a London sky, pink, sky-blue, that has wound
itself in the sun's hejab, in fold on fold
veiled its own dark grounds, she too could be found,
head in the clouds, while ours are fringed with gold?

THE DROUGHT GARDEN

Where does it grow
if not here not here

       here in the green
       the green?

What did you wish for
wish for wish

       if not for the heat
       the heat?

What will you plant
in the dust the dust

       where delphinium grew
       in the blue and grey

delphinium grew
in the green?

       I will plant in the dust
       geranium red

on either side of
steps stone steps

       in the backyard
       of a dream a dream

in the backyard
of a dream

SNOWDROPS

Amongst all that
kindling, ground ivy,
under brambles

and broken branches,
a clump of
snowdrops glistened

as if the snow
had never melted.
Whitewashed

frontages, daisies,
silver birches –
spring sunlight

fell on them
and showed me
it's not just

colour we long for
but also the purity
– the poetry? – without it.

PHOTO OF THE POET

I was shocked to see he parted his hair
on the side and plastered it over the top
and felt immediately sorry for him
for the way his heart went and hair went

were one and the same thing and it seemed,
for a man who was happily married and vain,
an explanation for the all the vague desires
he had made into poems and tamed.

I remember him licking his knife
twice, in two poems, and it was hard to tell
if he was faithful, if his wife was faithful
now, after all these years, but it seemed

he was for his poetry had the sadness,
the accommodation of an after-affair.
I remember a dinghy in cold, still water,
a simile that has lost its mooring and swims

searching for its likeness in the ether –
always the wrong, always the cold partner.
His poems seemed to end on a page
then, turned over, continue like his hair.

With anyone else I would have said,
end them there. But there was something
touching in the way they persevered
into a region softer, a net of instability

wind could have lifted, a continuum
more real than the closures younger poets
go for, riding pillion, staring out
of their photos hairy-armed, full-face.

TRIPLE BYPASS

for Scott Verner

He sits by the bed. Even now, he smiles
like a child both taken aback and dazzled
to be alive, to be himself. He calls
Gary Gerry. Painkillers have affected
his memory. He smiles delightedly
and elongates his neck like ET, grinning
from ear to ear. A nurse takes him to try
the stairs. He walks slightly behind her, limping.

It's not the sudden darkening of the sky
or the uneasy lull in conversation
or the warmth of the ward that makes him sleep
with his eyes open but the distant drone
of a motor that makes me think of weeping
and the tilt of the floor, of running away.

THE DARK SIDE OF THE MOON

for Mary MacRae

While Markie shunned light and human company,
scrabbled his bulk under the bath in fright,
took to drinking from the toilet bowl, Kitty
would fend off thistledown, tricks of the light.

Years later, I'd glimpse them too – was it wind,
ghost of a tail I could have sworn shot by?
No – a slippage of time, habit of mind,
lunar spots in the corner of my eye.

Low-lying shrubs, shade-loving plants, dry beds
in the valley below and a dull quiet lane
whose shade I hug now draw me downwards,

down to the floorboard dark where illness, pain,
flatten their fur and even sun freaks find
the dark side of the moon is just as kind.

GLOSE: THE SUMMER OF LOVE

But even in the summers we remember
The forest had its eyes, the sea its voices,
And there were roads no map would ever master,
Lost roads and moonless nights and ancient voices –
                              Donald Justice, 'Sadness'

That was the year in Shawshank Prison that Red
was paroled and hitched a ride to Zihuatanejo,
little place on the Pacific. As Andy said,
'a warm place with no memory' to go to
after the battles, burials – JFK buried
at Arlington, the Six-Day War, Biafra
born only to die an infant death – with no
family, home, no baggage. So there they fled –
two men with a past in that long hot summer.
But even in the summers we remember

– and who'd forget the summer of love, the rallies,
Be-Ins, fighting for peace armed with guitars,
the Sioux, South Dakota in facepaint and hippies
wearing carnations, bedsheets, paper stars
and us in black leotards for our first sally
onstage swanning around in star-struck poses,
Ruth so fond, Rory boyish, Tusse, Barra,
like a sun, a moon, Julian who died and Jimmy? –
yes, even in those days of wine and roses,
the forest had its eyes, the sea its voices.

Little did I dream when we did our audition
I'd marry Paul one day and have his kids.
While Puppet on a String won Eurovision,

the Shah was crowned, Elvis himself got married,
I was dreaming, as Andy was, of redemption,
of 'an entirely novel kind of star', a pulsar,
nebula, lightmap of some bright beloved.
Bright? Just as stars spun out of all proportion,
black holes were named, the Milky Way grew vaster
and there were roads no map would ever master.

Some of us fell from grace, others found fame,
fortune or sank quietly out of sight,
seen only by the forest. Back in Chalk Farm,
our rehearsal rooms, black-ceilinged, -floored, daylight
still flanked by blackout shutters and the same
backstairs, church portico, return bays, arches,
breathe through the dark thicket. I could take fright –
to end up here so lonely. That's why I came.
That's where I found you, friends, as age approaches,
lost roads and moonless nights and ancient voices.

BLESSING

Between the living and the dead,
may your memory be green.
In the book beside my bed,
may your signature be seen.

May your memory be green
for every lover, every spring.
May your signature be seen
inscribed on every living thing.

For every lover, every spring,
breathing clouds against the frost
inscribed on every living thing,
sees how every breath is lost;

breathing clouds against the frost,
because breath is always warm,
sees how every breath is lost
in the one beloved form.

Because breath is always warm,
Hafez, yours ignites the dark.
In the one beloved form,
it is still a burning spark.

Hafez, yours ignites the dark
in the book beside my bed.
It is still a burning spark
between the living and the dead.

GHAZAL

If I am the grass and you the breeze, blow through me.
If I am the rose and you the bird, then woo me.

If you are the rhyme and I the refrain, don't hang
on my lips, come and I'll come too when you cue me.

If yours is the iron fist in the velvet glove
when the arrow flies, the heart is pierced, tattoo me.

If mine is the venomous tongue, the serpent's tail,
charmer, use your charm, weave a spell and subdue me.

What shape should I take to marry your own, have you
– hawk to my shadow, moth to my flame – pursue me?

If I rise in the east as you die in the west,
die for my sake, my love, every night renew me.

If, when it ends, we are just good friends, be my Friend,
muse, lover and guide, Shamsuddin to my Rumi.

Be heaven and earth to me and I'll be twice the me
I am, if only half the world you are to me.

WEDDING VOW

Bride: Though the Barbary lion is extinct
and beside it love is a feeble thing,
                    I thee wed.

Groom: Though the skylark neither soars nor sings
of a joy whose race is just beginning,
                    I thee wed.

Bride: Though the cry violet has cried its last
and the first flush of youth has had its fling,
                    I thee wed.

Groom: Though the baobab's shade has grown so thin
and the elephant thirsts, remembering,
                    I thee wed.

Both: In the name of bird and beast, flower,
tree of life and song of love, with this ring
                    I thee wed.

HEARING VOICES

after Shakespeare's Sonnet 33

'Yes, you were, you were', I laughed, 'golden children!'
Through all those years of hubris, me taking pride,
As though it were my doing, in that golden,
Blameless childhood, you with no cause to hide
Anything more than boyhood's guilty pleasures.
But how you hid when the sky split, the voices came,
Each with a face you drew, wild familiars,
Grotesques that only talking to could tame.
Then on their heels crept silences: your childhood,
Mother, father, sister, all held at bay,
All suspect. Illness might be in the blood,
Even how we laugh in our DNA.
    Yet how we laughed, there in the sun that spread
    Through leaves and seemed to gild what my son said!

I am Spartacus, said Tony Curtis, just in time,
I am Spartacus, said another slave.
I am Spartacus, said another in the crowd behind
as the camera panned to the foothills and then

I am Spartacus said Hadley, rolling the r
and stressing the Spar, I am Spartacus
said a laughing nurse. I am Spartacus,
said Stanley, who always stole our strawberries,

I am Spartacus, said Tom, making sense.
And the camera stopped on sense. Then
I am Spartacus, said Tony Curtis just in time,
I am Spartacus, said another slave.

I am *Sparrr*tacus, said Hadley, I am Spartacus,
I am Spartacus, bobbed the laughing nurse.
I am Spartacus, said Stanley, who takes
me for Tom's grandmother, I am Spartacus,

said Tom, as if he really were. I am Spartacus,
said Curtis in the open air and behind him,
I am Spartacus, said a slave. I am Spartacus,
said another behind the slave behind him,

I am *Sparrrr*tacus, said head nurse Hadley
who'd gone through the system himself.
I am Spartacus, said Stanley, I am Spartacus,
said Tom, in that old blue shirt. Pause, hold

and cut to Curtis, Douglas all amazed;
Hadley, enunciating for England, the nurse,
in and out of shot but vertically, Stanley,
victim extraordinaire. Tom, last of the loop

and the last man in England to say
I am Spartacus straight from the heart –
Hello Spartacus, I say, visiting again,
or tried to but I'd forgotten the name.

Tuke Ward, Homerton Hospital

WHAT KIND OF TIGER?

Look! I said to Tom in my dream,
a tiger leaping through the air!
Not a stuffed toy but one that leaps
and bounds high above the palms,

flies through the air like fur, like pelt,
flakes, dissolves, melts into falling fire,
into melting stripes of sunset. Look,
my son, what has come for you, you

whose spirit longs for tigers. And I woke
knowing it wasn't mine or Tom's,
it was Rhoda's – her tiger that leaps

when the door is opened – it was
Rhoda's – Rhoda who kills herself
by leaping – Virginia's, Rhoda's tiger.

THE LIE

Into my dream walks a child and stands before me.
'What are you holding in your hands?' I ask.
'Nothing but their own softness', she answers.
'What are you holding in yours?' 'Mine are empty
where they should have been full. I've nothing to hide.'
I can tell by her smile she doesn't believe me.
It twists like a knife. She's expecting a baby
I'm not fit to go near, they'll say, a child
I dream is blonde. The baby talks. 'I'm amazed
she can talk', I say, 'she must have been born
knowing how to.' They'd lied about the date,
pretending it was June the 9th. 'Don't go yet.'
'I'm not going anywhere', she laughs in scorn,
yanking the door I had left open closed.

ONE DAY

She woke into sun, sun the great mathematician
of the sky apportioning pieces of a great, golden cake.
The skylights and the floor, walls and yellow counterpane,

gathered round like children at a party, holding their breath.
And she was grateful for this party, as clean and quiet as
a candle and for the kind old sun leaning over her shoulder

to cut the cake. But later that day, seeing her immersed
in a most wondrous book and the beauty of it throwing
another kind of beauty back on to her face, the sun

grew jealous as the soil is jealous of the flowers, the flowers
of the canopy and the canopy of the beautiful people
reading in its shade. He grew jealous of the shade itself.

So he cast his own in a steadiness who would have believed him
capable of until the words began to believe him as a child
believes her father and the letters skewed their little heads.

THE WASP NEST

She sleeps under eaves.
I went to find the noise
the children talked about,
the tiny feet behind the wall.

A wasp nest in the chimney.
The Council said what with the waiting list
and the season of their dying
it wasn't worth them coming at all.

They bothered her at night.
I sat on her bed, changing her linen.
One was buzzing at the window.
I let it out to fly before it died.

Dispirin, Paracetemol and Vicks,
Friars Balsam, Comfrey Ointment – what's this?
Germolene. Syrup of Figs, antihistamine.
I'll have to get some bee sting cream.

Wasp stings aren't so bad.
I make her bed. And smoothe away
the day I dread when medicine
no longer sings of childhood.

NOTES

In White Ink

p.62   'A Persian Miniature': Zahra's Paradise is Tehran's largest cemetery.

p.68   'Earls Court': quotation from Giacomo Puccini's *Madama Butterfly.*

p.80-81 'The Promenade': quotations from 'Who Are They', Delaware Indian Song (transl.1885)

p.89   'Plant Care': quotation from the Hadith of the prophet Mohammad.

Mirrorwork

p.157   'On Reading Rumi': quotations from *Quatrains of Rumi, Unseen Rain*, translated by John Moyne and Coleman Barks.

Entries on Light

p.201   'One sky is a canvas for jets and vapour trails': on seeing The Glory of Venice exhibition at the Tate Gallery.

p.204   'They go right through you, smells': *haft sin*, a tradition of the Iranian New Year, is a display of seven items beginning with the letter *sin.*

p.221   'Why does the aspen tremble': Khadija was the prophet Mohammad's first wife, Aisha his third, though he did not marry her until after Khadija's death.

The Chine

The Meanest Flower

p.347 'Ghazal: The Candles of the Chestnut Trees': the reference to 'Christ the apple tree' is from an 18th century American folk hymn.

p.349 'Ghazal: To Hold Me': refers to Rodolfo, Mimi's poet-lover in Giacomo Puccini's *La Bohème*.

p.350 'Ghazal: Of Ghazals': quotation from Agha Shahid Ali's ghazal 'Of Water' in his last book, *Call Me Ishmael Tonight*.

p.353 'The Mediterranean of the Mind': Michael Donaghy's last professional engagement, and his last reading, took place at Almàssera Vella where Christopher and Marisa North offered poetry courses in Spain. My course started the day that Michael and his family left and, during the days that followed, I wrote for him this poem of place, a place so infused with his presence. Quotations are from Federico García Lorca's lecture, *Play and Theory of the Duende*.

p.365 'The Middle Tone': epigraph from *Deep Song and Other Prose*, ed. and tr. Christopher Maurer.

p.367 'Scorpion-Grass': forget-me-not, also known as scorpion-grass due to its curved stem.

p.373 'Soapstone Retreat': a woodland river retreat for women writers in Oregon, founded by Judith Barrington and Ruth Gundle.

p.374 'On a Line from Forough Farrokhzad': foremost Iranian woman poet (1935-67). Her poem 'The Wind Will Carry Us' (*bad ma ra khahad bord*) inspired Abbas Kiarostami's eponymous film, which in turn suggested the imagery for this poem.

p.387 'Motherhood': misquotation refers to Shelley's question, given to Rhoda in Virginia Woolf's *The Waves: I will pick flowers; I will bind flowers in one garland and clasp them and present them – Oh! To whom?*

p.391   'On Lines from Paul Gauguin': first two lines are quoted in *Gauguin*, Lesley Stevenson. *And the Gold of their Bodies* is the title of Gauguin's 1901 painting of two Polynesian women.

p.394   'Ghazal: The Children': refers to Sebastiao Salgado whose photographs of migrant and refugee children featured in his exibition 'Exodus' at the Barbican Centre in London, 2003.

Child

p.407   'Iowa Daybook': quotation from *With Borges*, Alberto Manguel.

p.408   'Iowa Daybook': quotation from *Quarter Notes: Improvisations and Interiors*, Charles Wright.

p.410   'Iowa' Daybook': quotation from 'Patriotic Songs' in *Amen*, Yehuda Amichai.

p.420   'Afterword': E.A.Markham's epigraph, 'A Life', is from *Looking Out, Looking In: New and Selected Poems*.

The Weather Wheel

p.470   'Marrakesh I-VI': this sequence draws on *Matisse in Morocco: The Paintings and Drawings 1912-1913* exhibition catalogue. 'Marrakesh IV' quotes from the catalogue essay 'The Moroccan Hinge' by Pierre Schneider and also from Matisse's letter to Albert Marquet.

p.490   'The Soul Travels on Horseback': the poem draws on *Platero and I*, Juan Ramón Jiménez, tr. Salvador Ortiz-Carboneres.

p.493　'The Overmind': the poem draws on H.D.'s essay 'Notes on Thought and Vision', published together with 'The Wise Sappho'.

p.503　'Kusa-Hibari': quotes and draws from the essay of the same title by Lafcadio Hearn.

p.508　'On the Occasion of the 150th Anniversary': the phrase 'spark of the Gods' is taken from Friedrich Schiller's 'Ode to Joy', 1785.

p.513　'Bringing Down the Stars': quotations from *Glory*, Vladimir Nabokov.

p.526　'Granadilla I-VII': the sequence draws on *Guanches*, J.P.Camacho.

Afterwardness

p.542　'Dreamers': undocumented migrants who arrived in the U.S. as children. Their name is taken from the DREAM Act – Development, Relief, and Education for Alien Minors – which has never been signed into law.

p.543　'Afterwardness': *chaharbagh* (Persian, meaning 'four gardens') is a quadripartite garden based on the four gardens of Paradise mentioned in the Qur'an.

p.544　'Scripto Inferior': the 'underwriting' or faint traces of former texts on a palimpsest.

p.545　'Cafés': the quoted phrase is from *Biographia Literaria*, S.T. Coleridge.

p.549　'The Introvert House': architectural term for a house built around an inner courtyard.

p.550　'Outpatients':'The Narrows of the Arda River' (*Arda Boylari*) is a Balkan/Turkish folk song.

p.551　'Villajoyosa': the quoted phrase is from 'When Lilacs Last in the Dooryard Bloom'd', Walt Whitman.

p.553   'Dysphagia': difficulty in swallowing, which can be a side effect of antipsychotic medication.

p.564   'Twelve': the poem draws on the novel, *In a Land of Paper Gods*, Rebecca Mackenzie.

p.569   'The Street': the quoted phrase is from 'The Mask Now', Jorie Graham.

p.570   'Friends House': the quoted phrase is from Shakespeare's *Midsummer Night's Dream.*

p.571   'The Older Reader': *The Outrun, Under a Pole Star* and *In a Land of Paper Gods* are novels by Amy Liptrot, Stef Penney and Rebecca Mackenzie respectively.

p.577   'In Praise of the Sestet': quotations from *A Little Book on Form*, Robert Hass.

p.580   'One Summer Holiday': *Mara Beboos* was an Iranian song popular in the 60s.

p.581   'Facades': the term 'hidden immigrants' is taken from *Third Culture Kids*, David C. Pollock, Ruth E. Van Reken and Michael V. Pollock. I am indebted to the authors on whose themes I have drawn in some of these sonnets.

p.585   'My Sixth Birthday Party': *Aji maji la taraji* (Persian) roughly translates as 'abracadabra'.

p.586   'Junior School Production': the quoted phrase is from *The Nightingale*, Hans Christian Andersen.

p.587   'Azarinejad and Bear': the poem refers to *Bear Has a Story to Tell*, Philip C. Stead, and draws on an article captioned 'Iran's travelling cleric who reads to children' by Saeed Kamali Dehghan and a photograph in The Guardian, 29 August 2018.

p.589   'Mehrabad Airport ii': refers to Orhan Pamuk's The Museum of Innocence, after his eponymous novel.

ACKNOWLEDGEMENTS

Grateful acknowledgements are due to the editors of the following publications in which some of the previously uncollected poems, or earlier versions of them, have appeared:

Acumen, Brittle Star, AQA GCSE Anthology & Poetry Online 2010, Artemis, Brittle Star, Hwaet! (Bloodaxe, 2016), *Jubilee Lines* (Faber & Faber, 2012), *K.G. Confidential: A Festschrift for Katherine Gallagher* (Circle Time Press, 2015), *Not Only the Dark: 160 Poems on the Theme of Survival* (Categorical Books, 2011), *Of Love and Hope* (Avalanche Books, 2010), *On Shakespeare's Sonnets: A Poets' Celebration* (Bloomsbury Arden Shakespeare, 2016), *Poetry London, Poetry Review, The Critical Muslim, The Guardian, The North, The Poet's Quest for God* (Eyewear, 2016), *The Scores, Wasafiri.* 'Malih at St. Mary's' was commissioned by Julia Copus for The Royal Literary Fund's Reading Round Festival 2015.

I would like to thank my seminar group who commissioned the artist Christina Edlund-Plater to respond to my work with a felt artwork and for her permission to use the image on the cover.

My warmest thanks, as ever, to my publisher Michael Schmidt and to John McAuliffe, Andrew Latimer and all the team at Carcanet.

INDEX